Childhood Studies

The nature of childhood, the consideration of whether a certain age denotes innocence or not, and the desire to teach good citizenship to our children are all issues commonly discussed by today's media. This book brings together a variety of perspectives on the study of childhood: how it has been treated historically and how such a concept is developing as we move into a new century.

The book is divided into five main sections, as follows:

- Part One sets the scene and provides the reader with an overview of attitudes towards childhood;
- Part Two surveys the contribution of literature from the nineteenth and twentieth centuries;
- Part Three examines educational issues, such as children's play, language acquisition and spiritual development;
- Part Four looks at cultural representation and children in film;
- Part Five offers further help for study and research.

This book draws on a number of academic disciplines, including education, literature, language, theology, cultural studies and history. It will be of particular use to students and tutors of Childhood Studies courses and all those studying for a teaching qualification. Teachers of children aged 4–12 years old will find its contribution to their continuing professional development extremely helpful.

Jean Mills is very experienced as both a classroom practitioner and lecturer. She is currently Principal Lecturer, Head of the English Department and Programme Leader for the BA in Childhood Studies at Westhill College, University of Birmingham. **Richard Mills** taught for many years in schools before moving into higher education. He is currently Research Fellow at Westhill College, University of Birmingham. Both editors have published widely in their fields.

Childhood Studies

A Reader in perspectives of childhood

Edited by Jean Mills
and Richard Mills

London and New York

First published 2000
by Routledge
11 New Fetter Lane, London EC4P 4EE

Simultaneously published in the USA and Canada
by Routledge
29 West 35th Street, New York, NY 10001

Reprinted 2002 by RoutledgeFalmer

RoutledgeFalmer is an imprint of the Taylor & Francis Group

Typeset in Palatino by Taylor & Francis Books Ltd
Printed and bound in Great Britain by Biddles Ltd, Guildford and King's Lynn

British Library Cataloguing in Publication Data
A catalogue record for this book is available from the British Library

Library of Congress Cataloging in Publication Data
Childhood Studies: a Reader in perspectives of childhood / edited
by Jean Mills and Richard Mills.
Includes bibliographical references and index.
1. Children – research. 2. Child development – research.
3. Children – attitudes. I. Mills, Jean. II. Mills, Richard W.
HQ767.85.C483 2000 99-39732
305.23´07´2–dc21 CIP

ISBN 0–415–21414–9 (hbk)
ISBN 0–415–21415–7 (pbk)

Our Millennium Baby is dedicated to present and past students and tutors of Westhill College which, after a ninety-year independent history, now moves into a new relationship with Birmingham University.

J.M.
R.W.M.

Contents

Contributors

All contributors are, or have been, either full-time or part-time colleagues at Westhill College, University of Birmingham, where the BA in Childhood Studies is well established alongside teacher-education and other humanities courses.

Stuart Hanson was a Youth and Community Worker before completing a degree in Media and Cultural Studies as a mature student in 1992 at the University of Birmingham. He subsequently worked there in a variety of research posts, and elsewhere as a part-time lecturer, including Westhill. He is currently a Lecturer in the Department of Cultural Studies and Sociology. His research interests are in cinema as a social and cultural practice, the development of multiplexes and postwar British cinema (in particular the 1960s). His previous publications include 'Spoilt for Choice? Multiplexes in the 90s', in Robert Murphy (ed.) *British Cinema in the 1990s*, published in 2000.

Alison Johnson first came to work at Westhill in 1994, after teaching at primary and secondary level and completing an MA in special applications of linguistics. She currently teaches on the BA, MA and PGCE courses, and she is Programme Leader for the MA in English Studies. Her main research interest and PhD work is in the grammatical and computational analysis of questions and answers in interviews. Her other language interests include: text and discourse analysis; language acquisition; stylistics; critical discourse analysis; and language in education. She is the author of *English for Secondary Teachers: An Audit and Self-Study Guide*, 1998, Letts.

Jean Mills has taught since the 1970s in nursery, infant and junior schools in England, and lectured in higher education in Canada and Australia. She is the author/editor of several books on primary education, including some with Routledge. She was Deputy Director of the Language Support Service in a large local authority before moving into Westhill, where she is currently Principal Lecturer, Head of the English Department and Programme Leader for the BA in Childhood Studies. Her PhD research involves work with Muslim mothers and their bilingual children.

Richard Mills taught for ten years in English schools before moving into higher education. Having lectured in Pakistan and Australia, he became Principal Lecturer, Head of the English Department, and Director of the BA programme at Westhill. His doctoral thesis with Birmingham University was entitled 'Adult Perspectives of Childhood'. He is the author/editor of some twenty books on education, including several with Routledge. He took early retirement in 1997 in order to concentrate on writing and research, and he hopes he has done the right thing.

Jack Priestley began his teaching career at the Glaisdale secondary school in Nottingham. He then went to Zambia to teach at the Malcolm Moffat Teacher Training College at Serenje, some 250 miles north east of Lusaka. On returning to England he taught for a short while in a Primary school before joining the staff at St Luke's College, Exeter, later merged with Exeter University. He has published numerous papers and articles on moral and religious education. His doctoral thesis was entitled 'Moral Education and Religious Story'. In January 1991 he became Principal of Westhill. He retired, somewhat early, in 1997 and returned to Exeter where he is now a University Research Fellow in the School of Education.

Maxine Rhodes is a Senior Lecturer in Social History and joint research officer at Westhill, where she teaches on a variety of BA (Humanities) courses. Her research interests, which included her doctoral thesis, lie in the development of the midwifery profession and the changing culture of childbirth in the inter-war years. She also teaches for the Open University on DA 301 Family and Community History, and is a keen supporter of widening participation in higher education through open access.

Fay Sampson is the author of nineteen children's novels, eight novels for adults and three educational books. She began by teaching mathematics and was librarian in a Zambian teacher-training college. Her wide range of children's fiction includes the award-winning, *The Watch on Patterick Fell*. She has been a writer-in-residence for schools and libraries, has taught creative writing (at Westhill and elsewhere), and gives talks and workshops for both children and adults. She lives in Devon and is active in writers' societies.

Susannah Smith is a Senior Lecturer in Education at Westhill. Prior to this she spent a number of years teaching in primary schools in Birmingham and Northampton, and completed research into children's play for her MA. Her current research interests lie in early years education, particularly early literacy, and issues related to equal opportunities. She is presently researching for a PhD in the area of gender differences in early reading development.

Neill Thew has been working at Westhill College for the past five years, where he teaches on a variety of BA (Humanities) courses. Prior to that he taught at Oxford and London Universities. He has recently been involved in researching his PhD into the literary and artistic communities based in Paris during the 1920s and 1930s, and is currently writing up a series of interlinked projects relating to sexuality and representation. His teaching and research interests are mainly in twentieth-century literature and literary theory, with a particular focus on psychoanalysis.

Acknowledgements

We would like to record our warm appreciation to our contributor colleagues for their involvement in this book. They responded very positively to all our requests and met all deadlines (well, most of them).

We are grateful to Skoob books for permission to quote from Peter Abbs's poem at the end of Chapter 1.

Some of our students reversed roles and commented on early chapter drafts, and we wish to thank John Bolton, Gaynor Gaynor, Andrea Hicks, Sally Merritt, Samantha Poole and Claire Thomas for being risk-takers.

We have been particularly glad of the support and encouragement of Routledge staff, including Helen Fairlie, Nina Stibbe and Jude Bowen. They know something that many a management consultant has yet to learn, namely, that praise works better than blame.

Introduction

Jean Mills and Richard Mills

In all the books I had read childhoods were either idyllic or deprived. Mine had been neither.

(Alan Bennett, *Writing Home*, 1994)

The glossy, collage-like cover of a book by Colin and Tim Ward, *Images of Childhood in Old Postcards* (1991), has thirteen representations showing one or more children. Eleven of these representations are photographs, one is a painting and one is a cartoon. This last is in the style of Lucie Mabel Atwell and shows a ginger-headed, short-trousered, pink-faced, wide-eyed young boy washing his hands in a bowl of water, while looking out at us, half, it seems, in anticipation or hope or approval. The painting is in the colours, if not the sentiment, of Newlyn painter Walter Langley and presents a young 1930s schoolboy, with cap set at a relaxed if not quite rakish angle, sitting with his back to a wall, smiling as he reads his rather dog-eared copy of *Tit Bits* (the children's magazine, not the later saucy newspaper).

Of the eleven remaining representations, one tinted photograph has a young female child in early Victorian dress playing mother (albeit balanced on a chair for the purpose), as she washes the hair of her younger brother who is bent over a bowl

1

of water, also balanced on a chair. The words 'Little Mother' are printed on the wall behind the children. Three photographs are images of pretty, beautifully dressed, smiling girls. Another is of a seemingly wistful, perhaps bored or maybe petulant, girl in gypsy mode with a bundle tied on her arm, apparently lost in her own thoughts.

Six photographs remain: one shows an apparently sturdy, resolute boy sitting on steps by the side of his apparently equally sturdy and noble collie, both staring away at the same distant perspective; another one is of a tousle-headed boy dressed in French army uniform and with a lighted cigarette in his mouth; another is of the family snap variety with a naked child in a tin bath on the living room carpet; another appears to be of a boy posing in an advertisement for new boots; another shows a smiling older brother and sister, with a seemingly apprehensive younger sister in a juvenile trio which could prefigure a later photograph of mother, father and child. The last photograph shows an Edwardian drawing room with a sailor-suited young boy sitting in a chair being caressed (or is it strangled?) by a slightly older, smiling sister.

Only thirteen pictures, but already many more possibilities exist for interpretation. To begin with, the pictures themselves, and the predominantly sepia colour of a book cover obviously designed to attract browsers, are redolent of the past, of nostalgia, of a golden age, of innocence, of loss. Features of elegance, charm, steadfastness, dependability, independence, cuteness, insouciance, playfulness, wonder and yearning seem to be represented. Children appear as individuals but also in such poses as may suggest family life or later adult occupations. In short, the cover proclaims that all readers will identify in some way with the photographs, picture postcards and commentary inside; that there are shared assumptions between compilers and reader; that the world of childhood is varied and worth investigating.

In such investigation, a key premise is that childhood is socially constructed; it does not exist in pristine form, like some pearl merely waiting to be discovered. It is, rather, dependent on recall, interpretation, intuition, empathy and re-presentation. Whatever the original experience of childhood was like – and it will have varied in detail for every one of us – its reconstruction from combinations of memory, report, received wisdom at second or third hand, render it a different order of experience. Things are not what they seem. One postcard within the Wards' book makes this point quite neatly. The photograph shows an apparently weak but, perhaps, determined young boy in Edwardian smock, standing in a pose with a hoop. The accompanying message reads as follows:

> Dear Mrs Robins, You must not go by looks, as this sober looking little boy is not in the least little bit what he looks, if you could see him at home you would think him the essence of roguishness.

In other words, appearances are deceptive and, in any event, in this instance we are dependent on the judgement of the postcard writer, her view of the little boy and her understanding (and ours) of the term, 'essence of roguishness'. Photographs, like any other form of *evidence*, need interpretation, with commentary on substance, form and context, accompanied by a readiness in response to be non-dogmatic, tentative and all-inclusive. The interpreter, too, will be subject to assessment and evaluation.

Such considerations are relevant to this book, which seeks to be wide-ranging in incorporating insights from a range of separate disciplines. Such inter-disciplinary enquiry is crucial, given the nature of the subject, and this Reader draws mainly on the disciplines of literature, education, theology, media and cultural studies, and history. The study of childhood cannot be contained within the straitjacket of one approach; it needs varying perspectives.

Part One sets the scene and provides an overview of attitudes towards childhood as a background for the chapters which follow. Part Two surveys the contribution of nineteenth- and twentieth-century literature, both from a literary critical and a creative point of view. Part Three examines certain educational perspectives, notably those connected with children's play, language and the spiritual domain. Part Four scrutinises the representation of children within the mass media, concentrating particularly on film and, to a lesser extent, television. Part Five takes readers beyond the pages of this text and offers help for further study and research.

We have written the book for all students involved in studying childhood as an academic concern, and for teachers and students in teacher training, whether on undergraduate or post-graduate courses. We have put particular stress on referencing and recommended reading so that students will be able to follow up their particular interests. Selections from the *Review Questions and Tasks* at the end of each chapter should be appropriate either for 'in-house' or distance-learning students, for individual or for small group work.

Part One

Overview

Chapter 1

Perspectives of childhood

Richard Mills

Summary

This first chapter sets out to establish some of the key themes of any investigation of childhood. It lists the disciplines which may be involved in studying the phenomenon; the difficulties in defining what childhood is and who children are; and the factors affecting the various social constructions of childhood. The chapter offers six possible perspectives and describes how each of these comes about (i.e. children as innocent/as apprentices/as persons in their own right/as members of a distinct group/as vulnerable/as animals). Some of these perspectives are mirrored in a variety of ways in the chapters which follow but, as the appendix shows, there are many more possible constructions of childhood, each with its own interests and limitations.

Tread softly because you tread on my dreams.

W.B.Yeats, 'He Wishes for the Cloths of Heaven' (1899)

This book is not about childhood, but about perspectives of childhood and children. As explained in the introduction, such is the nature of childhood that its study cannot be confined within one academic discipline. It must draw on such areas of study as are felt to be appropriate, and these might include, in large or small degree: anthropology, art, computing, education, history, literature, medicine, philosophy, physiology, psychology, psycho-analysis, psychotherapy, sociology, statistics, or theology.

So much for the tools of enquiry but, however wide or narrow one's subject, defining terms remains crucial and, in this search for definition, the word 'childhood' presents problems. Does the investigation relate to boys, or girls, or both (Waksler, 1991: 234, 244)? Are they in rural or urban areas? (Cunningham contrasts the two states 1991: 150ff.) From which social class do they come? (This is a key issue for Humphries *et al.*, 1988: 35.) Are they contemporary children or from the past? (Ariès, 1996, maintains that child-hood did not begin until the seventeenth century; Pollock, 1983 and others forcibly dispute this.) Do the children come from the United Kingdom or elsewhere in the world? (La Fontaine, in Richards and Light, 1986: 10ff., sees cross-cultural comparisons as crucial.) How old is a child? (Gamage, 1992, states that the early childhood period is between birth and ten years; the social historian Walvin, 1982: 11, decides it is age fourteen and under; Miles, 1994: 263, reports childhood as including the years up to eighteen, as a matter of international law, binding on the twenty countries which rati-fied the United Nations agreement of 1990.)

These are some of the questions relating to the actual people involved. What of the phenomenon itself? What are some of its distinguishing features? Is childhood a state of powerlessness and adaptation to a lack of power (as Waksler maintains, 1991: 69)? Or a time and condition of secrets and shame (according to Postman, 1983: 80)? Or dependency (Shipman, 1972: 13)? Can it not simply be regarded as a period of biological, intellec-tual, and social development; as a time for the 'accumulation of experience' (Wadsworth, 1991: 7), leading to self-definition (1991: 12)? In these terms, is it not best linked with a series of school transitions such as: nursery–infant–junior–secondary, in the state system, and nursery–kinder-garten–prep–public school in the private system (see James and Prout, 1990: 233)? Or, should it be perceived as a category of child such as 'The Country Child' (Dudgeon, 1992)? If the talk is in terms of categories, do the terms 'institutional' and 'normative' (Wringe, 1981: 88) offer a useful perspective? The former refers to the legal or quasi-legal status of child-hood, and the latter to an expectation of certain capacities of children.

Perhaps approaches such as these outlined are too mundane and func-tional. If so, should an approach be adopted which seeks to capture the timeless essence of childhood in some kind of mystical manner, uniting 'a mythical past with a magical present' (James and Prout, 1990: 229)? One way into such a world is through fiction and the work (in English, at any rate) of such writers as J.M. Barrie, Lewis Carroll, Kenneth Grahame, Charles Kingsley, C.S. Lewis, A.A. Milne and J.R.R. Tolkien. The world these writers create is timeless and (despite certain potential terrors) safe and contained. In extraordinary and individual ways, these authors are regarded as having captured something elusive and indefinable (see Wullschläger, 1995, for a fascinating commentary on five of these writers). It is not the world of modern children's authors, such as Leila Berg, Edward Blishen, Roald Dahl, Anne Fine, Philippa Pearce and Robert Westall (see Meek *et al.*, 1977; Styles *et al.*, 1996; Tucker, 1991), who seek to represent more immediate 'real' experiences; it is beyond time, and often archetypal. In this regard it either creates for us, or reflects to us, something which we cannot replicate for ourselves. As George Eliot observed in *The Mill on the Floss*:

> Is there anyone who can recover the experience of his childhood, not merely with a memory of what he did and what happened to him ... but with an intimate penetration, a revived consciousness of what he felt then – when it was so long from one Midsummer to another?
>
> (1985: 123)

Such, then, are the problems of defining childhood, with its shifting visions, its lack of watertight compartments, its illusory and elusive nature: what Steedman refers to as its 'extraordinary plasticity' (1995: 7). It is clear that childhood or, rather, childhoods, are social constructions, cultural components inextricably linked to variables of race, class, culture, gender and time. In sociological terms, 'To recognise that "child" is a role is to suspend the assumption that childhood has some absolute, real, transcendent existence beyond the social' (Waksler, 1991: 146). It needs to be seen as 'a shifting social and historical construction ... a continually experienced and created social phenomenon which has significance for its present, as well as the past and future' (James and Prout, 1990: 231).

The eclecticism apparent earlier in the range of relevant disciplines will now be apparent as some of the key social constructions of childhood are outlined. These are presented in no hierarchical order and the intention at this stage is to keep them fairly discrete, although in reality they cannot be isolated but are interlinked and overlapping, in the manner of a Venn diagram. The constructions I have chosen are:

- children as innocent
- children as apprentices
- children as persons in their own right
- children as members of a distinct group
- children as vulnerable
- children as animals

Children as innocent

> They are idols of heart and of household;
> They are angels of God in disguise;
> His sunlight still sleeps in their tresses,
> His glory still gleams in their eyes.
> (Dickinson, 'The Children')

The notion of the child as innocent has had, and still has, a powerful hold on the imagination. Its origin or appeal seems to reside in one or more (or possibly an undifferentiated amalgam), of the following perspectives:

* child as theological construct
* child as being in need of protection
* child as a force for good

Child as theological construct

From a sociological point of view, the term 'theological construct' would be quite acceptable; from a religious point of view it might be more debatable, since what is being addressed is nothing less than the essence of human life. As Shipman has suggested, up until the twentieth century child-rearing and education in the western world had been dominated by two contrasting, and hardly compatible, Christian viewpoints: 'One view stressed the angelic, unsullied, natural goodness of children. The other stressed their devilish, potentially evil, self-willed nature' (1972: 8). As a sample of the first view, Shipman quotes from the essayist, John Earle, subsequently Bishop of Salisbury, who in 1628, at the age of eighteen, wrote in *Microcosmographie*:

> The child is the best copy of Adam before he tasted of Eve or the apple; and he is happy whose small practice in the world can only write his Character. He is Nature's fresh picture newly drawn in oil, which time, and much handling, dims and defaces. His soul is yet a white paper unscribbled with observations of the world, wherewith, at length, it becomes a blurred notebook.
>
> (Shipman, 1972: 9)

It is a view for which some justification could be found in the New Testament of the Bible and which foreshadowed later thinking. Words such as 'best', 'fresh' and 'white', denote a quality of purity and newness which found powerful endorsement in much late eighteenth-century and nineteenth-century writing, not least in Rousseau, who announces his personal manifesto early in *Émile* by stating: 'God makes all things good; man meddles with them and they become evil' (1762: Book 1, p. 5).

However they might disagree theologically about Original Sin or Original Innocence, both Earle and Rousseau are united in believing that something goes wrong, that the new beginning promised in childhood somehow founders. Postman is specific about the polarity. He writes:

> In the Protestant view, the child is an unformed person who, through literacy, education, reason, self-control and shame, may be made into a civilized adult. In the Romantic view, it is not the unformed child but the deformed adult who is the problem. The child possesses, as his or her birthright, capacities for candour, understanding, curiosity and spontaneity that are deadened by literacy, education, reason, self-control and shame.
>
> (1983: 59)

John Locke's metaphor of the 'tabula rasa', the clean slate (1693), clearly fits the first of these polarities in that it assumes an incremental build-up of knowledge, skills and attitudes through the acquisition and practice of literacy. For Rousseau, the child was within 'a state of nature' and, given the absence of adverse circumstances, that would be sufficient to develop what Postman calls 'the childhood virtues of spontaneity, purity, strength, and joy, all of which came to be seen as features to nurture and celebrate' (1983: 59).

The controversy, which goes back to the early Christian church, still has significance for the secular twentieth century, although the language has changed and the debate is more pragmatic, focusing not so much on essence but on practical import: namely, how should parents and professional educators treat young children? Hannah More faced this issue in 1799 in her book *Strictures on the Modern System of Female Education*, and asked the question:

> Is it not a fundamental error to consider children as innocent beings, whose little weaknesses may, perhaps, want some correction, rather than as beings who bring into the world a corrupt nature and evil dispositions, which it should be the great end of education to rectify?
>
> (Brown, 1993: 44)

The question, albeit in different terms, is still with us. Should parents follow the advice of John Wesley 'to break the will of your child, to bring his will into subjection to yours' (quoted by Hendrick in James and Prout, 1990: 38), or should a more sensitive, subtle, enabling route be followed? Expressed in that loaded form, the choice is perhaps fairly simple, but as we shall see throughout this book, such is the multi-faceted nature of the enquiry into the essence of human nature that the ground appears constantly to be shifting: one discipline offers insights which might seem to conflict with those from another discipline, one set of practical experiences is often at variance with another set, and new knowledge, particularly in the area of genetics (see Jones, 1994: 68ff), can enforce radical reappraisal of previously held convictions.

In short, the philosophical and ideological stances taken by parents, carers, and educators, whether precisely articulated or merely implicit, will determine how children are treated. That is a key premise of this present work.

Child as being in need of protection

It is axiomatic that, however the period of childhood is defined, children are in need of physical protection and nurture for their well-being. This is true of the young of any animal species. However, within the literature of childhood innocence, protection has a different significance. It refers to the preservation of a state of ignorance, of unknowingness, about certain areas of life which adults feel should best remain secret from those inhabiting the world of childhood.

Indeed, based on this premise, the movement out of childhood is seen as the gradual acquiring of secret knowledge. The transition from childhood in the western world is thus not some sudden act of ritualised initiation, as in some societies. Rather, it is a slow, incremental build-up of knowledge and experience, passed from adult to child over a period of time. In this sense, it is akin to an inheritance acquired not in one lump sum but rather in differing amounts and at different times. By this analogy, the precise date by which the inheritance has been received is uncertain, but there comes a point at which both donor and recipient acknowledge that it has occurred.

What, then, is the secret knowledge? For Postman, these secrets are to do with sexual relations, money, violence, illness, death, social relations and language; in other words there is, he believes, 'a store of words not to be spoken in the presence of children' (1983: 49). Two of these 'secrets' dominate the literature of protected childhood: death and sexual relations.

Such was the medieval world, according to Ariès, that the concept of childhood, in the sense of being cut off from adult secrets, did not exist. Basing his assertions on evidence from the world of painting and iconography, Ariès claims:

> Medieval art until about the twelfth century did not know childhood or did not attempt to portray it. It is hard to believe that this neglect was due to incompetence or incapacity; it seems more probable that there was no place for childhood in the medieval world.
>
> (1996: 31)

Children and adults lived out their lives, it appears, in such close proximity that secrets would have been impossible, even if thought desirable. Such may still be the case in certain rural Third World contexts.

However, by the nineteenth century in Europe, if not long before, there was a distinct attempt to hide or soften the reality of death by employing euphemisms, metaphors, religious promises, expressed in the literature of the age:

> Thus, a dead baby brother is seen as a butterfly bursting out of its chrysalis, a dying child worries about forgetting her prayers or wishes not to be adorned with flowers after her death because her Saviour's head was crowned with thorns, and several children yearn to be reunited in death with lost ones ... Tales of exemplary death-beds of children and of the flight to heaven of a child's soul were also designed to ease the grief of real parents in an age when the infant mortality rate was high, and to comfort them with the thought that the spiritual purity of their child would ensure eternal bliss.
>
> (Brown, 1993: 185)

The modern cynic could easily dismiss such sentiments as literary flights of fancy, or Victorian hypocrisy, or simple wish-fulfilment. There may indeed be elements of all of these, but the fact remains that one could easily identify modern equivalents by which adults seek to mitigate the harshness of loss (of pets, for instance, let alone relatives). Wallbank makes this link down the ages when she writes:

> Perhaps the adult wish to protect a child from exposure to the two taboo subjects of sexuality and death is a natural one. <u>It is natural to want children to be happy, to allow them a period of innocence before they take on the cares of adulthood.</u> The vocabulary of death does seem harsh, too brutal to offer to a little child. It involves using words like death – and dying – and grave – and funerals – and body – and burning – and burying. Perhaps also, few adults have reached a full understanding and acceptance of their own mortality and that of those they love.
>
> (in Varma, 1992: 69)

This last suggestion is powerful. Perhaps in protecting children from adult secrets, we are in effect trying to protect ourselves also; to keep at bay unpalatable truths; to escape vicariously into a more secure world than the one we know we and they inhabit. The psychology of repression is full of such dark secrets, especially in the area of sexuality, and it is here that the maintenance of childhood innocence is seen by some to be paramount. This is reflected strongly in both nineteenth-century literature and twentieth-century popular mythology.

In focusing on the concept of the innocent child, Brown refers specifically to the way in which girls were portrayed in books of the last century. They were:

> the embodiment of untainted innocence and spirituality and were favoured as the angelic instruments of redemption and regeneration by female and male authors alike. It is equally significant that such little girls often die young, thus

being denied the possibility of development, which might expose them to worldly influences, in order to preserve their purity intact.

(1993: 183)

Indeed, as Avery shows in her surveys of 1965 and 1975, Victorian literature is full of examples where innocence, and particularly sexual innocence, can only be preserved by death at an early age. Contact with 'the world' would bring death of a different kind, and here there is a link between nineteenth-century fiction and twentieth-century anxieties. This latter unease is reflected in a spate of books whose titles presage doom by announcing or predicting childhood loss. They include:

- *Betrayal of Innocence: Incest and its Devastation* (Forward and Buck, 1981)
- *The Death of Innocence* (Janus, 1981)
- *The Erosion of Childhood* (Polakow, 1992)
- *The Disappearance of Childhood* (Postman, 1983)
- *The Erosion of Childhood* (Rose, 1991)
- *The Rise and Fall of Childhood* (Sommerville, 1982)
- *Children Without Childhood* (Winn, 1984)

Postman's thesis is that innocence can only thrive on secrets and shame, and that, with the advent of the all-pervasive, all-intrusive medium of television and other means of mass communication, no privacy can survive: 'Nothing is mysterious, nothing awesome, nothing is held back from public view' (1983: 97). Children, as adults, have easy access via television to a treatment of 'the defence budget, the energy crisis, the women's movement, crime in the streets ... to incest, promiscuity, homosexuality, sadomasochism, terminal illness, and other secrets of adult life' (1983: 81). The contemplation of such a lost world is a matter of infinite sorrow to Postman:

> To have to stand and wait as the charm, malleability, innocence, and curiosity of children are degraded and then transmogrified into the lesser features of pseudo-adulthood is painful and embarrassing and, above all, sad.
>
> (1983: xiii)

This is powerful, persuasive, emotive prose. However, at least two arguments against it need to be considered. One is the general notion that children, as all people, only absorb information that makes sense to them, information that they can understand and that fits in with their world view and experience. In other words, according to this notion, children's very ignorance acts as a protective barrier to unpalatable knowledge.

Such an argument has some force. However, a stronger case can be made for the view that the concept of sexual innocence can itself be a danger. Kitzinger identifies three strands of this danger:

First, the notion of childhood innocence is itself a source of titillation for abusers. ... Second, innocence is a double-edged sword in the fight against sexual abuse because it stigmatizes the 'knowing' child. ... The third ... is that ... to deny children access to knowledge and power ... actually increases their vulnerability to abuse. The twin concepts of innocence and ignorance are vehicles for adult double-standards.

(in James and Prout, 1990: 160–1)

Slightly earlier, in 1988, Humphries *et al.* had examined the concept of ignorance from a decidedly down-to-earth, social class-oriented, sociological point of view, appropriate for the Channel Four television series which the book accompanied. First acknowledging the influence of such writers as Angela Brazil and Enid Blyton in portraying fictional asexual childhoods which, in turn, were reflected in the clothes worn by real boys and girls of the time, the television programme proceeded to highlight social class differences. Girls in particular were singled out as suffering from sexual ignorance:

Many had no idea what was happening when their periods started; some thought they were dying or that it was a punishment from God. Most mothers made no attempt to prepare their daughters for menstruation, while those who did tended to pass on a feeling of shame and a sense that periods were unclean. Sanitary towels were not in general use by working-class girls, who at best used pieces of rag or sheeting.

(1988: 157)

The key challenge, which remains with us, is how to minimise children's vulnerability while, at the same time, allowing them space and time in which to enjoy the pleasures of their childhood.

Middle-class Victorian England had little doubt as to how this might be accomplished. It was by drawing on the centrality of the family and family life, as each verse of Mrs Hemans's poem 'The Homes of England' makes clear, combining and merging love of home with patriotism as she refers to: 'The stately homes of England ... The merry homes of England ... The blessed homes of England ... The cottage homes of England ... The free fair homes of England' (1876: 441).

Implicitly endorsing such a view of the power of the home, if not positively equating that domestic setting with the national context, is the following assertion from the author of *Boys and Their Ways* (1880):

A quiet, methodical, religious home in which the parents are actuated by a high sense of duty, in which all the members are linked together by love's golden chain, in which a place is found for everything and everything is in its place, so that the mind is insensibly trained in habits of discipline and order, in which happiness constantly prevails, because tempers are subdued and wills controlled by the very spirit of the scene; such a home exercises an influence which lasts until death.

(Avery, 1975: 129)

Similar sentiments have been expressed by Jonathan Sacks who, as Chief Rabbi, testified powerfully to the value of the family not only as the key social institution but also as the unit uniquely qualified to nurture future generations. He commented:

> The family is where we acquire the skills and language of relationship. It is where we learn to handle the inevitable conflicts within any human group. It is where we first take the risk of giving and receiving love. Of all the influences upon us, the family is far the most powerful. Its effects stay with us for a lifetime. It is where one generation passes on its values to the next and ensures the continuity of a civilisation. For any society the family is the crucible for its future.

(1995: 13)

Sacks's metaphor of the crucible is significant. It suggests a melting pot, a vessel in which ingredients are being tested and formed, a living, changing experiment, out of which will emerge something new and, possibly, different.

Interestingly, Postman also sees in the family a solution to the problems of stability, culture maintenance and security. He does not reproduce those sentiments of a past age, with their stress on religion, duty, order, hierarchy, training and submission, but he yearns for parents who will serve children by 'defying the directives of their culture. ... Those parents who resist the spirit of the age will contribute to what might be called the Monastery Effect, for they will help to keep alive a humane tradition' (1983: 153). Postman's metaphor of the monastery certainly suggests security, but security by way of seclusion, of separateness, of being cut off from the secular, media-dominated world.

Bruno Bettelheim, having in his own life experienced in the Nazi concentration camps some of the worst suffering that this world can impose, proposes something far more fundamental in his quest for security and preservation of innocent values. The solution for him lies not in a social institution, however crucial, but rather more in the psyche of individual boys and girls, men and women: in other words, in the power of the fairy tale both to reveal and conceal simultaneously, to bring readers face to face with a reality they can cope with and an experience which will forewarn and fore-arm them to face subsequent fears and trials. Offering a wealth of characters with whom children may identify and a range of archetypes, incidents, emotions and trials which grip and stimulate the imagination, the genuine fairy tale, according to Bettelheim, reaches a part of the human psyche which other experiences do not reach. He claims: 'The fairy tale ... confronts the child squarely with the basic human predicaments' (1991: 8). If Bettelheim is correct, then the fairy story offers a way whereby the discontinuity between childhood and maturity might be avoided, whereby the essence of childhood might be treasured and passed on, not in a spirit of jealously guarding an old, worn-out, spluttering spirit, but more in positive celebration of a living inheritance.

From family barricade to television censorship to a diet of fairy tales; put crudely like that, the 'solutions' may seem rather bizarre. What is significant, however, is that the experience and hence the preservation of childhood, whatever writers mean by the phrase, is perceived as worthy of the greatest attention by parents and professional educators.

Child as a force for good

The notion here is that, by virtue of their childhood innocence, their promise of hope, their unalloyed vulnerability, children are somehow a force for good in the world. The concept is probably linked initially with the Platonic idea of perfection of form, namely, that the outward attractiveness indicates an inner quality of goodness. Whatever the validity of such a philosophical stance, the fact seems to be that the young of any species are automatically attractive to the older members of that group. This may indeed be crucial for the survival of that species.

It is significant that much nineteenth-century literature which involved child heroes and heroines inevitably portrayed them as physically attractive, as judged by the norms of the day. Certain physical attributes denoted innocence, as Avery records:

> The child hero was pretty ... it had suddenly become very important to have curly hair, blue eyes, and pearly teeth, and too often this was linked in the author's mind with innocence ... 'What the Earl saw' (from *Little Lord Fauntleroy*) 'was a graceful childish figure in a black velvet suit, with a lace collar, and with lovelocks waving about the handsome, manly little face, whose eyes met his with a look of innocent good-fellowship.' ... 'My Sweetheart is sweet.' (from Samuel Rutherford Crockett's *Sweetheart Travellers*, 1895). 'To look into her eyes is to break a hole in the clouds and see into heaven ... For my Sweetheart is but four years old, and does not know that there is a shadow on all God's world. To spend a day with her in the open air is to get a glimpse into a sinless paradise. For there is no Eden anywhere like a little child's soul.'
>
> (1965: 176, 178).

It would be all too easy to dismiss such sentimentality as Victorian claptrap, but brief reflection on twentieth-century attitudes within the media (see Chapters 7 and 8 of this volume) reveal something very similar in terms of the way 'stars' are presented. Child protagonists of popular appeal will invariably be physically attractive. Either that, or their attraction will lie in some inner quality which they possess or in some promise which they represent. Many television advertisements portray children as symbolic of future hope, of generational continuity, of security in a shifting world. Such an adult-centric viewpoint highlights the value and attractiveness of children for what they will become, for their potential as human resources. For the purposes of manipulative commercial television, this view does not value children as persons in their own right.

Nevertheless, children are intrinsically attractive. They are also seen as innately wise, with an insight that belies their years, and with the capacity to teach truths to their elders. Again, one looks to the nineteenth century for powerful expression of this viewpoint and finds in the Avery surveys convincing endorsement, albeit perhaps crudely expressed in some cases. So, for instance, the drunkard is saved by the spiritual child; smoking is denounced by the concerned daughter as injurious to her father's health; the family assembled for the operation to save a blind child's eyes is comforted by Emily, the ideal girl (1965: 36); Harry, the ideal boy, has an 'honest, good-natured countenance which makes everybody love him, is never out of humour, always obliging, shares his dinner with the needy, and is always, always kind to animals' (1975: 37); Cedric (Little Lord Fauntleroy) converts his grandfather, the Earl, from curmudgeon to local benefactor.

Perhaps these are unsophisticated stereotypes (although the 1995 BBC television series of *Little Lord Fauntleroy* managed to offer a reasonably acceptable interpretation). Either way, an altogether richer nineteenth-century literary creation expressing the theme of innocent child as spiritual guide is to be found in the work of George Eliot (see Chapter 2 of this book), herself by no means the stereotypical female Victorian novelist of evangelistic fervour.

For her novel of 1861, *Silas Marner*, Eliot chose as her epigraph a quotation from Wordsworth's poem 'Michael', asserting that: 'A child, more than all other gifts / That earth can offer to declining man, / Brings hope with it and forward-looking thoughts'. Marner suffers betrayal (by his fiancée and best friend) and loss (of his gold) and becomes a recluse. After many years of suffering (reflecting the Shakespearean notion of redemption through sorrow), Marner, the short-sighted weaver (all significant details, of course) discovers one New Year's Eve a bundle of gold on his hearth, mysteriously arrived while he had stepped outside his cottage to hear the church bells. Where formerly he had stored up material gold, now he worships golden-haired Eppie with true, altruistic, self-effacement. He is redeemed by the child, as he acknowledges: 'Eh, my precious child, the blessing was mine. If you hadn't been sent to save me, I should ha' gone to the grave in my misery. ... It's wonderful – our life is wonderful' (Chapter 19).

In Eliot's case, the love generated is not that from God. It is more secular, more of this world rather than of the next:

> There was love between him and the child that blent them into one ... In old days there were angels who came and took men by the hand and led them

away from the city of destruction. We see no white-winged angels now. But yet men are led away from threatening destruction: a hand is put into theirs, which leads them forth gently towards a calm and bright land, so that they look no more backward; and the hand may be a little child's.

(Chapter 14)

Perhaps this is an appropriate link between the Victorian age and the twentieth century, for George Eliot appears to be saying that we are moving out of a narrowly specific religious period into a much more humanistic, but nevertheless supportive, time. And the agent of redemption is a child, not in former narrow threatening evangelistic terms, but in something altogether warmer and richer and welcoming.

Children as apprentices

Train up a child in the way he should go; and when he is old, he will not depart from it.

(Proverbs 22:6)

The term 'apprentice' is an industrial concept, stemming from the days when young people (more often than not, young boys), underwent a period of several years of transmission-type learning, during which time they acquired the practical skills to work alongside their mentor and, ultimately, to step into his shoes. Little if anything was required of them in terms of initiative. The process was barely reciprocal, but rather was static and one-sided. In this chapter, the metaphor is stretched to include a view of childhood as a period of socialisation and of acculturation, but also to suggest a richer relationship between teachers and taught, whereby learners are enabled to develop their own personalities and to take an active role themselves in influencing the process of culture transmission.

Anthropologists and sociologists have consistently shown that all societies develop systems, by means of formal and/or informal institutions, for passing on appropriate knowledge, skills and attitudes and for the maintenance of acceptable patterns of behaviour. Such patterns vary from society to society and from age to age. Erasmus (1466–1536), for instance, in what has been termed the Early Renaissance period, gave precise advice to both adults and children about how to spit and how to wipe one's nose in public. In Ireland over two centuries later, Emily, Countess of Kildare prescribed a good diet, sea bathing and much physical affection both for the upbringing of her own children and for that of others (see Tillyard, 1994: 237). In the 1950s world of Alan Bennett, 'children do not refer to relatives by anything so naked as their name' (1994: 23). In modern middle-class Pakistan, it is unacceptable to smoke in front of one's elders.

Such an odd collocation of detail makes the point that social class is a major determinant of what is, and is not, acceptable, and that there are hardly any limits by which regulatory practices may be circumscribed. What remains consistent across ages, cultures and social classes is that a view of cultural transmission which is static assumes that all power for impact lies with the adults.

A more modern view (as Shipman, 1972; Richards and Light, 1986; Waksler, 1991, and others, have indicated) is that the learner who is being socialised is by no means a passive agent, a sponge-like recipient. Rather, there is interaction between all the parties concerned, so much so that what emerges, at least in a dynamic society, is something new and different. If it is a difference acceptable to both parties, then there is little if any dysfunction within that society. If it is radically different, in a way which alarms either party, then the young are labelled by those who are older as 'deviants'.

Such a concept of emergent, developing, living culture is powerfully in tune with a re-definition of the term 'apprentice'. Indeed, the last two decades in the United Kingdom have virtually demanded a re-evaluation of the term if it is to remain in current use. Just as the notion of 'a job for life' has disappeared, so too has the notion of static, unchanging transmission which appeared to depend on a cocoon-like context for its realisation.

In summary, socialisation is reciprocal, dynamic and contextualised; it is not one-sided, static and *in vacuo*; it is all-embracing, from personal morality to public duty. Its chief institutional focus in Western society is the school, which endeavours in a variety of ways to resolve those hostile tensions just described. Universal literacy and numeracy are regarded as crucial not only in developing the economy, alongside social welfare, but also in the maintenance of a political democracy. For such a democracy to be fair to all its citizens, there needed to be a concept of national childhood, where former social class and urban–rural divisions would be rendered irrelevant.

Inevitably, the stress in school education lay on the preparation of future citizens, and the literature of child development (witness the very name) connects biological growth with social and educational progress. The whole process reached its apotheosis in England with the development of a National Curriculum, encompassing a range of Levels determined for specific years and comparing children of the same age. This model of education is linear and hierarchical; its stress is on the future, not the present. Schooling is perceived as a series of hurdles, each leading to another, ever onward and upward.

Perhaps the notion of clear stages of progression in the acquisition of knowledge has been underpinned by the pervasive theories of Jean Piaget (see Chapters 4 and 5 in this book), whose thinking has long been absorbed into teacher-training courses and, until fairly recently, been widely accepted. The theory of pre-determined stages has taken over from the less defined, more open-ended, notion of varieties of sets of experiences, each of which contributed in some way towards the development of the individual person and were valid in their own right, not merely for possible future benefits.

Such a view would be entirely consistent with an old definition of apprenticeship. It does not accord with the concept of a partnership approach envisaged at the beginning of this section. Neither does it give any credibility to the value of childhood in its own right. In seeking a middle way of accommodation, it would seem that the two concepts of *stasis* and *kinesis* need to be held simultaneously; that the period of childhood, just like the period of middle age, is regarded as both an independent time and a staging post.

With this in mind, it is appropriate to move from the social to the personal, from a view of children as apprentices trained, albeit with their compliance and involvement, to take their part in society to a view which emphasises their individual personality, their unique emotional and psychological development.

Children as persons in their own right

I rejoiced in being what I was.

(Roethke, 'The Rose', 1964)

This perspective which, like the others, cannot be wholly self-contained and discrete, is intended to indicate a view of childhood which stresses personal, individual features and the integrity, uniqueness and value of each child, both as a child and as an emergent adult. If too much attention is paid to what the child will become, then childhood itself is devalued. A balance needs to be maintained between these two tensions of being and becoming.

We have known for some time, notably through the work of Iona and Peter Opie, that children can and do act as perfectly competent social beings in contexts which are familiar and acceptable to them. What may have been a feature, though, of this realisation is the adult perspective that such socialisation is merely practice for what comes later; that child rules merely prefigure adult concepts of justice and fairness; that, in short, all is preparation for becoming. It is indeed extremely difficult to overlook this view, for obvious reasons. However, Waksler's sociological readings attempt to do just that and, in page after page of her observations and the observations of her contributors, readers have it impressed upon them that:

> Children can be viewed as fully social beings, capable of acting in the social world and of creating and sustaining their own culture.
>
> (1991: 23)

> The children I observed did not necessarily act in accordance with adult expectations of what working at an activity should look like.
>
> (1991: 193)

It was a world in which there were no lasting achievements, no possessions and no competition. It was a world of mutually exploring whatever here-and-now possibilities presented themselves – music, toys, trampolines, dressing, eating – all again novel, open and without delineable horizons for interpretation.

(1991: 160)

Such comments may have a natural attraction for those who have felt the need to re-evaluate children's status in society and to re-assess the quality and power of their early experience. Waksler's research method is that of a participant observer, trying to enter the world of childhood on the children's level, indeed, as a child. This, of course, is impossible, but the attempt, sustained over many months, bears vivid testimony to the differing perspectives of adults and children and to the need for appropriate recognition of the integrity and validity of the children's world.

Such a point is fundamental for the development of an appropriate pedagogy for young children, a pedagogy which acknowledges that, far from being uniformly empty uniform jugs waiting passively to be filled, they are, rather, different-sized, differing vessels whose different contents will be mixed with differing amounts of whatever is new. Such a stress on the development of each individual person promotes a recognition of value at each stage. Children of whatever age are no more, nor less, important than adults. As Newell says, in his argument against corporal punishment: 'Hitting people is wrong, and children are people too' (1989: ix).

They are also growing people, not merely physically but also emotionally and psychologically and, in this regard, may be valued as persons in their own right since such growth is not obvious to an observer. It occurs in the brain; it is secret and, unlike physical height, unmeasured. But it takes place, nevertheless, stealthily, and children need private mental space for it to occur. How it best occurs, whether through play, socialisation, story, myth, instruction, family life, is not the issue here and there would be many giving contrary advice on the matter. What would be less in doubt is the view, expressed in Milton's 'Paradise Regained', that: 'The childhood shows the man as morning shows the day' (1671: Book IV. l. 220).

Children as members of a distinct group

This above all; to thine own self be true:
And it must follow, as the night the day,
Thou canst not then be false to any man.

(Shakespeare, *Hamlet*, I. 3. L. 82–4)

A strong theme running through *Hamlet* is the question of identity and role, and the epigraph above comes at the end of a lengthy piece of advice by the old courtier Polonius to his son, Laertes, about relationships and how one should behave, both as an individual and in groups in society. Given the ultimate unknowability of the reality of childhood, there is something attractive in the notion that children are members of a group which, in key regard, is different from the group inhabited by adults. This view makes all kinds of assumptions, notably about the commonality of child and adult experiences. The imposition of a label (such as 'children', 'middle-aged', 'retired', 'the black/white community', 'students') can have the same effect as any stereotyping device; namely, it can easily discourage further thought about the individuals who are assumed to compose 'the group'. It can also provide a convenient mechanism by which disparate and possibly disturbing, thoughts can be side-stepped, allowing the mind the comforting illusion that anarchic and elusive experience has been tamed.

So, again, as with the perspectives on childhood described earlier, this view also needs to hold at least two strains in tension. One is the retention of the crucial notion, at least in western educational thought, of the particular individuality of each child. The other is the notion that certain people, of a certain age, in a certain context, do share certain experiences and may legitimately be thought to inhabit, at least partially, similar worlds. If this were not the case, it would be impossible to talk of childhood.

With this proviso, if we assume that a group is partly defined by the exclusivity of its shared knowledge and experience, what is it that children possess which is distinct? What world, lost to adults, do they inhabit?

To begin with, there is much evidence that, in terms of cognition, attitudes to causality and interpersonal relationships, young children can be satisfactorily demarcated from adults, thereby allowing those in authority (i.e. adults) to specify what children need. In this respect, the United Nations 'Declaration of the Rights of the Child' is interesting for what it reveals, not particularly of children's so-called 'needs', but of the attitudes of its authors and of the context out of which it came. Deconstruction of its first paragraph would centre on such matters as the value judgements and assumed sets of shared beliefs, the lack of definition of large terms, the inadequacy of sociological and cultural awareness, and the linguistic insensitivity. The Declaration begins:

> The child, for the full and harmonious development of his personality, needs love and understanding. He shall, wherever possible, grow up in the care and under the responsibility of his parents, and in any case in an atmosphere of affection and moral and material security; a child of tender years shall not, save in exceptional circumstances, be separated from his mother.
>
> (United Nations, 1959: 198).

This is not to say that children do not have needs. They do, as does everyone else. It is, rather, to signal that the identification and articulation of those needs is far from being a simple matter.

In fact, the concept of 'needs' could be seen merely as shorthand for indicating authors' beliefs about childhood requirements. Different sets of views could be advanced which highlight, let us say, cultural/social class relativity, or personal psychological development.

A completely different approach which does not attempt to ascertain what children need, from an adult and developmental perspective, seeks to investigate the childhood world much as a culturally sensitive anthropologist might seek to understand the ways of an alien tribe. Such an approach is described by Tucker (1985: 6); Harré, in Richards (1986: ch. 13); Tizard, in Richards and Light (1986: ch. 11); Humphries (1988: 118); and James and Prout (1990: ch. 10). It seeks to learn about the ways in which children conduct their social relationships, to discover what their fears, interests and beliefs are and how these impact upon their lives, and to understand children's ideas and to take them seriously. Some regard the work of the Opies, already referred to, as pioneering in this regard. Others see it, however pioneering, as part of a now outmoded approach. They argue for an approach to childhood which fuses history and sociology and which accurately portrays childhood as it is. They plead for a stance which is not imperial and patronising; which does not seek to minimise complexity; which respects definitions by those within the group (i.e. children), rather than by those outside (i.e. adults).

It is for this that we value such twentieth-century prose fiction writers as Nina Bawden, Richmal Crompton, Roald Dahl, William Golding, Penelope Lively, Mark Twain and E.B. White (see Chapter 3 of this book, and Townsend, 1990). Where fairy stories deal in archetypes in a timeless, non-locatable context, these writers and others, create contemporary worlds which are recognisably modern, Western and child-centred. Each type, in some way, speaks to children.

Children as vulnerable

> The days of childhood are but days of woe
>
> (Southey, 'The Retrospect', 1795)

Predominant images on television and in newspapers of children in certain Third World countries are not of secure youngsters within loving, extended family networks, since those would hardly be considered newsworthy. The images that predominate, in a visually dramatic manner, are those of black Oxfam boys and girls with staring eyes and distended stomachs; of Brazilian street children haunted and hunted by police death squads; of Nicaraguan eight-year-old guerrilla fighters practising military drill with wooden replica guns; of young Afghan carpet weavers visually impaired by close work for long hours in appalling conditions; of Thai child prostitutes soliciting wealthy visitors as part of the flourishing tourist trade; of mutilated members of organised begging syndicates in India; of homeless refugee orphans on dusty roads or in bare institutions of country after country.

With such insistent media coverage, a differentiation is perceived between Western childhood which appears as generally wholesome and life-enhancing, and non-Western childhood, which is pitiable in image, if not in reality. If Kitzinger is to be believed, there is a strong racist element in such portrayal. As she says: 'Racism means that while a white child can represent "Childhood" the black child is only used to represent *black* child-hood, or "The Third World" or "Foreign" or "Starvation"' (1990: 158).

Such media distortion for Kitzinger is not the whole story, but merely symptomatic of the powerlessness of vulnerable children. This is a picture which reflects nineteenth-century England as well as twentieth-century Third World, and the economic exploitation brought about by the industrial revolution has been well documented in fiction and fact. Indeed, from the first Factory Act of 1802 to the present day, one could view much legislation as an ever-developing understanding of the need to protect children from cruelty on the one hand, and lack of consideration, on the other.

One assumes such legislation to have been at the heart of health reform and there is much evidence, often of a personal and anecdotal kind, that the need was great. Here, for instance, is oral historian Kathleen Dayus writing of slum conditions in the 1920s:

> Many young children died in the large families in these slums – of whooping cough, measles, chicken pox, diphtheria. It was no wonder these young children couldn't survive in these crowded conditions, breathing in the fumes from the stagnant canal that ran along the backs of these courts, where many of them went to play.
>
> (Dayus, 1993)

Such a comment links the twentieth-century worlds of north and south, and reminds us that injustice and lack of care are unconfined by time or geography. Child as vulnerable is not merely a Third World image or an outmoded Victorian concept. It can also be seen as a 1990s British reality, whether the stress is on any one of the following:

- playground bullying
- domestic violence
- sexual abuse
- consumerist advertising exploitation of childlike innocence
- racial harassment

Indeed, beginning her book with an account of the (televised) abduction and subsequent murder in 1993 of two-year old James Bulger by two ten-year old boys, Miles proceeds to catalogue a range of statistics indicating various ways in which children in the United Kingdom and in the United States have been, and are being, victimised. Even if the selection of some of her dates and statistics, together with some of the value judgements

25

accompanying them, might be questionable, the accumulation of data is such that a strong polemical case is made out, arguing that the situation is fast deteriorating and that the adults are to blame. This conclusion is fore-shadowed in the emotive title of her book, *The Children We Deserve: Love and Hate in the Making of the Family* (1994).

In the main, Miles writes about children who are physically able-bodied, even though some of them may be emotionally and psychologically scarred. What of the so-called 'special needs' children who, through some physical or mental condition, may be denied a full or appropriate place in society? Surely these are more vulnerable than many others?

Without denying the validity of their childhood experiences or adopting a patronising attitude, it does seem legitimate to regard them as more vulnerable, in the sense that many of them inhabit a world to which they have to accommodate more than do most children, and which hardly accommodates to them.

Such children are within the psycho-medical construction of childhood and, therefore, outside or on the periphery of mainstream society. Perhaps they experience, in extreme form, those fears, anxieties, uncertainties and vulnerabilities to which all people are subject.

Indeed, merely to scan the contents list of Varma's edited collection (1992) is to be reminded, not only of the hidden world inhabited by many 'victims', but also of how many different kinds of victim there may be. Any twentieth-century construction of childhood would be incomplete without this representation. It is a perspective on childhood which may sit ill with more positive stances, and is all the more valuable for that.

Child as animal

> David ... if I have an obstinate horse or dog to deal with ... I beat him
> (Dickens, *David Copperfield*, 1850)

Apart from the obvious biological fact that humans have much in common with animals, there seem to be two main influences which appear to have emphasised the relationship. One is the advocacy of certain writers on child-rearing practices (and how different that phrase is from a translation such as, 'How To Bring Up Your Baby'). The other influence seems to be that of certain sociologists who equate socialisation with civilisation, and who assume a less than human state in their young subjects.

A powerful influence in the 1930s on the upbringing of children was F. Truby King who advocated a rigid system and routine designed to result in the mastery of the child by the mother: 'A real Truby King baby is one whose mother brings it up strictly according to the Truby King system' (1934: 4). The emphasis in King's advice was on discipline, structure, authority and rigidity, analogous to training a dog or breaking in a horse (even if with less of the terror generated by Mr Murdstone for David

Copperfield in the epigraph above). King conveyed absolute conviction in the rightness of his methods:

> A real Truby King baby is completely breast-fed till the ninth month, with a gradual introduction to solid foods. Truby King babies are fed four-hourly from birth, with few exceptions, and they do not have any night feeds. A Truby King baby has as much fresh air and sunshine as possible, and the right amount of sleep. His education begins from the very first week, good habits being established which remain all his life. He is not treated as a plaything, made to laugh and crow and show off.
>
> (1934: 4)

One cannot fail to notice the brand loyalty emphasis ('Truby King baby'), in alliance with male authority and the puritanical element of the last sentence. There is no scope here for tentativeness and variation, no sense that we are dealing with individual persons who have preferences, personalities and idiosyncrasies. But inexperienced parents were, to judge from the sales of King's books, only too ready to be told what to do, despite any misgivings they might have had. These misgivings were addressed by later 'child experts' such as Dr Spock, whose stress is on warm relationships, individual judgement and personal confidence, fun and enjoyment within the mother–baby bond. Such a bond exists in some form or other between most animal creatures, but to stress the animal connections is to undermine the human relationships. Thus, Darwin writes: 'I was at first surprised at humour being appreciated by an infant only a little above three months old, but we should remember how very early puppies and kittens begin to play' (1877: 285).

A hundred years later, Schaffer writes of the 'bonnet-reared child' and the 'pigtail parent' (1977: 110). Bonnets and pigtails are species of monkey, the former being gregarious and the latter exclusive. Later still, Nanny Smith, dispensing advice to *Daily Telegraph* readers, writes: 'At two years, babies are like little animals – if they want something they will take it and if they are frustrated they will push and hit' (21 January 1995).

Such remarks across the years offer some small testimony to the link in adult perception between children and animals, but they are insignificant when compared with the impact of Victoire, the famous wild boy of Aveyron, documented initially in the journals of Jean Itard (1801) and later in François Truffaut's film *L'Enfant Sauvage* (1969). Here was a feral child, quite at home in the wild, having apparently adjusted satisfactorily to life in a non-human setting. Here, too, was an eighteenth-century French educationist, determined to teach Victoire human communication skills and behaviour. Their encounter was lengthy and well-documented; their experiment was a failure, in that Victoire was unable to adapt to the human environment. No doubt Itard would similarly have failed had he been the one required to adapt. Whatever the lessons to be drawn from the case, the

27

human–animal dimension seems to have captured the imagination (both in film and in print) and the relationship of mankind to the animal world became further embedded in mythology.

Victoire was regarded by Itard as incomplete. Young children in modern society are often so regarded by those professionally responsible for their education and upbringing.

Book learning, along with language and reason; the products of a creative and civilised culture; a record of history and a sense of its significance; an ability to reflect upon experience; control of emotions and desires; a sense of morality and justice: these are some of the features which distinguish humans from animals. Where such ingredients are absent from a construction of childhood, the scope for diminishing human nature is expanded. The concept of a self-fulfilling prophecy is pertinent here. As Trigg puts it:

> Perhaps just as important as the kind of beings we are is the kind we think we are. The ideas we have of ourselves govern the way we live our lives ... Ideas of human nature are the most potent ideas there are.
>
> (1994: 169)

Such labels provide, I believe, the necessary balance between limitation and open-endedness. They are, moreover, rich enough in metaphor and association to be capable of legitimately absorbing a range of insights and perspectives, and this will be demonstrated throughout this book.

Above all, perhaps, they are not tied to an historical period and, in this regard it is worth attempting to define the current emphasis and to say which of these categories seems to predominate in the late twentieth century. This issue will emerge in detail in later sections of this Reader. Suffice it to say at this point that, while a highly positive picture emerges about the relatively recent past, 'the current historical moment' may be described as one of 'child panic' (Wallace, 1995: 285).

If any consistency of view may be discerned, it seems to lie in the process of trying to catch the indefinable essence of childhood, rather than in any result one might obtain; the journey, not the destination, is significant. Inevitably, like the phenomenon they seek to describe, commentators are elusive. Psychoanalyst Adam Phillips, for instance, writes: 'Adulthood, one could say, is when it begins to occur to you that you may not be leading a charmed life' (1993: 82). Educationist Philip Gamage (1992) speaks of the: 'happiness, creativity, immediacy, serendipity' of an individual child. Novelist Thomas Keneally writes of his book, *Homebush Boy*: 'The past is ever-present, like a train running on a parallel track, and we can see the old faces clearly in the windows opposite' (Falcone, 1995: 3).

It is this strange harmony of 'stasis' and 'kinesis' that is reflected in the categories I have chosen and which have been described above. To continue the scientific language for a moment, defining childhood might be analogous to defining energy, that is, something which cannot be created or destroyed but is merely changed from one form to another. The search is not for the 'reality' of childhood, for that itself is an illusion. As Peter Abbs puts it in his poem of 'The Other Child':

> I cannot find the child I was. Nothing
> Coheres. Or coincides. Or rhymes.
> The school door's locked; the place is out of bounds.
> A pensive boy inside does not turn round.
>
> (1995)

Appendix

Further perspectives

There are many possible ways in which social constructions of childhood may be labelled. I will list four sets, apart from those I have described in detail.

Benton (1996) cites seven representations:

- 'the polite child'
- 'the impolite child'
- 'the innocent child'
- 'the sinful child'
- 'the authentic child'
- 'the sanitized child'
- 'the holy child'

He justifies such labels with support from the two disciplines of art and literature and, in doing so, acknowledges, although not uncritically, the seminal work of Ariès (1960). In building on this work, Benton helps to redress the balance of neglect of a most interesting area of investigation, i.e. the representation of children in art. He draws on paintings by Blake, Hogarth, Steen, Reynolds, Gainsborough, Millais and others to illustrate (literally) how children and childhood have been variously perceived, and how the skills of literary criticism may be appropriately applied to consideration of paintings.

Brown (1993) describes six constructs:

- 'the child of reason'
- 'the child of faith'
- 'the exploited child'
- 'the child at home'
- 'the childhood self'
- 'the child of conflict'

The focus for Brown's work is nineteenth-century English literature and particularly the novels of female writers whom she considers to have been neglected in this regard, such as George Eliot, Charlotte Brontë, Elizabeth Gaskell, Juliana Ewing and Maria Edgeworth. A key justification for this approach lies in Brown's assessment of Victorian consciousness, including the social and spiritual concerns of the age, the marginalising and power-lessness of women, which promoted the need for self-recognition and assertion in some acceptable form, and the 'lingering nostalgia for their own lost childhood in the face of the increasing materialism of the indus-trial age' (1993: 61).

Hendrick (in James and Prout, 1990: 35–59) looks more to traditional historical sources and, in his survey from 1800 to the present day, chooses the labels of:

- 'the romantic child'
- 'the evangelical child'
- 'the factory child'
- 'the delinquent child'
- 'the schooled child'
- 'the psycho-medical child'
- 'the welfare child'
- 'the psychological child'
- 'the family child and the public child'

Most of these categories reflect the historical tradition from which they stem, and there is little obvious overlap with either Benton or Brown. Acknowledging the 'numerous perceptions of childhood, which have been produced over the last two hundred years or so', Hendrick grounds each of his constructs firmly in their historical time and context; they are responses to 'the social, economic, religious and political challenges of their respec-tive eras' (1990: 36).

Jenks identifies the following categories:

- 'the child as savage'
- 'the natural child'
- 'the social child'
- 'the Dionysian child'
- 'the Apollonian child'

In the first three cases, the main impetus for such categorisation is sociological and anthropological, rather than artistic, literary or historical. As Jenks puts it: 'Any view of the child reflects a preferred, but unexplored, model of the social order' (1996: 9). The last two cases, which Jenks characterises as 'images' rather than 'literal descriptions' (1996: 74), owe more to religion and aesthetics (but see also Neill Thew's comment on Jenks in Chapter 7 of this volume).

It is clear that many permutations are possible, depending on:

- the sources from which they are drawn;
- the consistency within and between the concepts;
- the purposes they seek to achieve;
- the level of personal and academic satisfaction they provide for the writer.

In three of the four instances just cited, there is a strong chronological element. It is not unvarying, but it is too noticeable to be overlooked. In my proposed categories, there is no reflection of a chronological sequence since my intention is to present a contemporary view. Perhaps the image of a prism is appropriate, where the various angles of vision produce differing perceptions. But more than this, what is seen depends on the viewer and the viewer's experience. Whatever we search for and find is, to some degree, determined by who we are and what our interests are.

Review questions and tasks

1 Six perspectives of childhood have been described in the chapter. What are the main characteristics of each one?

2 Which academic disciplines seem to have been most significant in arriving at each of the six perspectives?

3 In what ways, if any, does each of the six perspectives match your own personal experience?

4 To what extent, if any, do you share:

    a Bettelheim's views on the value of fairy stories?
    b Postman's beliefs on the dangers of television?
    c Truby King's attitudes towards the rearing of children?
    d Abbs's notion of the impossibility of recovering childhood?

5 In seeking to understand the world(s) of childhood, which kind of writing do you believe has more to offer and why: fact or fiction?

6 Tape record an interview with a friend in which you ask about childhood experiences and memories. On listening to the tape, make notes on your thoughts and impressions and, if possible, discuss these with your friend.

Further reading

James, A. and Prout, A. (eds) (1990) *Constructing and Reconstructing Childhood: Contemporary Issues in the Sociological Study of Childhood*, London: Falmer Press. First published in 1990 and now in its second edition of 1997, this edited work draws on the research of eleven scholars who represent the disciplines of anthropology, history and sociology, and have between them a range of European, North American and South American experience. As such, it not only provides a thorough grounding in what these disciplines have to offer but also in the research methods by which those offerings came about, juxtaposing qualitative and quantitative data in digestible form.

Ransom, D. (ed.) (1998) *Eye to Eye: Childhood*, Oxford: New Internationalist. In large format, with life-affirming colour photographs, this mainly prose anthology draws on the work of major writers from Africa, South America, the Middle East and the Far East. Jung Chang, Anita Desai, Nadine Gordimer, Camara Laye, Arundhati Roy and Wole Soyinka are among the best known, but there are many others who reflect on their own real or fictional childhoods. Above all, perhaps, Ben Okri provides an introduction which is full of teasing, tantalising ideas and assertions. Here is a taste, as Okri writes:

> Childhood is the Nile of life; it is the Eden, the Atlantis; the living emblem of mysterious places, vanished origins, lost beginnings, all that haunts because never to be found again. It is the celebrated place of innocence, of the first evils, of the first falls, of the first sufferings, of the first floods, and of the first civilisations within each human spirit.
>
> (1998: 11)

Rosen, M. (ed.) (1994) *The Penguin Book of Childhood*, London: Viking Penguin. This rich anthology spans four thousand years, from an ancient Egyptian inscription of advice ('Spend no day in idleness') of 2000 BC to a *Guardian* newspaper report of 1994 about children left alone after school. It also spans most continents and many cultures with prose, drama, poetry and song extracts from young children and adults, rich and poor, happy and unhappy. Such a wide compass highlights the universality of much childhood experience, and the sense of common humanity. For those concerned about falling standards, here is Socrates (469–399 BC): 'Children today love luxury too much. They have execrable manners, flaunt authority, have no respect for their elders … What kind of awful creatures will they be when they grow up'?

Waksler, F.C. (ed.) (1991) *Studying the Social Worlds of Children: Sociological Readings*, London: Falmer Press. This edited collection is mainly the work of sociologists, but also has material from teachers and freelance writers. Its strength lies in its attempt to enter the world of children, by participant observation, by tape recording and transcription and by empathic involvement and understanding. Accordingly, many of the chapters draw directly on children's words and actions and attempt, in a qualitative manner, to see things from the children's perspective. As Waksler herself comments: 'Phenomenology emphasises the importance of conducting studies from the point of view of those being studied and encourages researchers to suspend judgements about those studied' (1991: 239).

Wullschläger, J. (1995) *Inventing Wonderland: The Lives and Fantasies of Lewis Carroll, Edward Lear, J.M. Barrie, Kenneth Grahame and A.A. Milne,* **London: Methuen.** As the sub-title indicates, this book links the biographies and invented worlds of the great British male figures of the Golden Age of children's literature. It does not do so in any simplistic way of matching art with life but, nevertheless, does highlight some intriguing similarities in the lives of these significant Victorian and Edwardian eccentrics. This helps us to focus on some of the major concerns in their writing. Four of the five had unhappy or unfulfilled childhoods and, invariably, problematic adult lives. They suffered rejection of some sort, often with devastating consequences. They were uneasy with adult or, in some cases, female company and, correspondingly, at ease with children. The exception is A.A. Milne, who had a very happy childhood, but then ironically suffered in later years with the burden of Pooh's disproportionate fame, while his son suffered from mockery as the eponymous Christopher Robin.

References

Abbs, P. (1995) *Personae,* London: Skoob Books.

Ariès, P. (1996) *Centuries of Childhood,* London: Pimlico, first published in France in 1960.

Avery, G. (1965) *Nineteenth-Century Children: Heroes and Heroines in English Children's Stories 1780–1900,* London: Hodder & Stoughton.

—— (1975) *Childhood's Pattern: A Study of the Heroes and Heroines of Children's Fiction 1770–1950,* London: Hodder & Stoughton.

Bennett, A. (1994) *Writing Home,* London: Quality Paperbacks Direct.

Benton, M. (1996) 'The Image of Childhood: Representations of the Child in Painting and Literature, 1700–1900' in *Children's Literature in Education,* vol. 27, no. 1, March, 35–61.

Bernstein, B. and Brannen, J. (1996) *Children, Research and Policy,* London: Taylor & Francis.

Bettelheim, B. (1991) *The Uses of Enchantment: The Meaning and Importance of Fairy Tales,* Harmondsworth: Penguin. First published in Great Britain by Thames & Hudson, 1976.

Boyden, J. (1990) 'Childhood and the Policy Makers: A Comparative Perspective on the Globalization of Childhood', in A. James and A. Prout (eds), *Constructing and Reconstructing Childhood. Contemporary Issues in the Sociological Study of Childhood,* London: Falmer Press, ch. 9, 184–215.

Brown, P. (1993) *The Captured World. The Child and Childhood in Nineteenth Century Women's Writing in England,* Hemel Hempstead: Harvester Wheatsheaf.

Carpenter, H. (1985) *Secret Gardens: A Study of the Golden Age of Children's Literature,* London: Allen & Unwin.

Carpenter, H. and Prichard, M. (1995) *The Oxford Companion to Children's Literature,* Oxford: Oxford University Press.

Coe, R.N. (1984) *When the Grass Was Taller: Autobiography and the Experience of Childhood,* New Haven, CN: Yale University Press.

Cottingham, M., Brookes, B. and Stewart, S. (1997) *A Sporting Chance: Tackling Child Labour in India's Sports Goods Industry,* London: Christian Aid.

Coveney, P. (1967) *The Image of Childhood: The Individual and Society, a Study of the Theme in English Literature*, Harmondsworth: Penguin; first published in 1957 as *Poor Monkey*.

Crockett, S.R. (1895) *Sweetheart Travellers*, quoted by G. Avery (1965).

Cunningham, H. (1991) *The Children of the Poor*, Oxford: Blackwell.

—— (1995) *Children and Childhood in Western Society Since 1500*, Harlow: Longman.

Dainville, Père de (1940) *La Naissance de l'Humanisme Moderne*, quoted by N. Postman (1983).

Darwin, C. (1877) 'A Biographical Sketch of an Infant', *Mind*, vol. 2, 285–94.

Davin, A. (1996) *Growing Up Poor: Home, School and Street in London, 1870–1914*, London: Rivers Oram Press.

Dayus, K. (1993) *The People of Lavender Court*, London: Virago.

Dickens, C. (1850) *David Copperfield*, Oxford: Oxford University Press, 1987.

—— (1854) *Hard Times*, Oxford: Oxford University Press, 1987.

Dickinson, C.M. (*n.d*) 'The Children', in B.E. Stevenson (ed.), *The Home Book of Verse*, New York: Holt, Rinehard & Winston, 1962, 250–1.

Donaldson, M. (1978) *Children's Minds*, Glasgow: Fontana Collins.

Doyle, C. (1995) *Helping Strategies in Child Sexual Abuse*, London: Whiting & Birch, in association with the National Children's Bureau.

Dudgeon, P. (1992) *The Country Child: An Illustrated Reminiscence*, London: Book Club Associates and Headline.

Eliot, G. (1985) *The Mill on the Floss*, Harmondsworth: Penguin, first published 1860.

—— (1944) *Silas Marner*, Harmondsworth: Penguin, first published 1861.

Elkind, D. (1989) 'Developmentally Appropriate Education for 4-Year-Olds', *Theory into Practice*, vol. 28., no. 1, 47–52.

Erasmus, D. (1532) *De Civilitate Morium Puerilium*, in J.K. Sowards (ed.), *Collected Works of Erasmus*, vol. 25, Toronto: University of Toronto Press, 1985.

Falcone, B. (ed.) (1995) *The Good Book Guide*, vol. 84, London: Peter Braithwaite.

Forward, S. and Buck, C.(1981) *Betrayal of Innocence: Incest and its Devastation*, Harmondsworth: Penguin.

Gamage, P. (1992) 'Quality: the Tension Between Content and Process', *Standing Conference on Education and Training of Teachers* (SCETT), Occasional Paper No. 1.

Goldson, B. (1997) 'Childhood: An Introduction to Historical and Theoretical Analyses', in P. Scraton (ed.), *'Childhood' in 'Crisis'?*, London: University College of London Press, ch. 1, 1–27.

Goode, D.A. (1991) 'Kids, Culture and Innocents', in F.C. Waksler (ed.), *Studying the Social Worlds of Children: Sociological Readings*, London: Falmer Press, ch. 11, 145–60.

Harré, R. (1986) 'The step to social constructionism', in M. Richards and P. Light (eds), *Children of Social Worlds: Development in a Social Context*, Cambridge: Polity Press, ch. 13, 287–96.

Hart, W.A. (1993) 'Children are not Meant to be Studied,' *Journal of Philosophy of Education*, vol. 27, no. 1.

Hemans, F.D. (1876) *The Poetical Works of Mrs Hemans*, London: Frederick Warne & Co.

Hendrick, H. (1990) 'Constructions and Reconstructions of British Childhood: An Interpretative Survey, 1800 to the Present', in A. James and A. Prout (eds), *Constructing and Reconstructing Childhood: Contemporary Issues in the Sociological Study of Childhood*, London: Falmer Press, 35–59.

Heywood, J. (1970) *Child in Care*, 2nd edn, London: Routledge & Kegan Paul.

Higgins, R. (1992) 'The Secret Life of the Depressed Child', in V.P. Varma (ed.), *The Secret Life of Vulnerable Children*, London: Routledge, ch. 1, 1–19.

Hilton, M. (ed.) (1996) *Potent Fictions: Children's Literacy and the Challenge of Popular Culture*, London: Routledge.

Holland, P. (1992) *What is a Child? Popular Images of Childhood*, London: Virago.

Humphries, S., Mack, J. and Perks, R. (1988) *A Century of Childhood*, London: Sidgwick & Jackson.

Hunt, E.H. (1981) *British Labour History, 1815–1914*, London: Weidenfeld & Nicolson.

Itard, J.M.G. (1801) *Of the First Developments of the Young Savage of Aveyron*, in L. Malson (ed.), *Wolf Children and the Problem of Human Nature*, New York: New Left Books, 1972.

James, A. and Prout, A. (eds) (1990) *Constructing and Reconstructing Childhood: Contemporary Issues in the Sociological Study of Childhood*, London: Falmer Press; 2nd edn, 1997.

Janus, S. (1981) *The Death of Innocence*, New York: Morrow.

Jenks, C. (1996) *Childhood*, London: Routledge.

Jones, S. (1994) *The Language of the Genes*, London: Flamingo.

Joseph, S. (1993) 'Childhood Revisited: Possibilities and Predicaments in New Research Agendas', *British Journal of Sociology of Education*, vol. 14, no. 1, 113–21.

Keneally, T. (1995) *Homebush Boy*, London: Hodder.

King, F. Truby (1934) *Mothercraft*, Sydney: Whitcombe and Tombs.

Kitzinger, J. (1990) 'Who Are You Kidding? Children, Power and the Struggle Against Sexual Abuse', in A. James and A. Prout (eds), *Constructing and Reconstructing Childhood: Contemporary Issues in the Sociological Study of Childhood*, London: Falmer Press, ch. 8, 157–84.

La Fontaine, J. (1986) 'An Anthropological Perspective on Children in Social Worlds', in M. Richards and P. Light (eds), *Children of Social Worlds: Development in a Social Context*, Cambridge: Polity Press, ch. 1, 10–30.

Locke, J. (1693) *Some Thoughts Concerning Education*, cited in G. Boas, *The Cult of Childhood*, Dallas, TX: Spring Publications, 43.

MacCabe, C. (1995) 'Tradition, Too, Has its Place in Cultural Studies', *Times Literary Supplement*, 26 May, 13.

Mackay, R.W. (1973) 'Conceptions of Children and Models of Socialisation', in F.C. Waksler (ed.), *Studying the Social Worlds of Children: Sociological Readings*, London: Falmer Press, ch. 3, 23–37.

Masterman, L. (1986) *Teaching the Media*, London: Comedia.

Mause, L. de (ed.) (1991) *The History of Childhood: The Untold Story of Child Abuse*, London: Bellew; first published 1974.

Mayhew, H. (1851) *London Labour and the London Poor*, in P. Quennell (ed.), *Mayhew's London*, London: Hamlyn, 1969.

Meek, M., Warlow, A. and Barton, G. (1977) *The Cool Web: The Pattern of Children's Reading*, London: Bodley Head.

Miles, R. (1994) *The Children We Deserve: Love and Hate in the Making of the Family*, London: HarperCollins.

Milton, J. (1671) 'Paradise Regained', in *The Poetical Works of John Milton*, London: Collins.

Moore, M., Sixsmith, J. and Knowles, K. (1996) *Children's Reflections on Family Life*, London: Falmer Press.

Mussen, P.H., Conger, J.J. and Kagan, J. (1963) *Child Development and Personality*, New York: Harper & Row.

Newell, P. (1989) *Children Are People Too: The Case Against Physical Punishment*, London: Bedford Square Press.

Opie, I. and Opie, P. (1959) *The Lore and Language of Schoolchildren*, Oxford: Oxford University Press.

—— (1984) *Children's Games in Street and Playground*, Oxford: Oxford University Press.

Phillips, A. (1993) *On Kissing Tickling and Being Bored: Psychoanalytic Essays on the Unexamined Life*, London: Faber & Faber.

Piaget, J. (1926) *The Language and Thought of the Child*, London: Routledge & Kegan Paul.

—— (1958) *The Child's Construction of Reality*, London: Routledge & Kegan Paul.

Plewis, I. (1996) 'Young Children at School: Inequalities and the National Curriculum', in B. Bernstein and J. Brannen (eds), *Children, Research and Policy*, London: Taylor & Francis, ch. 7, 136–48.

Plotz, J. (1988) 'The Disappearance of Childhood: Parent-Child Role Reversals', *Children's Literature in Education*, vol. 19, no. 1, 67–79.

Polakow, V. (1992) *The Erosion of Childhood*, Chicago: University of Chicago Press.

Pollock, L. (1983) *Forgotten Children: Parent-Child Relationships from 1500 to 1900*, Cambridge: Cambridge University Press.

Postman, N. (1983) *The Disappearance of Childhood*, London: W.H. Allen.

Ransom, D. (ed.) (1998) *Eye to Eye: Childhood*, Oxford: New Internationalist.

Richards, M. and Light, P. (eds) (1986) *Children of Social Worlds: Development in a Social Context*, Cambridge: Polity Press.

Roethke, T. (1964) 'The Rose', in B. Roethke (ed.), *The Collected Poems of Theodore Roethke*, London: Faber & Faber, 1968, 205.

Rose, L. (1991) *The Erosion of Childhood: Child Oppression in Britain, 1860–1918*, London: Routledge.

Rosen, M. (ed.) (1994) *The Penguin Book of Childhood*, London: Viking Penguin.

Rousseau, J.J. (1762) *Émile*, trans. B. Foxley, London: Dent & Sons, 1961.

Sacks, J. (1995) 'Finding Our Way Back to the Family', *The Independent*, 6 March, 13; based on *Faith in the Future*, London: Darton, Longman & Todd.

Schaffer, H.R. (1977) *Mothering*, London: Open Books.

Scraton, P. (ed.) (1997) *'Childhood' in 'Crisis'?*, London: University College of London Press.

Shakespeare, W. (1604) *Hamlet*, ed. G.B. Harrison, Harmondsworth: Penguin, 1962.

Shipman, M.D. (1972) *Childhood: A Sociological Perspective*, Windsor: National Foundation for Educational Research.

Singleton, R. (ed.) (1995) *The Facts of Life: The Changing Face of Childhood*, Ilford: Barnardos.

Smith, J. (1995) 'Nanny Smith Answers Questions From Parents', *Daily Telegraph*, 21 January, *The Telegraph Magazine*, 9.

Sommerville, C.J. (1982) *The Rise and Fall of Childhood*, London: Sage.

Southey, R. (1795) 'The Retrospect', in *Poems of Robert Southey*, ed. M.H. Fitzgerald, London: Oxford University Press, 1909, 405ff.

Spock, B. (1955) *Baby and Child Care*, London: Bodley Head.

Stacey, C. (1989) 'How to Get Ahead', *Options*, November, 26–7.

Steedman, C. (1990) *Childhood, Culture and Class in Britain: Margaret McMillan, 1860–1931*, London: Virago.

—— (1995) *Strange Dislocations: Childhood and the Idea of Human Interiority, 1780–1930*, London: Virago.

Styles, M., Bearne, E. and Watson, V. (eds) (1996) *Voices Off: Texts, Contexts and Readers*, London: Cassell.

Tillyard, S. (1994) *Aristocrats: Caroline, Emily, Louisa and Sarah Lennox 1740–1832*, London: Chatto and Windus.

Tizard, B. (1986) 'The Impact of the Nuclear Threat on Children's Development', in M. Richards and P. Light (eds), *Children of Social Worlds: Development in a Social Context*, Cambridge: Polity Press, ch. 11, 236–57.

Tomlinson, J. (1991) 'Attitudes to Children: Are Children Valued?', *Early Years*, vol. 11, no. 2, Spring, 40.

Townsend, J.R. (1990) *Written for Children*, London: Bodley Head; first published 1965.

Trigg, R. (1994) *Ideas of Human Nature: An Historical Introduction*, Oxford: Blackwell.

Troyna, B. and Hatcher, R. (1992) *Racism in Children's Lives: A Study of Mainly White Primary Schools*, London: Routledge, in association with The National Children's Bureau.

Tucker, N. (1985) 'The Experience of Childhood in Adult and Children's Literature', *School Librarian*, vol. 33, no. 1, 5–11.

—— (1991) *The Child and the Book: A Psychological and Literary Exploration*, Cambridge: Cambridge University Press; first published 1981.

United Nations (1959) 'Declaration of the Rights of the Child', in *Resolution 1386 (XIV), Yearbook of the United Nations*, New York: United Nations, 198.

Varma, V.P. (1992) *The Secret Life of Vulnerable Children*, London: Routledge.

Vipan, T. (1994) 'Dealing With Domestic Violence', *Children Today*, Autumn/Winter, pp. 6–7.

Wadsworth, M.E.J. (1991) *The Imprint of Time: Childhood, History and Adult Life*, Oxford: Clarendon Press.

Waksler, F.C. (ed.) (1991) *Studying the Social Worlds of Children: Sociological Readings*, London: Falmer Press.

—— (1996) *The Little Trials of Childhood and Children's Strategies for Dealing with Them*, London: Falmer Press.

Wallace, J. (1995) 'Technologies of "the Child": Towards a Theory of the Child-Subject', *Textual Practice*, vol. 9, no. 2, Summer.

Wallbank, S. (1992) 'The Secret World of Bereaved Children', in V.P. Varma (ed.), *The Secret Life of Vulnerable Children*, London: Routledge, 62–75.

Walvin, J. (1982) *A Child's World: A Social History of English Childhood*, Harmondsworth: Penguin.

Warner, M. (1995) *From the Beast to the Blonde: On Fairy Tales and Their Tellers*, London: Vintage.

Williams, C. (1993) 'Who are "Street Children"? A Hierarchy of Street Use and Appropriate Responses', *Child Abuse and Neglect*, vol. 17, no. 6, November–December, 831–41.

Winn, M. (1984) *Children Without Childhood*, Harmondsworth: Penguin.

Wolff, S. (1989) *Childhood and Human Nature: The Development of Personality*, London: Routledge.

Woodhead, M. (1990) 'Psychology and the Cultural Construction of Children's Needs', in A. James and A. Prout (eds), *Constructing and Reconstructing Childhood: Contemporary Issues in the Sociological Study of Childhood*, London: Falmer Press, 60–77.

Wringe, C.A. (1981) *Children's Rights: A Philosophical Study*, London: Routledge & Kegan Paul.

Wullschläger, J. (1995) *Inventing Wonderland: The Lives and Fantasies of Lewis Carroll, Edward Lear, J.M. Barrie, Kenneth Grahame and A.A. Milne*, London: Methuen.

Yeats, W.B. (1899) 'He Wishes for the Cloths of Heaven', in A.N. Jeffares (ed.), *W.B. Yeats. Selected Poetry*, London: Macmillan, 1965, 35.

Part Two

Literature

Chapter 2

The child in nineteenth-century literature

Jean Mills

Summary

This chapter surveys the theme of childhood in literature, initially by noting early representations, then by focusing on the contribution of selected nineteenth-century authors within the context of two significant constructs of the period: original sin and original innocence. It proceeds to develop the focus in detail by examining three mid-century fictional autobiographies: *David Copperfield*, *Jane Eyre* and *The Mill on the Floss*. Finally, there is a commentary on a particular aspect, the child's imagination, and how it is represented through the image of the child as reader.

> The two slight youthful figures soon grew indistinct on the distant road – were soon lost behind the projecting hedgerow. They had gone forth together into their new life of sorrow, and they would never more see the sunshine undimmed by remembered cares. They had entered the thorny wilderness, and the golden gates of their childhood had for ever closed behind them.

Thus George Eliot, in closing the second book of *The Mill on the Floss* (1860: 178), offers us a perspective on childhood that operates on several levels and seeks to control our imaginative response in several ways:

- she guides our viewpoint in the manner of a film camera, by directing our attention to the figures of Maggie and Tom Tulliver disappearing into the distance;
- she adjusts our emotional response by calling for our compassion with the words 'slight' and 'youthful';
- she echoes the theme of lack of fulfilment by the terms 'indistinct' and 'lost';
- she gives us the view of the characters of their predicament which is again a blend of a visual and an emotional response: 'they would never more see the sunshine undimmed by remembered cares';
- she takes for granted that there is a separation between the world of the child and the adult;
- she suggests, by the intertextual reference to Milton's 'Paradise Lost' ('golden gates'), that the childhood state is a lost Garden of Eden to which one can never return;
- she metaphorically evokes the notion that life is a journey by placing her figures on a road in which the central figures travel from one stage to the next, or, in this case, face a series of trials. 'Children ... are "on their way" (the journey metaphor is a recurrent one)' (Rose, 1992: 13).

These elements combine to convey a tone of nostalgia and regret.

I have opened this chapter in this way for several reasons. I intend to go on to highlight particular themes that are reflected here, and to draw your attention to some of the features of different writers. But, as in the extract above, I want to do this by encouraging you from the start to examine texts closely. I want also to indicate ways in which you, as reader, can approach the subject of childhood in texts of the nineteenth century.

However, as the chapter heading indicates, this is by no means a straightforward undertaking. Before the themes can be addressed, certain issues in dealing with this topic must also be resolved. One immediate concern is the size of the undertaking. Images of children appear not just in a part of one novel but in a range of prose and poetry over a period of one hundred years, a period when, it is estimated, 40,000 novels were published, with 'an extraordinarily large number [remaining] in the common currency of popular, rather than scholarly, reading habits' (Cunningham, 1992: 93).

The first issue, then, is choice; a choice for me in providing a focus for you, reader, (as Brontë or Eliot might say in authorial mode) and a choice for you when, after reading this chapter, you wish to explore the area further. Thus, does one choose 'classic' prose and poetry from the canon of English literature – material by Wordsworth, Coleridge, Dickens, Emily Brontë – or does one introduce previously neglected and underrated authors and genres? Should I attempt a survey of the whole period, or use one author as an exemplar?

As the references at the end of the chapter indicate, others have made this choice before me and, in doing so, they both provide you with excellent sources to pursue your interests in greater depth and also indicate a change in critical approaches. Thus, Coveney (1967) focuses almost exclusively on such figures as William Blake, Charles Dickens, Henry James and D.H. Lawrence, while Brown (1993) concentrates on the number of women writing prose for children, as well as adults, and also considers autobiographical works (as does Coe, 1984). Selection can denote ideology. As Brown says of Coveney in her survey of previous critical texts, 'it is deeply disturbing that ... the other women writers he discusses are always compared in pejorative terms' (1993: 2). For Banerjee, 'the original title of his [Coveney's] work, *Poor Monkey*, reveals his bias and he is widely misread' (1996: xviii). These other sources, then, must be read with an appreciation and acknowledgement of their particular standpoints.

So to my selective focus. Since, as we have already seen, it is impossible to be comprehensive in a chapter of this length, my alternative aim is to indicate ways of reading certain texts and, at the same time, to highlight what I consider to be key images in them. I thus intend:

- to consider the portrayal of children prior to the nineteenth century (which is covered more extensively by Banerjee, 1996, and Pattinson, 1978);
- to note the climate of ideas which influenced that portrayal subsequently;
- to comment on child perspectives;
- to concentrate on the contribution of three mid-period novelists: Charlotte Brontë, Charles Dickens and George Eliot, in the novels, *Jane Eyre* (1847), *David Copperfield* (1850) and *The Mill on the Floss* (1860), all drawing on autobiography, all writing within the genre of the *bildungsroman* – the novel of growth – and all, as we will see below, reflecting Wordsworthian and/or evangelical influences;
- to present my own commentary on a feature of all three novels, namely, children as readers.

Beginnings

Let us return to the George Eliot passage above. Are the elements I have picked out innovations, or are they rather not 'new things but in new ways'? Such is the controlling authorial presence of this writer, the conventions she employs and, possibly, one's response to 'classic' literature that one could be tempted to focus exclusively and unreflectingly on that period of early to late nineteenth-century England when the figure of the child 'emerges from comparative unimportance to become the focus of an unprecedented literary interest' (Coveney, 1967: 29), 'and the theme of childhood became [an] immensely popular literary topic(s)' (Brown, 1993: 1).

In particular, such is the familiarity of the responses evoked by this passage and the way these notions are embedded, particularly in British culture, that it is possible to ignore earlier powerful portrayals of children in literature, the ways in which child figures are used to engage our emotions and to disregard examples of particular motifs. The number and variety of child figures in nineteenth-century writing should not mislead us into thinking that children did not appear in a significant way at all prior to this, or that English literature has a cultural monopoly of this theme. Homer in *The Iliad* (700 BC) describes Hector taking leave of his wife and baby son before he fights Achilles outside the walls of Troy:

> As he finished, glorious Hector held out his arms to take his boy. But the child shrank back with a cry to the bosom of his girdled nurse, alarmed by his father's appearance. He was frightened by the bronze of the helmet and the horsehair plume he saw nodding grimly down at him. His father and his lady mother had to laugh. But noble Hector quickly took his helmet off and put the dazzling thing on the ground. Then he kissed his son, dandled him in his arms and prayed to Zeus.
>
> (translated Rieu, 1986: 129)

Fleetingly, we have the point of view of this baby, but in particular, by the use of the child figure, the poet enlists our sympathy and conveys the qualities of Hector and the poignant universality of a doomed warrior's farewell.

Children also appear, of course, in the Bible; in the work of Roman authors, such as Plutarch and Horace; in pre-Romantic English writers such as Chaucer, Shakespeare, Marvell and Gray (Pattinson, 1978: 21ff.); and in the rich resource of folk and fairy tales of many cultures (Warner, 1995; Zipes, 1997). Similarly, as Banerjee points out (and as we are reminded in Chapter 1 of this book), it was not only nineteenth-century authors who addressed the relationship between early childhood experience and the nature of the adult that the child becomes: 'Thus, in *Robinson Crusoe*, [1719] the young Crusoe is at fault for neglecting his parents' advice'. Moreover,

'Defoe's later novels testify more conspicuously to his intense concern with the parent/child relationship, since the central characters are increasingly likely to be affected by childhood events, and are judged by their behaviour towards their own offspring' (Banerjee, 1996: 2). Similarly for the novelist Henry Fielding, there appears a clear correlation between his eponymous hero Tom Jones's innocence and early good nature, and the generous and open-hearted youth he becomes.

Context

The issue then, I would suggest, is not so much one of novelty or originality but more one of quality, quantity and particularity. It is the range and the complexity of depictions of children and childhood, particularly in English literature, that demand our attention from the late eighteenth century onwards. In turn, these depictions indicate a change in the climate of ideas and the 'complicated cultural status of childhood in nineteenth-century England' (Andrews, 1994: 1) that Coveney characterises as a 'revolution in sensibility' (1967: 29).

In reading these texts, we have to recognise the social and cultural context. Nineteenth-century writers were drawing on, and reflecting, other potent ideologies such as the eighteenth-century cult of the 'noble savage', whereby 'the belief that man's greatest happiness and moral nobility was to be found in his original state, "the state of nature", and that his subsequent history – the history of advancing civilisation – has been one of gradual moral degeneration' (Andrews, 1994: 10). This became 'a picturesque prototype of the complicated, contradictory conception of childhood' (1994: 11). The notion is reflected in Wordsworth, particularly in 'Ode: Intimations of Immortality from Recollections of Early Childhood' (1807):

> ... trailing clouds of glory do we come
> From God, who is our home:
> Heaven lies about us in our infancy!
> Shades of the prison-house begin to close
> Upon the growing Boy,
> But He beholds the light, and whence it flows ...
> At length the Man perceives it die away
> And fade into the light of common day

It also appears in his idealised children of nature, such as 'Lucy Grey' and 'The Idle Shepherd-Boys' (1800), and the connection between the savage and the child is often made explicit:

> Oh many a time have I ...
> stood alone
> Beneath the sky, as if I had been born

> On Indian Plains, and from my mother's hut
> Had run abroad in wantonness, to sport,
> A naked savage, in the thunder shower
> Fair seed-time had my soul
>
> ('The Prelude', Book 1, 300)

The tension in this concept, between nostalgia for a lost Golden Age of innocence on the one hand, and fear of natural, possibly degenerate and uncontrollable impulses or external forces, on the other, is seen in the later polarisation of attitude between what has been characterised as 'the two great streams of Victorian morality' (Houghton, cited in Andrews, 1994: 20). This is the notion of original innocence, which can be thought of as Rousseau's development of an aspect of the noble savage, and the evangelical doctrine of original sin, whereby all are born already corrupted and must attain redemption.

These polarities, as noted in Chapter 1 of this Reader, find their echoes repeatedly in the depiction of children in this period and in our own, in the claims for the special vision and purity of childhood innocence in Dickens, for example, and in repression, consciousness of sin and physical correction of children's wickedness by such figures as the Murdstones (*David Copperfield*) and Brocklehurst (*Jane Eyre*). This emphasis in *Jane Eyre* reflects Charlotte Brontë's own distress as a young woman:

> My eyes fill with tears when I contrast the bliss of such a state brightened by hopes of the future with the melancholy state I now live in, uncertain that I have ever felt true contrition, wandering in thought and deed, longing for holiness which I shall *never, never* obtain – smitten at times to the heart with the conviction that your Ghastly Calvinistic doctrines are true – darkened in short by the very shadow of Spiritual Death!
>
> (Barker, 1995: 284)

Neither notion replaces the other; the two continue to co-exist.

Children's perspectives

The concept of 'original innocence' derived from Rousseau and the Romantic poets (Brown, 1993: 5), emphasised that children were significant in their own right since they had 'natural purity and sensibility and innate tendencies to virtue … and have their own way of thinking and seeing things' (Brown, 1993: 4). There is, partly in consequence of this, a major departure in the depiction of children. Writers move from describing child experience from the outside to an insistence on speaking from within, so that, as a result, a series of child voices appears in literature from the late eighteenth century onwards. This shift both signals the change in attitude to the significance of childhood experiences and allows writers to work in new territory. Simply by introducing these voices, writers emphasise that children have something special to say and should be listened to in their own right. There is such an insistence on the child's vision that a way into these texts is to attend closely to this voice.

For each writer, the perspective can be slightly different and operates in three ways. Adult writers can act as ventriloquists in assuming a child's voice; they can include a child's voice within their own commentary; or they can refer to their own childhood experience. So, for Blake, the child voices we hear in 'Songs of Innocence' and 'Songs of Experience' are 'The Little Black Boy', 'The Chimney Sweeper', 'The Little Vagabond', 'Infant Sorrow' and 'The Schoolboy', and while, in the case of the first two, both figures are used to convey a critique of religion, both also speak of a specific and oppressed child being separated from parents and, in the case of the chimney sweep, of the oppressive nature of the work. They convey a particular sympathy in speaking to other children.

Similarly, Wordsworth in poems such as, 'We are Seven' and 'An Anecdote for Fathers', uses two voices in contrasting an adult's 'wisdom' with a child's expression of truth:

> O dearest, dearest boy! my heart
> For better lore would seldom yearn,
> Could I but teach the hundredth part
> Of what from thee I learn.

Furthermore, for Wordsworth a crucial connection is between child and adult experience, as expressed in 'The Rainbow', and it is worth looking closely at this poem to tease out the themes we are about to address.

> My heart leaps up when I behold
> A rainbow in the sky:
> So was it when my life began;
> So is it now I am a man;
> So be it when I shall grow old,
> Or let me die!
> The Child is father of the Man;
> And I could wish my days to be
> Bound each to each by natural piety.

Firstly, once again there is the insistence on visual perception and the physical leap of emotion within the speaker that it stimulates. Next, there is the common link between that feeling in the child and adult and the wish that there will never be a disruption in that capacity, which is semi-religious ('natural piety') in its response. Thus Wordsworth, in linking child and adult experience, raises two issues: he confronts questions of growing up and maturity, and he emphasises the particular power of imagination and vision in childhood which the adult must retain. These notions William Empson, in his innovatory commentary on 'golden age' (i.e. pastoral) literature, observes:

> run through all Victorian and Romantic literature ... [The writers] kept a sort of tap-root going down to their experience as children. Their idea of the child [was], that it is in the right relation to Nature, not dividing what should be unified, that its intuitive judgement contains what poetry and philosophy must spend their time labouring to recover.
>
> (1995: 209)

Children in novels

It is in this area that certain later novels draw their particular strengths and, for this purpose I am going to look more closely at *David Copperfield*, *Jane Eyre* and *The Mill on the Floss*. First, of course – since we are pursuing this theme – perspective is powerfully conveyed because each work draws upon the author's own life. This is extended in the case of the first two works, which are written in the first person and purport to be autobiography, what Rose refers to as 'the importance of a centrally cohered narrator' (1992: 148). Thus, David Copperfield: 'Whether I shall turn out to be the hero of my own life, or whether that station will be held by anybody else, these pages must show' (ch. 1, p. 49). *Jane Eyre* is subtitled *An Autobiography*, and caused controversy at the time because Charlotte Brontë, among other things, had drawn upon her own school experience in the depiction of Lowood.

On the other hand, while *The Mill on the Floss* is not written ostensibly as autobiography, it opens with an ambiguous narrator who insists on the reality of the scene described. Is this figure male or female? Is she talking of herself in presenting to us the little girl by the river and recalling herself as a child figure? Thus, each of these works blurs the relationship between the author and the narrator. Where do the life experience of the author and the portrayal of the fictional character meet?

This has two effects on us as readers. We feel called upon to respond to the authenticity of these experiences since they lay claim to being particularly 'realistic', and we are drawn into sympathy with the central characters since we see the world through their eyes. Critically, knowledge of the actual biographies of these authors has sometimes proved a distraction in distinguishing what they are saying about themselves from what they saying about childhood. That is to say, the task of the biographer is to understand the life; the task of the critic is to understand the work: 'And though the life of a great writer has a meaning which cannot be ignored, it should not be made identical with what is written' (Beer, 1986: 87). As Andrews notes: 'the habit of drawing largely on the biographical record, when considering Dickens' treatment of childhood, reduces the complexities of his attitudes to a matter of personal idiosyncrasy' (Andrews, 1994: 1).

Let us, then, examine the perspectives of the children in these novels. In conveying the child view, each author also gives us a physical viewpoint and this necessarily involves an overtone which characterises the child narrator. The author both conveys the freshness of the child's view and uses this within the overall scheme of the book in conveying character and themes. Here is Dickens:

> There comes out of the cloud, our house – not new to me, but quite familiar, in its earliest remembrance. On the ground floor is Peggotty's kitchen, opening into a backyard ... and a quantity of fowls that look terribly tall to me, walking about in a menacing and ferocious manner. There is one cock who gets up on a post to crow, and seems to take particular notice of me as I look at him through the kitchen window, who makes me shiver, he is so fierce ... Here is a long passage – what an enormous perspective I make of it! ... A dark store-room opens out of it, and that is a place to be run past at night.
>
> (ch. 2, p. 62)

This description not only captures the familiar terrors of a young child but, in introducing the particular sensitivities of David Copperfield's personality, foreshadows his reaction to other intimidating characters (the waiter who eats his dinner; the coachman who orders him off the best seat; the manipulative Heap; the sinister Littimer).

Similarly, in *Jane Eyre*:

> I looked up at – a black pillar! – such, at least, appeared to me, at first sight, the straight, narrow, sable-clad shape standing erect on the rug; the grim face at the top was like a carved mask, placed above the shaft by way of capital ...
> Presently he addressed me –
> 'Your name, little girl?'
> 'Jane Eyre, sir.'
> In uttering these words I looked up: he seemed to me a tall gentleman, but then I was very little; his features were large, and they and all the lines of his frame were equally harsh and prim.
>
> (ch. 4, p. 33)

Again, the physical perspective is not mere description of a tiny child facing a large adult, but part of the texture of a book where the inflexible nature of those who would crush Jane's spirit is given physical manifestation. The black pillar of the Brocklehurst figure is later paralleled in another figure of repression, the white pillar of St John Rivers. Moreover, Tom and Maggie Tulliver's view (in *The Mill on the Floss*) of their aunt Glegg, 'as the type of ugliness,' is undercut and put into its attitudinal context by Eliot's comment that 'no impartial observer could have denied that for a woman of fifty she had a very comely face and figure' (ch. 7, p. 47).

The introduction of these physical perspectives encourages us to see the world through these children's eyes, and also links them to the subsequent adult. 'The author who launches hero or heroine early in life can count on a special kind of goodwill in the reader' (Tillotson, 1962: 298). This introduces a related interest of these writers, namely, the charting of the development of these central figures and a concern with their subjectivity. The very qualities they have as children are manifest in the ways they meet the challenges of later life. The child remains alive in the adult. David Copperfield's trust and naïvety (foreshadowed in his father 'taking the birds on trust' when he bought their house called 'The Rookery' (ch. 1, p. 54)) persists into his young adult life. Jane Eyre's sharpness of retort, frankness and perspicacity remain with her throughout the book and, indeed, attract Rochester to her. The savagery and reserve, sensitiveness and sharpwittedness 'that we are to know in Jane at eighteen are hers at ten … She is as tough in happiness as in misery' (Tillotson, 1962: 303). Maggie Tulliver's inconsistent rebelliousness and intense need to be loved and admired appear in the little girl who cuts off her hair, pushes Lucy in the pond and who runs away to the gypsies, and in the young woman who continues to meet Philip Wakem and who almost absconds with Stephen Guest.

David Copperfield

In Dickens, particularly, the insistence on this keen vision and on keeping the values of the child alive in the adult is seen in its most developed form.

> I believe the power of observation in numbers of very young children to be quite wonderful for its closeness and accuracy. Indeed, I think that most grown men who are remarkable in this respect, may with greater propriety be said not to have lost the faculty, than to have acquired it; the rather, as I generally observe such men to retain a certain freshness, and gentleness, and capacity of being pleased, which are also an inheritance they have preserved from their childhood.
>
> (ch. 2, p. 61)

In fact, in a whole series of ways *David Copperfield* could be said to be a book about childhood and to exemplify many of the concerns centred around children and childhood that appear in Dickens's other work and which are thus central to this discussion. First, David is the first child character of Dickens that we see growing up. These include, among a very extensive range of types in his books prior to *David Copperfield*, Oliver Twist, Little Nell, Smike and Paul Dombey. The last three of these die and thus induce our pity (Smike), preserve their unsullied innocence (Little Nell), or carry an indictment of cold and materialistic parenting (Paul

Dombey). It is thus a commonplace to view *David Copperfield* as a *bildungsroman*. But what are the qualities that David has to develop as he attains adulthood?

These we discover either in positive portrayals of other characters or see brought out in David's relationships with others. Thus, a key area where such qualities are highlighted is in the issue of child-rearing, of which there are several examples in the book, and in which both positive and negative features are depicted. There is the early, unrestrained, affectionate idyll of life with Peggotty and Clara; the Murdstone code of 'firmness' and the physical manifestation of this repression; the warmth of Mr. Pegotty's boathouse; the chaos of the Micawbers; the comment of Betsey Trotwood on her own raising of David:

> 'But what I want you to be, Trot,' resumed my aunt, 'I don't mean physically, but morally; you are very well physically – is a firm fellow, a fine firm fellow, with a will of your own. With resolution,' said my aunt, shaking her cap at me, and clenching her hand. 'With determination. With character that is not to be influenced, except on good reason, by anybody or anything. That's what your father and mother might both have been, Heaven knows, and been the better for it'.
>
> (ch. 19, p. 332)

There is, moreover, David's own oft-repeated comment on his relationship with the child-like Dora, as the prompting of an 'undisciplined heart' (ch. 53, p. 838).

We have, therefore, an ambivalent series of associations of affection, trust and open-heartedness with immaturity, or the child-like state, while self-discipline, control and repression are associated with maturity, or the adult state. The issue for the grown-up David is to resolve the two in a 'disciplined heart' (whatever that might be) that neither crushes the spirit nor wallows in disorder and avoids adult responsibilities, a problem that is solved for him in terms of this plot by the convenient death of Dora and his marriage to Agnes.

Moreover, this issue of child-rearing, and therefore how maturity might be attained, is rendered more problematic by the fact that no family that is both conventional, stable and nurturing is represented in the book. David starts life having, in effect, two mothers: Clara, who is both child-like and childish, and Peggotty, who has traditional maternal qualities and who, in effect, mothers them both. He then acquires a (wicked) step-father; goes on to assume a parenting role with the Micawbers ('A curious equality of friendship, originating, I suppose in our respective circumstances, sprung up between me and these people, notwithstanding the ludicrous disparity in our years' (ch. 11, p. 219)). He is finally brought up by the fairy godmother figure of Betsey Trotwood, who is already a surrogate parent to Mr Dick.

Furthermore, it is made clear at David's first meeting that the idealised family in Mr Peggotty's upturned boat is not a traditional family unit. 'I was very much surprised that Mr Peggotty was not Ham's father, and began to wonder whether I was mistaken about his relationship to anyone else there' (ch. 3, p. 83). In other words, there is an implicit distrust or unease here about the ability of traditional families to nurture children and an explicit attraction to fantasy and whimsy when portraying happy families.

This brings us to other manifestations of children in this book that have echoes in Dickens' other work. He presents many characters for which the roles of adults and children have either been reversed or are blurred. By focusing on these, we can delineate once more what the attributes of both states appear to be. Thus, for example, the childlike features of female characters such as Clara, Dora and *Little* Emily are stressed. All are orphans, all are dependent and helpless, doubly so in this text because they are female. The first two fail in their adult responsibilities as wives and mothers, and the girlish vanity that was initially attractive becomes a source of frustration for their partners.

Alternatively, a figure such as Agnes, although physically a child when we first meet her, never appears anything other than mature, calm and reflective, and the parent (like David above) to her own father (as is the central figure in *Little Dorrit*). On the other hand, there are adults who carry childlike qualities into adulthood which are a positive source of strength. It is Mr Peggotty's simplicity, emotional candour, capacity for love and integrity that enable him to search for Emily. It is Mr Dick's ability to see the truth in a relationship and not to be embarrassed about resolving a breach that allows him to reconcile Dr and Annie Strong: 'A poor fellow with a craze, sir … may do what wonderful people may not do' (ch. 45, p. 721). It is Mr Micawber, for all his lack of personal responsibility, who can theatrically assume moral responsibility to expose fraud and deceit.

What does all this tell us? Overall, of course, it suggests that Dickens is not presenting a 'single coherent and stable idea of childhood. And if there is no coherent idea of childhood can there be a coherent idea of adulthood?' (Andrews, 1994: 146). I suggest that, in spite of the issue appearing to be unresolved, overall Dickens is presenting a world in which the domains of child and adult are not easily separated, and that childhood is a condition with particular redemptive qualities.

Reading and imagination

Furthermore, to bring us back to our discussion of 'vision', it is a world where imagination is a powerful attribute. Imagination in Dickens's sphere is associated with perspective and observation, and all, as we saw earlier, are characterised as significant childlike attributes. Thus, it is the imaginative empathy of Mr Dick, Micawber and Mr Peggotty that brings about the triumph of good. More importantly, David himself is portrayed as a particularly imaginative child whose fancy is nourished by reading and stories. This obviously has central significance in a book that is about someone who grows up to become an author, but it also brings us back to *Jane Eyre* and *The Mill on the Floss*, where the imagination and integrity of the central characters are similarly sustained by reading.

The role of reading and stories is thus twofold in these novels. It is part of the texture of the books in that it supports the characterisation and the working out of the main themes, but stories are also part of the vision of these books, structurally and metaphorically. 'Like metaphor, they allow meaning to emerge without settling' (Beer, 1986: 91).

Thus, as Andrews (1994: 152) notes, David is sustained by his imaginary world on several occasions: when the Murdstones take over; when he tells stories to Steerforth at Salem House; when he starts work at Murdstone and Grinby's. Moreover, he is also a character who sees the world through fancy and story, as witness his comment on the Peggotty boat: 'If it had been Aladdin's palace, roc's egg and all, I suppose I could not have been more charmed with the romantic idea of living in it' (ch. 3, p. 79). However, as a further aspect of the narrative technique, the book itself engages with, and is enriched by, echoes of other texts. So Betsey arrives in Chapter 1 as a bad-tempered fairy godmother to the birth of a child at midnight who has the magical attribute of a protective caul. Is this child, then, to be particularly blessed? Will he undergo adversity only to ultimately succeed? Similarly, like his favourite heroes from eighteenth-century fiction, David undergoes a series of journeys and picaresque adventures. We thus have an account where the imaginative qualities of the author are also attributes of the main character, and the intertextual echoes are reflected in the narrative structure in an endorsement of a unity of vision.

There is a similar symbiosis between the imagination of the central character-narrator and the author in *Jane Eyre*. When we first meet Jane she has retired to read a book about arctic birds, so that we immediately encounter themes of escape and flight and the motif of cold as opposed to the heat and passion which will appear later. Jane is:

> 'a creature dependent, captive, yet with the liberty of adventure in imagination' – a window to look out of, a book to read and pictures on which to build fancies. The double impression of constraint and freedom is burnt into the mind in those first few paragraphs
>
> (Tillotson, 1962: 300)

Jane, like David, is sustained by fairy stories, in her case from Bessy the maid, and is characterised by her own supernatural qualities while the novel itself draws upon echoes of Cinderella and Bluebeard. 'Jane's first meeting with Rochester is a fairytale meeting. Charlotte Brontë deliberately stresses mythic elements' (Gilbert and Gubar, 1984: 351). Yet, if the texts that spring to mind in *David Copperfield* are fairy stories and eighteenth-century picaresque tales, in *Jane Eyre* it is even more pertinent to note the overt allusions to *Pilgrim's Progress* as a comparable narrative of trial, struggle and ultimate vindication, in what Gilbert and Gubar describe as a 'borrowing of the mythic quest-plot' (1984: 336).

In Maggie Tulliver, too, we have an avid reader for whom reading is part of the characterisation: 'There were few sounds that roused Maggie when she was dreaming over a book.' (bk 1, ch. 3, p. 11) There is an intensity and passion about Maggie's desire for knowledge that is seen, in turn, in her other actions (Beer, 1986: 87). 'Oh What books ... How I should like to have as many books as that' (bk 2, ch. 1, p. 135).

It is apt also that the first book we find her reading is Defoe's *History of the Devil* with its account of a witch's trial by water: 'if she swims she's a witch, if she's drowned – and killed, you know – she's innocent, and not a witch, but only a poor silly old woman' (bk 1, ch. 3, p. 13). Again, this reference serves several functions: it prefigures Maggie's actual fate while highlighting her dilemma. As a 'small mistake of nature' (ch. 2, p. 9), Maggie cannot survive in this society with its conventional expectations of women, and part of this is that reading and learning are constantly typified as unnatural female attributes: 'a woman's no business wi' being so clever' (ch. 3, p. 13). 'They've a great deal of superficial cleverness; but they couldn't go far into anything. They're quick and shallow' (bk 2, ch. 1, p. 140). If she suppresses her true nature, she becomes 'a poor silly old woman' and can only triumph through death.

As with Jane Eyre, this female aberration is seen in terms of magic: '"Ah, now I see how it is you know Shakespeare and everything, and have learned so much since you left school; which always seemed to me witch craft before – part of your general uncanniness", said Lucy' (bk 6, ch. 3, p. 364). Maggie herself rejects the antithesis of the blonde and dark heroine in conventional novels: '"If you could give me some story, now, where the dark woman triumphs, it would restore the balance. I want to avenge ... all the rest of the dark unhappy ones"' (bk 5, ch. 4, p. 312).

As the titles of separate Books of *The Mill on the Floss* chosen by George Eliot indicate ('The Downfall', 'The Valley of Humiliation', 'Wheat and Tares', 'The Great Temptation', 'The Final Rescue'), along with another text chosen by Maggie, *The Pilgrim's Progress*, this narrative also follows a pattern of struggle, temptation, (ambivalent) reconciliation and vindication in which the heroine's intellectual and spiritual growth is nurtured by literature. This literature is mediated by the friend-guide Philip Wakem, with his re-telling of classical myths, and by the spiritual guide Thomas à Kempis, whose *The Imitation of Christ* speaks so powerfully to Maggie of renunciation after her father's bankruptcy.

It is an intriguing matter and a fitting close for this chapter, where the qualities of the imagination and the link between child and adult experience have been addressed, that for each of these authors their vision of childhood is focused by the imaginary world of other texts.

Summary

To close, then, let me set out the main points which I hope you have absorbed from this chapter.

- First, it essential that you continue to examine texts closely. Whatever readings or standpoints you may then employ, this is the basic technique of literary criticism.
- Although this is a very significant period for the depiction of children in literature, we must not ignore depictions from other historical periods, from different cultures and from contemporary world literature.
- The range and complexity of portrayals in this period should be viewed within the social and cultural climate of the time, in particular relating to notions of innocence, redemption, child vision, maturity.
- Individual authors, although working within this climate of ideas and influences, nevertheless approach them with their own unique imaginative responses.
- Finally, reader, I hope that, if you have not done so before, you are now drawn to these great texts as a preliminary to exploring further the image of the child.

Appendix

Plot summaries

Some readers may not be familiar with the three books cited. Plot summaries are provided here as an aid to orientation and a stimulus to reading the books themselves.

David Copperfield

This novel, like some others of Dickens, was originally published in monthly parts during 1849–50. This is reflected in the structure, length and features of plot and characterisation, which have some of the qualities of modern soap operas.

The novel opens with an account of the hero's birth to his youthful, recently widowed, mother and the visit of his father's aunt, Betsey Trotwood, who flounces off on finding that the baby is a boy and not the girl she had expected. The idyllic early days of David with his mother and Peggotty, his nurse, are described, which continue with a visit to Peggotty's family in Yarmouth where David meets her brother, Daniel, and niece and nephew, Little Emily and Ham, who all live in an upturned boat. On return, the idyll ends as David encounters his mother's new husband, Edward Murdstone, and his sister, Jane. David is sent away to school and hero-worships an older boy, Steerforth. The repressive ways of the

Murdstones result in the death of David's mother and in David's being sent to labour in a London warehouse. He lodges with the eccentric Micawber family. On their leaving, the neglected David runs away to Dover to find his Aunt Betsey, who also fosters the childlike Mr Dick. Betsey adopts David and sends him to school in Canterbury where he lives with Betsey's lawyer, Mr Wickfield, and his daughter Agnes, and encounters the sinister clerk, Uriah Heep. David grows up to try several professions, but settles upon being a writer. He marries the attractive but childish Dora Spenlow, realises her deficiencies but is none the less desolated by her early death. In a series of climaxes, the villains, Heep and Steerforth (who has seduced and abandoned Emily) are dealt with, and David, older and, we trust, wiser, marries the faithful Agnes.

Jane Eyre

Jane Eyre is an orphan living with her aunt, Mrs Reed, and her cousins. After turning on her cousin, John, as he bullies her, she is locked in the 'Red Room', where her uncle died, and experiences a kind of fit. On her recovery, she is sent away to Lowood School, a charitable institution where the harsh regime, implemented by the trustees who are represented by Mr Brocklehurst, is intended to crush the spirit and suppress the fleshly desires of the girls. Here Jane encounters the model of the saintly Helen Burns, who dies as a result of this treatment. Reforms of the system are put in place, and Jane grows up to leave Lowood and to take up the position of governess to the ward of the master of Thornfield Hall, Edward Rochester. Although it is made clear that Jane is quite plain, attracted by her independence of mind, Rochester proposes and is accepted. However, during the service on their wedding day it is revealed that Rochester has a deranged wife, Bertha, living in the attic of the house. Rejecting the chance to become Rochester's mistress, Jane flees and is eventually taken in by the Rivers family at Marsh End. Again she receives a proposal, this time from the frigid St John Rivers. Almost at the point of consenting, Jane hears, supernaturally, the voice of Rochester calling her. She returns to Thornfield to find it a blackened ruin and Rochester disfigured during a fire started by Bertha, who perished with the house. In the famous lines of Chapter 18, 'Reader, I married him', Jane and Rochester contract a marriage on more equal terms, and live, we suppose, happily ever after.

The Mill on the Floss

Maggie and Tom Tulliver live at Dorlcote Mill. In the opening chapters, Tom returns from school to the delight of Maggie, who adores him, it may be said, far more than he does her. The different natures of Tom (a 'Dodson', his mother's family) and Maggie (a 'Tulliver') are explicitly contrasted during a visit of the Dodson aunts. It is in reaction to these aunts that Maggie carries out her impulsive acts of rebellion. Mr Tulliver, however, is determined to buy Tom a classical education to pit him, when older, against rascally lawyers, especially Wakem, with whom he is in constant litigation. Tom's schooling at the Reverend Stelling's is seen as utterly inappropriate for his practical and unimaginative nature, although not for fellow pupil Philip Wakem, the crippled son of the lawyer, to whom Maggie is drawn. Maggie, in contrast, although a quick and voracious reader, does not warrant an expensive education because she is a mere girl. In time, Mr Tulliver is bankrupted by his litigious pursuits, the family is dispossessed, Tom forbids Maggie to have contact with Philip and they are further estranged when she is compromised by Stephen Guest, her cousin Lucy's fiancé. However, Tom and Maggie are reconciled, drowned and buried together after she attempts to rescue him from the Mill during an unprecedented flood.

Review questions and tasks

1   Three authors, Banerjee, Brown and Coveney, have made a significant contribution to the study of this topic. Choose one of them and read their introductory chapter. What are the main points made:

    a   about the representation of children in literature;
    b   about the contribution of other critics? (Note, both Banerjee and Brown draw upon Coveney).

2   In Blake's 'Songs of Innocence and Experience', there are several poems that are paired thematically either by topic ('The Lamb' and 'The Tyger'; 'Infant Sorrow and 'Infant Joy') or by title ('The Chimney Sweeper'; 'Holy Thursday'; 'Nurse's Song'). Choose two of these poems and make a detailed comparison.

3   Discuss Wordsworth's view of childhood and its relationship to his poetic vision in 'Ode on Intimations of Immortality' and Book One of 'The Prelude'.

4   Study the first four chapters of David Copperfield ('I am Born'; 'I Observe'; 'I have a Change'; 'I fall into Disgrace'). What do we learn: about David; about the portrayal of the various parent figures (Clara, Peggotty, Murdstone, Jane Murdstone, Daniel Peggotty); about Dickens's techniques as a writer?

5   Read the 'Lowood' chapters of Jane Eyre (5–10) and compare them to a biographical account from a life of Charlotte Brontë.

a   In what ways are the two accounts different?
b   What appears to be the particular point of view of the biographer? (See J. Barker (1995) *The Brontës*, London: Phoenix; E. Gaskell (1971) *The Life of Charlotte Brontë*, Dent; L. Gordon (1994) *Charlotte Brontë. A Passionate Life*, Chatto & Windus).

6   In 'Book First' of *The Mill on the Floss'*, 'Boy and Girl', the relationship between Tom and Maggie Tulliver is established, both thematically and as characters.

a   What key terms are used about each when they are first introduced (Maggie in Chapters 2 and 3, Tom in Chapter 4)? What do these suggest about some of the themes of the book and how they are presented?
b   Look closely at the scenes of Maggie's rebellions (the hair cutting, Chapter 7; pushing Lucy in the pond, Chapter 10; running away to the gypsies, Chapter 11). What do these incidents tell us about Maggie and about the society in which she lives?

Further reading

Andrews, M. (1994) *Dickens and the Grown-Up Child*, **Basingstoke: Macmillan.** An excellent exploration of an aspect of Dickens's treatment of children in which the work of other critics in this fairly well-tilled field is also addressed. The opening two chapters usefully re-examine (see Coveney) the unresolved tensions in late eighteenth- and nineteenth-century attitudes to primitivism, as seen in debates on the Golden Age and the noble savage. These confusions are related to Dickens's own treatment of childhood and maturity which is put into its cultural context rather than merely being treated as 'his inability to come to terms with his own childhood experiences' (p. 26). Andrews then proceeds to examine Dickens's exploration of maturity in some of his essays and to categorise his multifarious representations of children under such headings as 'Little Mothers and Housekeepers', 'Premature Little Adults' and 'The Child-like Gentleman'. The topic of Christmas, and depictions in *Dombey and Son* and *David Copperfield*, are then discussed in detail.

Banerjee, J. (1996) *Through the Northern Gate: Childhood and Growing up in British Fiction 1719–1901*, **New York: Lang.** Banerjee's stated aim in her introduction is to 'set the record straight' (p. xviii) on the depiction of children in nineteenth-century fiction by showing the legacy of the eighteenth-century novel and by counteracting, in her view, the notion that the prevailing image of Victorian children is as being moribund and weak. That she is not entirely successful in sustaining these themes throughout her book does not mean that it is not nevertheless a very useful and detailed resource in examining a wide range of authors (the well-known 'classic' writers as well as such figures as Mrs Craik, Margaret Oliphant and Charlotte Yonge) and genres (ecclesiastical writings, literature for children, and diaries and social commentaries).

Brown, P. (1993) *The Captured World: The Child and Childhood in Nineteenth-Century Women's Writing in England,* **Hemel Hempstead: Harvester Wheatsheaf.** (See the appendix 'Further perspectives' to Chapter 1 in this Reader.)

Coveney, P. (1967) *The Image of Childhood. The Individual and Society: a Study of the Theme in English Literature,* **Harmondsworth: Penguin (first published as** *Poor Monkey,* **1957).** This book, now unfortunately out of print, has achieved almost classic status, and some subsequent writers sometimes use it as a yardstick by which their own position is measured (see Brown, 1993; Banerjee, 1996) and others refer to it somewhat uncritically (see Hendrick, 1990). Although by contemporary standards it is a book very much of its period (note the foreword by F.R. Leavis and the mannered prose) and the focus is narrow, covering mainly classic and almost overwhelmingly male authors, Coveney directs attention to 'the very immensity of the number of books about children' (p. 11) and to the change in sensibility that this signalled. He traces the influence of Rousseau and the succeeding image of the 'romantic' child in Blake, Wordsworth and Coleridge, and the transformations and development of this image in Dickens and other nineteenth-century authors, through to the early twentieth century with Sigmund Freud, James Joyce, D.H. Lawrence and Virginia Woolf. Generally, Coveney's commentary on the cultural setting needs reappraising and reviewing in a more critical light.

Rose, J. (1992) *The Case of Peter Pan or The Impossibility of Children's Fiction,* **Basingstoke: Macmillan.** This book is quite different from those above in focusing almost exclusively on children's fiction, a notion that it problematises early on as: 'fiction the child produces or fiction given to the child?' (p. 12). Rose goes behind her title to examine *Peter Pan* as a cultural phenomenon which highlights many of our concepts and fantasies of childhood, such as notions of innocence, identity, nostalgia and 'the integrity of the child's self expression and growth' (p. 136). In doing so, she discusses historical and modern children's fiction and contemporary critical commentaries. As such, it can be read in its own right, but Rose's commentary also brings a novel perspective to the issues discussed in my chapter in this book and to the works cited above.

References

Andrews, M. (1994) *Dickens and the Grown-Up Child,* Basingstoke: Macmillan.

Banerjee, J. (1996) *Through the Northern Gate: Childhood and Growing up in British Fiction 1719–1901,* New York: Lang.

Barker, J. (1995) *The Brontës,* London: Phoenix.

Beer, G. (1986) *George Eliot,* Bloomington: Indiana University Press.

Binyon, L. (ed.) (1931) *Poems of Blake,* London: Macmillan.

Brontë, C. (1847) *Jane Eyre,* London: Penguin, 1994.

Brown, P. (1993) *The Captured World: The Child and Childhood in Nineteenth-Century Women's Writing in England,* Hemel Hempstead: Harvester Wheatsheaf.

Coe, R.N. (1984) *When the Grass Was Taller: Autobiography and the Experience of Childhood*, New Haven, CN: Yale University Press.

Coveney, P. (1967) *The Image of Childhood. The Individual and Society: a Study of the Theme in English Literature*, Harmondsworth: Penguin.

Cunningham, G. (1992) 'The Nineteenth Century Novel', in *The Bloomsbury Guide to English Literature*, London: Bloomsbury.

Dickens, C. (1850) *The Personal History of David Copperfield*, London: Penguin, 1985.

Eliot, George (1860) *The Mill on the Floss*, London: Dent, 1950.

Empson, W. (1995) *Some Versions of Pastoral*, London: Penguin, first published 1935.

Gilbert, S. and Gubar, S. (1984) *The Madwoman in the Attic: The Woman Writer and the Nineteenth-Century Literary Imagination*, New Haven, CN: Yale University Press.

Hutchinson, T. (ed.) (1926) *The Poems of Wordsworth*, London: Oxford University Press.

Pattinson, R. (1978) *The Child Figure in English Literature*, Athens: University of Georgia Press.

Rieu, E.V. (trans.) (1986) *Homer: The Iliad*, Harmondsworth: Penguin.

Rose, J. (1992) *The Case of Peter Pan or The Impossibility of Children's Fiction*, Basingstoke: Macmillan.

Tillotson, K. (1962) *Novels of the Eighteen-Forties*, London: Oxford University Press.

Warner, M. (1995) *From the Beast to the Blonde*, London: Vintage.

Zipes, J. (1997) *Happily Ever After? Children, Fairy Tales and the Culture Industry*, London: Routledge.

Chapter 3

Childhood and twentieth-century children's literature

Fay Sampson

Summary

This chapter traces the changing emphases in children's fiction during the twentieth century. It looks to novels of childhood as a golden age; to novels in which children are the heroes of great adventures; to a growing inscription of social realism and the mirroring of children's everyday lives; and to the trend away from absolutism towards greater ambivalence about oneself and others. In the discussion on trends in publishing, there is a recognition that the concept of the child-as-reader is as important as that of the child-in-fiction. The varying approaches authors may take, and the different effects these produce, are illustrated from the writer's own experience as a reader and writer of children's fiction.

> In literature childhood is an invention, a creation, a state constructed. The literature of childhood properly is either historical fiction, or an aspect of imaginative reconstruction. Childhood itself is a fairytale taking place in a chaos. Childhood is not aware of itself as childhood.
>
> (Ben Okri, 1998)

The very concept of a separate literature for children is itself a construction of childhood. It asserts that children are different from adults. It sets a value on them which says that books should be provided to meet their interests and needs.

C.S. Lewis has defined three ways of writing for children:

* writing for the assumed tastes of children, perceived as different from those of adults;
* telling the story to a particular child, and adapting it to their responses;
* writing a universal story in a style appropriate for children (Walsh, 1979: 196).

I would add one variation:

* writing for the child-self within the author.

I hope to show how these approaches produce different emphases in the image of childhood and how the balance has shifted in the twentieth century. As a writer of children's fiction, I shall draw on my own experience to illustrate how different ways of writing are read by both children and adults, who incorporate them in varying ways into their constructions of childhood.

Enchanted childhoods

The twentieth century opens with the child-within-the-author as the predominant mode. Kenneth Grahame entitled the nostalgic memoir of his childhood, *The Golden Age* (Grahame, 1896). His *The Wind in the Willows* (Grahame, 1951) is not really a children's book, but a middle-class adult's nostalgia for a rural idyll, a flight from the industrial and proletarian present. That nostalgic unwillingness to let go of the past reaches its peak in James Barrie's *Peter Pan* (Barrie, 1928). Peter is the boy who lives in the Never-Never Land and will never grow up, and he would like to prevent the children of the Darling family from doing so.

The sense of an enchanted land is a recurring theme in Edwardian writers. It is the Secret Garden in Frances Hodgson Burnett's novel of that name (Burnett, 1911). It is the top of the Forest in A.A. Milne's Pooh stories (Milne, 1928). These are places sacred to childhood, where an adult is an intruder. Burnett, optimistically, and Milne, pessimistically, show there is a need to grow beyond this, but their association of childhood with the enchanted idyll remains.

Yet within this sentimental idealisation, something interesting is happening. In *The Secret Garden*, Mary is an ugly, ill-tempered orphan who is helped by a rural working-class boy, Dickon, to bring the abandoned garden back to life. In the process, she herself blossoms, physically and psychologically. Together, they help the self-pitying invalid Colin to walk and laugh. Milne makes his own son, Christopher Robin, the human child in the Pooh books. But the fictional Christopher Robin behaves like a wise adult, appearing on the scene to solve problems and pronounce judgement, the role assigned to adults in earlier didactic fiction for children. It is the toys who are really the children: endearing, funny, ignorant, inadequate. The construction of the child here is not – as it largely was in real life – someone-to-whom-things-happen, but someone-with-power to decide, to act, to effect change.

This was not totally new. The Jack of folk tales slays giants. George MacDonald's nineteenth-century books about the princess Irene and the miner's son showed children affecting the fate of a kingdom (MacDonald, 1994). But Burnett's garden and Milne's forest provide enclosed worlds in which the child reigns supreme.

E. Nesbit's fictional families in her realistic books about the Bastable children and the fantasy romps involving those ill-tempered and unpredictable spirits of magic, the Psammead and the Phoenix, seem at first sight a long way from sentimentalism (Nesbit, 1959, 1982, 1990). Edward Lear's *Book of Nonsense* in 1846 had a seismic effect on children's literature, proclaiming that childhood could be fun. The self-contained, often anarchic escapades of Nesbit's children exploit this liberty. But, although they romp through cities and countryside, and across centuries and continents, these exploits still, in their own way, happen within a secret garden. They must at all costs be kept secret from adults, who would spoil the fun. Children are different from adults.

Most of Arthur Ransome's *Swallows and Amazons* series appear so realistic that they may be read as DIY manuals for sailing, camping and natural history (Ransome, 1931). Yet in a sense, they too take place in a self-contained, enchanted world. Here the emphasis is not on the celebration of childhood, but on the assumption of adulthood. Children captain sailing craft, run households, negotiate treaties. It is a child's dream of adulthood, the mirror image of Barrie's adult dream of childhood.

As is usual with family stories, a range of characters is offered. The reader can choose which to empathise with in order to try out personal dreams. As a child, I identified with both the timid, imaginative Titty, who was like my real self, and Nancy Blackett, the pirate captain, who was what I wished to be. I thought Titty's elder sister, Susan, was a minor character. It is only re-reading the books as an adult that I realise she is just as important to the story and offers a construction of girlhood as housewifely, motherly, yet competent at handling a boat and living out of doors. As children, we read and re-read those constructions of childhood which reinforce our preferred image, and filter out those which do not.

What is normal?

All of these writers make the assumption that childhood is definitively middle-class and white. The rustic Yorkshire lad Dickon, in *The Secret Garden*, plays a powerful part in the transformation, both of the garden and of Mary and Colin. Yet he is constructed as the 'other'. His life in a small cottage with a family of fourteen amazes Mary, an only child. His ability to talk to animals and coax them to come to him is idealised to the point where he resembles Grahame's heavily-censored image of the bucolic god Pan in *The Wind in the Willows*. Dickon is the rural idyll personified. However flattering the portrait, we see him from Mary's point of view. His faultless goodness and wisdom would make it hard for a child to empathise with him, even if invited to do so.

A more problematic approach to the 'other' is typified in the work of Enid Blyton (Blyton, 1963). The golliwog is the troublemaker in the toy cupboard. The villains of her adventure stories are likely to be working class or foreign. Readers of such authors were not only offered a concept of normality as Anglo-Saxon and middle class, but encouraged to despise and distrust what, for many, was their true normality.

A ground-breaking story from the 1940s was Eve Garnett's *The Family from One-End Street*, which centred on the children of a dustman and a cleaner living in a small terraced house in an industrial city (Garnett, 1942). Working-class children had already appeared as chief protagonists in the nineteenth century: Tom the chimney sweep's boy in *The Water Babies* (Kingsley, 1994); Diamond the coachman's son in *At the Back of the North Wind* (MacDonald, 1964). But *The Water Babies* is the story of Tom's salvation from his godless past, and Diamond, like Dickon, is idealised, the Victorian image of the beautiful child. The family from One-End Street are down-to-earth, in and out of trouble, as much as the middle-class Bastables or Blacketts. They are to be enjoyed as they are, not held up as exemplars or in need of reformation. Yet, reading this book now, we may still feel the narrative stance is that of an amused observer of the exotic 'other', rather than an assumption of their circumstances as normality.

Those in the book world constantly debate the need to provide children with literature which projects their own experience. But this is not a simple matter of labelling the protagonists 'working class' or 'black'. As a working-class child in the 1940s, I read *The Family from One-End Street* with enjoyment. I was sufficiently class-conscious to appreciate its setting as a refreshing change. But I still did not feel that the reality depicted was my own. Though I could remember weekly baths in a zinc tub in front of the fire, I lived in a village, and my father listened to symphony concerts and read Dickens to us. Nor did I recognise this construction of childhood – the large family, the naughty brothers, the older girl staggering under the weight of the baby – as to any great degree mine. Garnett offers a different, somewhat stereotyped but not untruthful model of a working-class childhood, in an industrial city and with no pretensions to anything other than its own culture.

Representations of class, race, gender and disability are important in expanding the range of models of childhood available, but we need to beware not to let such broad classifications obscure the diversity they encompass. Middle-class childhood is itself not a monolithic concept. Ransome's Walker family, whose cheerful and enabling Australian mother used to sail in Sydney Harbour, contrasts with the model of childhood portrayed in *The Secret Garden*, in which Mary sees so little of her socialite mother that she thinks of her as 'the Memsahib', and Colin's father cannot bear to see his invalid son. The most important constructions of childhood may be in the emotional truth we recognise in the characters, rather than in their physical circumstances. The bookish Titty Walker and the adventurous Nancy Blackett were far more formative in shaping my idea of myself than Garnett's working-class children.

However, it was recognised by the 1950s that more of the reality of working-class children's lives needed to be inscribed in the fiction they were reading, though in an unpatronising way. Leila Berg's *Little Pete Stories* does not stress the boy's social background; what matters is the adventure he is engaged in (Berg, 1970). Over the next decades, that enlarged awareness began to take in ethnic diversity, feminist aspirations and a consciousness of disabled children in the community. Macmillan's Nippers series was one of the imprints which emerged in the 1970s to meet this need. Garnett's detached third-person narrator has given way to a greater focalisation from the child's point of view. A rural primary school model was offered in William Mayne's *No More School*, although he also wrote about life as a cathedral chorister (Mayne, 1955, 1977). Nina Bawden made a blind girl the heroine of *The Witch's Daughter*. Her supposed disability becomes the key to saving her friends (Bawden, 1969). Gene Kemp's *The Turbulent Term of Tyke Tiler* overturns the reader's assumptions about male and female (Kemp, 1977).

Other writers turned to animal stories, as writers have done for millennia, to inscribe a universal experience. Russell Hoban's *A Baby Sister for Frances* deals, for instance, with an older sibling's jealousy, using a family of bears as a distancing tactic (Hoban, 1987). Books like these enable children to come to terms with the fears and mistakes of everyday life.

The heroic child

Another, more cataclysmic, type of book spread its banners after the Second World War. There had been forerunners in the 1920s and 1930s, with John

Masefield's *Midnight Folk* and *The Box of Delights* (Masefield, 1927, 1935), and J.R.R. Tolkien's 1930s creation *The Hobbit* has many childlike character-istics (Tolkien, 1966). The genre took off with C.S. Lewis's Narnia series in the 1950s (Lewis, 1959). Here 'ordinary' children, in Lewis's terms, enter a secondary fantasy world and are transmuted into adult kings and queens. The ultimate salvation of Narnia rests with the lion Aslan. Yet the children play important roles, sometimes causing evil but eventually helping to thwart it and restore Aslan's rule. In the 1960s and 1970s, this scenario produced a rich harvest of work from authors like Alan Garner (1971) and Susan Cooper (1984). From the USA came Madeleine L'Engle's *A Wrinkle in Time* and *The Wind in the Door* (L'Engle, 1967, 1975) and Ursula Le Guin's *Earthsea* trilogy (Le Guin, 1971). In each case, catastrophe threatens our primary world or a secondary one. The outcome depends on children.

These authors are writing in the shadow of the Second World War, in the knowledge of the holocaust and nuclear weapons. Alan Garner acknowl-edges his childhood perception of the war as a struggle between good and evil (Garner, 1997: 17). The North American writers were particularly conscious of the Cold War, with its dread of a Soviet communist conquest and its terror of full-scale nuclear war. The mythic models on which these novels draw can produce meaning at all kinds of levels: psychological, social and political, theological. Their enlisting of children as chief protago-nists, rather than the adult Arthur, Hercules or Siegfried of legend, offers children a vision of themselves as heroes, with the necessity of choosing sides. Typically, there is a figure of wisdom, who must be listened to if disaster is to be avoided: examples include Cooper's Merriman and L'Engle's Mrs Whatsit. But, equally typically, these adult figures say they have limited power to intervene. The future of the universe rests in the hands of the younger generation.

The heroism called for is not, in the best writers, a simple resort to the sword. Joy Chant, in *Red Moon and Black Mountain*, uses it but with evident regret (Chant, 1973). The hobbit Bilbo stops a war by giving away the greatest treasure he has found. Ged, in *A Wizard of Earthsea*, controls the devouring shadow only by embracing and naming it with his own name. Meg reverses the anti-creation of the Unnamers when she wills herself to name and love them. David Gooderham sees this as the final stage of development represented in children's literature, following fantasies of wish fulfilment, control, venture and competence. He calls it the 'fantasy of devotion' (Gooderham, 1995: 176).

In Narnia, it is necessary for the children to decide whether they are on Aslan's side or the Witch's, and the reader is left in no doubt when a child chooses the wrong side. This uncritical goodies-and-baddies, zap-the-alien mode is still alive and well. Brian Jacques's Redwall series, about a valiant community of mice, sells hugely (Jacques, 1990). In the 1970s, Catherine Storr could say about good and evil in children's books, 'The Good presents no difficulty; it is, of course, oneself' (Storr, 1977: 123). But others are leading children towards notions of ambivalence, about the world and themselves: Tolkien and Garner have good wizards whose twin brothers are in the service of evil. More recent writers have internalised this dichotomy. In Louise Lawrence's *Llandor* trilogy (Lawrence, 1995, 1996a, 1996b), the children are not the victims of evil. They themselves constitute the danger which has entered the land. The Black Mage Kadmon confounds their assumptions, first by proving to be their guardian, second by being himself tainted with evil. In the course of the trilogy, the message shifts from 'Beware whom you trust', to, 'You must learn *when* to trust me'. In the late twentieth century, children are increasingly endowed with the responsibility of questioning absolute authority.

The child in the marketplace

Books of this quality can be found in hardback editions on library shelves, as well as selling plentifully in paperback. But in the 1970s, a trend in book-selling got underway which has contributed to a shift in the way books are now published for children. Early in that decade John Rowe Townsend, addressing the Exeter Children's Literature in Education conference, could say that a hardback children's book from a reputable publisher would pay its way on library sales alone. Such books were chosen by librarians and teachers, using criteria of quality as well as sheer entertainment. If they perceived the need for books to represent the lives of working-class, black and disabled children more fully, they could use their purchasing power to support this.

During the 1970s, the growth of school book clubs significantly boosted paperback sales. Books were increasingly chosen by children themselves, possibly with the assistance of a parent, who would not usually have the same knowledge of more recent authors as a teacher or librarian, or use the same criteria. Squeezes on public spending have drastically cut the amount of money schools and libraries have available for book buying. The takeover of small publishing firms by large conglomerates has led to publishing decisions being influenced by accountants rather than by editors. 'Would we be proud to see this book on our list?' has been replaced by, 'Will it sell?'

Child-led publishing sounds healthy; teachers have long pointed out that some books, given awards by adults, linger on the shelves, unread by children. But it tends to privilege a literary construction of childhood different from that encouraged at the more challenging end of the market. Roald Dahl has understood this better than almost any other writer. His books sometimes disturb adults with their subversive child's-angle approach. In *James and the Giant Peach*, the aunts James dislikes are termi-nally flattened (Dahl, 1973). There is no suggestion that James needs to change or grow in understanding. The unwary publisher will assume that children only want books which present childhood as wish fulfilment. The fictional child wins, can overcome any difficulty, can beat any enemy. The better ones credit children with the wisdom to know that real life is not that easy. They take heart from the commercial success of writers like Anne Fine, who present sympathetic characters comically in need of a change of attitude (Fine, 1989). Her stories both entertain children and assume they can rise to a subjective challenge.

Humphrey Carpenter has observed that children's fiction at the beginning of the twentieth century celebrates childhood as the ideal state, while in the second half, it is about teaching children to grow up (Carpenter, 1985: 216). There is considerable truth in this at the quality end of the market. But it may become less true as market forces increase their authority over what may now be published. In the larger publishing houses, it is no longer sufficient for a book to make a profit; it must make a sizeable profit if that author is to remain on the list.

This trend makes it increasingly difficult for minorities to see themselves inscribed in fiction. Teachers and librarians have, in recent years, appreciated the need to stock books which feature black and Asian children. Editors in the 1970s and 1980s were on the look-out for authors like Farrukh Dhondy who could write such books authentically (Dhondy, 1978). But also in the 1980s, the marketing manager of WH Smith was telling a group of children's authors he found that books with a black child on the jacket would not sell. When teachers and librarians had greater purchasing power, bookshop sales were not crucial in determining what could be published. Now, computerised access to an author's previous sales record means that booksellers can tell publishers at manuscript stage whether they would stock such a book. Their response can determine whether a book is published or not. Models of childhood and child readers which accord with majority perceptions present less commercial risk. More off-beat alternatives may not get the opportunity to prove their popularity.

In the 1980s, I asked a much-respected children's editor, 'What sort of manuscript would you most like to see on your desk tomorrow morning?' She said, 'The one I'm not expecting'. She did not survive the takeover of her firm. Now, editors will more typically tell you the specifications for series which they have predetermined in-house, detailing the length, readership and type of subject matter. There is still room for originality within these slots, and the possibility remains for marvellous one-off novels, like Philip Pullman's trilogy *His Dark Materials*, which rewrites a youthful Eve's role in the Fall (Pullman, 1996, 1997, 1999). But the sales potential of originality is unpredictable. Increasingly, the models offered to children are being tailored by the publishers' perception of the kind of children who will buy them in large quantities. Ghost and mild horror stories abound.

A personal perspective

As a reflective practitioner of children's fiction, it is useful for me to site my own work in the shifting patterns of the twentieth century and to see how different modes of writing have favoured particular perspectives. In my children's books, I have employed a variety of approaches. Since my view of the world has not fundamentally changed over the years, there is an underlying consistency in the construction of childhood they present. But I am aware that my varying starting points have changed the emphasis and produced different responses in both adult and child readers.

I have resisted the lure to write simply for commercial reasons, to shape a book which fits the editor's, or my own, perceptions of childhood in general. Nor have I ever originated a novel by telling the story first to a particular child. My usual motivation is curiosity, typically, 'What would it feel like to be in that situation?' This internalising approach necessarily draws on my perception of my own childhood, which, from five to fifteen, spanned the 1940s. We were the cherished generation who, our parents hoped, would inherit the postwar society and build a better future for the world. We were encouraged to be idealistic, to have large visions, to believe that we could change the world. It is not surprising, therefore, that my writing, like others of my generation, has leaned towards the heroic model of childhood. But differing choices in envisaging the central protagonists have produced variations.

The particular child I have at times written for is myself. In *The Hungry Snow* (Sampson, 1980) I wrote about a girl in a Dartmoor village at the beginning of the twentieth century, who finds that a series of severe winters is leading to the suppression of female births. In the heroic mode, she intervenes to rescue one baby. *A Free Man on Sunday* (Sampson, 1987) introduces fictional children into the real-life drama of the mass trespass on Kinder Scout in 1934, when young people broke the law and claimed the right to walk the hills. These historical stories are set earlier than my own childhood, and the family circumstances are unlike mine, except in the broad sense of being working class. Yet the protagonists act and react to their situations as I imagine I would have done. Their relationship with their parents owes much to mine.

The feedback suggests that, for all the applicability of their idealism today and the proactive attitude of their protagonists, this way of writing has produced an adult's perspective of childhood remembered. These books have been warmly received by other adults, including some who took part in the Kinder Scout Trespass. *The Hungry Snow* has appeared on the adult shelves of the public library and in homes for the elderly. I have received fewer responses from children.

My first published book was *F.67* (Sampson, 1975), a near-future story in which British children become refugees in an African country. I modelled the boy and girl more or less on my own children. In *Chris and the Dragon* (Sampson, 1985), a humorous school story about the Christmas season, I also drew the inspiration for the principal character from real life. In fact, the model was a fourteen-year-old girl, who becomes in the book a nine-year-old boy, but the reality is the same: a warm-hearted likeable child who is always in trouble because of an inability to think out the consequences before acting.

These are observed realities, not lived ones. These children are not like me. Though *F.67* has a science-fiction opening, both books share the tendency of social realism to recognise the limited power of children to change the world in which they find themselves, unlike the more heroic tendency of fantasy or historical novels. These children affirm, sometimes celebrate, the condition of childhood, acknowledging the bruising effect of their powerlessness yet struggling to optimise their own lives within these constraints. The books strike a chord with children. If I am visiting a school, I know I can read from these books and expect a positive response. Each has been questioned by adult reviewers or teachers for their child's-eye priorities or the toughness of the experience they describe. I am told that children emphatically reject these adult perceptions. Such stories inscribe a model of childhood which is less idealistic, less nostalgic, less the internalised heroism of my child-self, and more attuned to the actual situations and interactions of contemporary children.

My third type of children's book is, as in Lewis's third mode, that which draws on universal themes of myth, inscribing a vision beyond either the author-as-child or the observed child. I place my *Pangur Bán* books in this category (Sampson, 1997). They are fantasy, set in Celtic times. The two chief focalising characters are a little white cat and a bloodthirsty princess. What threatens them in each of the six books is hardly the point; they are the perils and tests common to romance. What matters is the progress towards the resolution, the discoveries and changes this entails. This is what separates the mythic genre from the adventure series in which characters reappear in successive volumes, virtually unaltered by their previous experiences. The cat, Pangur Bán, is the Jack of folklore, representing the small, apparently powerless child, who has only his wits to rely on but who achieves more than he thought possible. Princess Finnglas is the heroic figure, who needs to be socialised to the reality of her world and has to learn that true nobility requires more than a sword. These figures are age-old. They inscribe both what a child is and can do now, and what that child may become. But their adventures are set in a larger dimension in which individual effort, however heroic, is not enough. They co-operate with a universal presence.

The responses I receive show that this category of my work provokes the deepest responses from both children and adults. I have been told of a teenage boy who has thrown away all his other children's books but kept this series; of a vicar who has a passage from it read in his church every Easter, because he cannot trust himself to read it without tears.

Anecdotal experiences like these comment on the construction of childhood as internalised, observed or shared. This is, of course, an oversimplification. My inscriptions of childhood, and the responses to them, overlap to a considerable degree. An author is, perhaps, the least reliable person to interpret her own work. But similar reflections are echoed by many famous children's writers. Gene Kemp is a keen observer of classroom culture; her books are a hit with a broad range of children. Leon Garfield claims to write only for himself. He may be seen to appeal particularly strongly to literary children and to adults who work with children's books. Alan Garner claims that every book he writes has its roots in myth (Garner, 1997: 137). He stirs deep responses across a spectrum of readers.

Again, I am oversimplifying to make a point. What is interesting is that no one of these perspectives of childhood appears to be more successful than another. *A Free Man on Sunday, Chris and the Dragon* and *Pangur Bán* were all shortlisted for national awards and they represent all three categories. Kemp, Garfield and Garner are all acclaimed, award-winning writers.

Future visions

When children's literature began as a separate genre around the seventeenth century, its sole purpose was didactic. Since then, we have learned to celebrate guilt-free childhood and explore ambivalence. What is imponderable in the current trend is its effect on the constructions of childhood that will emerge. Will they be conservative, with children, parents and grandparents buying what they already know? Will it still be possible for authors, and other professionals in the book world, to see what is missing from the picture and take steps to supply it? How far will it be influenced by other media – children's television, films, computer games – whose particular strengths are in action rather than in exploring character and motivation, and whose simplified plot lines lend themselves to polarisation?

Since women and girls buy more books than males, and middle-class females more than working-class females, we might expect that the influence of feminism towards stronger roles for girls will be maintained by market forces. The current concern for the poor performance of boys in school may heighten a call for more books inscribing a conventional image of masculinity. But the effect on publishers' lists of such a call will depend on the readiness of boys to be customers for them. Bettelheim's *Uses of Enchantment* shows that boys can identify with Cinderella (Bettelheim, 1978: 282), yet the common perception of society is that books about girls are unacceptable to boys.

I do not wish to argue that the shift in market influence from professional adults towards end-readers is absolute in its effect. Works of originality can be published within the familiar parameters of a series. Terry Pratchett has shown that comic science fiction can both be hugely popular and raise large questions about the human condition (Pratchett, 1993). It may be harder than it was twenty years ago for an innovative author to break accepted norms and propose new models of childhood and inspire an editor to back them, but the really sparkling original work can still break through.

It will be interesting to see how the growth of Internet publishing will alter the presentation of childhood in the twenty-first century. The Internet allows communication between author and reader with fewer intermediaries. In its most direct form, it greatly reduces editorial control. Ideological perspectives of all shades will have greater freedom from the constraints of commercial publishing. Readers may be exposed to a great deal of self-indulgent writing. Authors with experimental visions, however, may find it liberating.

Conclusion

Visions of childhood will vary with the questions each generation is asking itself, whether about duty or levity, feminism, race, class, the freedom to be a child or the challenge to grow up, the necessity to endure, to adapt or to effect change. They offer three broad choices, through which these images can be explored:

- childhood as experienced by the author;
- childhood as experienced by the reader;
- childhood as part of the universal experience of humanity.

Review questions and tasks

1   What are the pressures which have contributed to changing approaches to childhood in twentieth-century children's fiction?
2   What portrayal of childhood made the deepest impression on you in your own reading as a child? What concept of childhood was being projected through this image?
3   Discuss the relative merits of children's books which:

   a   celebrate childhood;
   b   enable the child to act the role of an adult;
   c   deal with the progress of a child towards adulthood.

4   Make a list of the experiences which you think need to be represented in the fiction available to a typical primary school class.

5 Discuss the possible effect of greater freedom to publish work through the Internet on the images offered in children's fiction.

6 Write the first chapter of your own book for children, along with a commentary on:
   - your thought-processes in writing for children;
   - the choices you had to make;
   - the ideas you rejected;
   - your level of satisfaction with the final outcome.
   - (If you are really satisfied, why not finish the book?)

Further reading

Butler, F. and Robert, R. (eds) (1986) *Triumphs of the Spirit in Children's Literature,* **Hamden, CN: Library Professional Publications.** Madeleine L'Engle's introduction quotes her injured granddaughter, who was 'healed by doctors and nurses, but also by the stories she heard that summer'. She declares, 'We grow through the things that stretch us, that hurt us'. This is a study of books which deal with the darker side of children's experience and offer routes to hope. It reflects a shift in children's literature from emphasis on physical drama to psychological trauma. This collection of essays is weighted towards North American novels, but considers some European examples.

Carpenter, H. (1985) *Secret Gardens: A Study of the Golden Age of Children's Literature,* **London: Allen & Unwin.** Carpenter begins with the Victorian fantasists, Kingsley, Carroll and MacDonald, but carries the tradition forward to Tolkien in the mid-twentieth century. His title expresses his theme: that the early children's books of this century are about a private dream, in contrast to the more recent trend towards books that help children grow up. He is particularly concerned with the implied relationship between the child and authority, whether parents or God, and the way in which these authors are working out their own preoccupations through children's books. He shows how the social awareness of the evangelical Victorians gave way to Edwardian middle-class assumptions, which remained dominant until the mid-twentieth century.

Chambers, N. (ed.) (1980) *The Signal Approach to Children's Books,* **Harmondsworth: Kestrel.** This is an anthology of work from the influential journal on children's literature, *Signal*. There are three particularly interesting articles. In 'The Seventies in British Children's Books', Elaine Moss widens the perspective of the subject away from the purely literary by considering trends in publishing and selling books, including the growth of school book clubs. She relates this to the child-centred emphasis of the 1970s and the growth of a multi-cultural society and feminist awareness, quoting Farrukh Dhondy's celebration of a story which 'doesn't see Asians as victims'. Aidan Chambers's 'The Reader in the Book' explores the idea of the implied reader. He discusses the effect of different narrative stances, of tone of voice, of whether the author is a watcher of children or is in collusion with them. In 'An Interview with Alan Garner', he relates these ideas to the work of a particular author. Garner cites his responses from children. The discussion moves to 'subversive' messages and children's ability to handle them.

Goldthwaite, J. (1996) *The Natural History of Make-Believe: A Guide to the Principal Works of Britain, Europe and America,* **Oxford: Oxford University Press.** All true children's stories, Goldthwaite says, make promises to their readers. 'Here you are, unhandy and short, and there is the big world that will one day be yours'. He traces the roots of children's literature in fairy tales and carries their themes forward to the 1970s. Given his refreshingly iconoclastic attitude to writers like C.S. Lewis, it is a matter for regret that he has not subjected the most recent generation of authors to the same scrutiny. His stance is every bit as ethical as Lewis's, but he has a compassion for the erring child. His contrast between Lewis's damnation of Susan, in *The Last Battle,* and Maurice Sendak's celebration of Max's anger, in *Where the Wild Things Are,* reflects the more complex understanding of children in the late twentieth century.

Haviland, V. (ed.) (1973) *Children and Children's Literature: Views and Reviews,* **London: Bodley Head.** The emphasis in this collection is on books which deal with challenges to children and which are themselves challenging. The contributors range from John Buchan to P.L. Travers, and the anthology includes C.S. Lewis's essay on 'Three Ways to Write for Children'. There is a general condemnation of blandness, and a high regard for children's potential as readers. Paul Heins quotes a *Horn Book* editorial: 'It is foolish to say "we ought only to give the child conceptions it can understand." His soul grows by wonder over things it cannot understand'.

Stephens, J. (1992) *Language and Ideology in Children's Fiction,* **London: Longman.** The concept of childhood in children's literature rests as much on the implied reader as on the children in the story. This book offers a study of the complex transaction negotiated in reading, involving author, implied author, narrator, events and existents, narratee, implied reader and actual reader. It examines the conventions of different genres and the socialising or alienating effect of varying narrative stances and tone of voice. Stephens notes a shift from the assumption of unchanging human nature to cultural relativism and the development of 'carnivalesque' books, creating 'roles for child characters which interrogate the normal subject positions created for children within socially dominant ideological frames'.

References

Barrie, J. (1928) *Peter Pan,* London: Hodder & Stoughton.

Bawden, N. (1969) *The Witch's Daughter,* Harmondsworth: Penguin.

Berg, L. (1970) *Little Pete Stories,* Harmondsworth: Penguin.

Bettelheim, B. (1978) *The Uses of Enchantment: The Meaning and Importance of Fairy Tales,* Harmondsworth: Penguin.

Blyton, E. (1963) *Tales of Toyland,* London: Dean.

Burnett, F.H. (1911) *The Secret Garden,* London: Heinemann.

Carpenter, H. (1985) *Secret Gardens: A Study of the Golden Age of Children's Literature,* London: Allen & Unwin.

Chant, J. (1973) *Red Moon and Black Mountain*, Harmondsworth: Penguin.

Cooper, S. (1984) *The Dark is Rising Sequence*, Harmondsworth: Penguin.

Dahl, R. (1973) *James and the Giant Peach*, Harmondsworth: Penguin.

Dhondy, F. (1978) *Come to Mecca and Other Stories*, London: Fontana.

Fine, A. (1989) *Goggle-Eyes*, London: Hamish Hamilton.

Garner, A. (1971) *The Weirdstone of Brisingamen*, London: Collins.

—— (1997) *The Voice that Thunders: Essays and Lectures*, London: Harvill.

Garnett, E. (1942) *The Family from One-End Street*, Harmondsworth: Penguin.

Gooderham, D. (1995) 'Children's Fantasy Literature: Towards an Anatomy', *Children's Literature in Education*, vol. 26, no. 3, 171–83.

Grahame, K. (1896) *The Golden Age*, London: John Lane/Stone & Kimball.

—— (1951) *The Wind in the Willows*, London: Methuen.

Hoban, R. (1987) *A Baby Sister for Frances*, London: Scholastic.

Jacques, B. (1990) *Redwall*, London: Random House.

Kemp, G. (1977) *The Turbulent Term of Tyke Tiler*, London: Faber.

Kingsley, C. (1994) *The Water Babies*, Ware: Wordsworth.

Lawrence, L. (1995) *The Journey Through Llandor*, The Llandor Trilogy Part 1, London: Collins.

Lawrence, L. (1996a) *The Road to Irriyan*, The Llandor Trilogy Part 2, London: Collins.

Lawrence, L. (1996b) *The Shadow of Mordican*, The Llandor Trilogy Part 3, London: Collins.

Lear, E. (1846) *Book of Nonsense*, London.

L'Engle, M. (1967) *A Wrinkle in Time*, London: Penguin.

—— (1975) *A Wind in the Door*, London: Methuen.

Le Guin, U. (1971) *A Wizard of Earthsea*, Harmondsworth: Penguin.

Lewis, C.S. (1959) *The Lion, the Witch and the Wardrobe*, Harmondsworth: Penguin.

MacDonald, G. (1964) *At the Back of the North Wind*, London: Macmillan.

—— (1994) *The Princess and Curdie*, London: Penguin.

Masefield, J. (1927) *Midnight Folk*, London: Heinemann.

—— (1935) *The Box of Delights*, London: Heinemann.

Mayne, W. (1955) *A Swarm in May*, London: Hodder & Stoughton.

—— (1977) *No More School*, London: Hamish Hamilton.

Milne, A.A. (1928) *The House at Pooh Corner*, London: Methuen.

Nesbit, E. (1959) *The Phoenix and the Carpet*, Harmondsworth: Penguin.

—— (1982) *The Treasure Seekers*, Harmondsworth: Penguin.

—— (1990) *Five Children and It*, London: BBC Books.

Okri, B. (1998) in D. Ransom, *Eye to Eye: Childhood*, Oxford: New Internationalist

Pratchett, T. (1993) *Only You Can Save Mankind*, London: Corgi.

Pullman, P. (1996) *Northern Lights*, London: Scholastic.

—— (1997) *The Subtle Knife*, London: Scholastic.

—— (1999) *His Dark Materials*, vol. 3, London: Scholastic.

Ransome, A. (1931) *Swallows and Amazons*, London: Cape.

Sampson, F. (1975) *F. 67*, London: Hamish Hamilton.

—— (1980) *The Hungry Snow*, London: Dobson.

—— (1985) *Chris and the Dragon*, London: Gollancz.

—— (1987) *A Free Man on Sunday*, London: Gollancz.

—— (1997) *Shape-Shifter/Pangur Bán*, Oxford: Lion.

Storr, C. (1977) 'Things That Go Bump in the Night', in M. Meek, A. Warlow and G. Barton (eds), *The Cool Web: The Pattern of Children's Reading*, London: Bodley Head.

Tolkien, J. R.R. (1966) *The Hobbit*, London: Unwin.

Walsh, C. (1979) *The Literary Legacy of C.S. Lewis*, London: Sheldon.

Part Three

Education

Chapter 4

Children at play

Susannah Smith

Summary

After an endorsement of the value of play by children, this
chapter seeks to define exactly what play is and to consider its
potential value. At each stage in the discussion, observation
notes ensure that the investigation is rooted firmly in real
events, real situations and real children. It is clear that play
involves learning through activities that are enjoyable, often self-
motivated and all-absorbing. It is both autonomous and social
and it can be therapeutic. To observe children at play is a delight
and a privilege.

> Play is indeed the child's work.
>
> (Isaacs, 1929)

Observing children at play is a fascinating experience, offering a window into their lives and into the things that are important for them. It is also an informative experience. Through watching children playing, we can learn about childhood. Play is fundamental to childhood, since it is the most natural means by which children develop and learn. It has been suggested that the work–play distinction is unnecessary in childhood, as the epigraph from Susan Isaacs asserts, but the more common belief is that play is for children what work is for adults. Certainly, play can be a challenging, tiring and rewarding occupation for children, as can work for adults.

In this chapter, the following areas of children's play have been identified for examination:

- children as active players
- children as learners
- children as social beings
- children as emotional beings
- children as autonomous players

These five areas will be discussed separately, but since childhood is a whole, some areas will inevitably overlap and more than one may be evident in any play observation.

Before considering any observations, however, we must examine what is meant by play. This is notoriously difficult, since the term incorporates a wide variety of behaviours. Consider the following: doing a jigsaw; playing a game of chess; cooking a pretend meal in a toy kitchen; making snails out of plasticene; painting a picture; skipping in the playground. What are the common features? Educationalists (Piaget, 1962; Garvey, 1977; Smith *et al.*, 1986) attempting to define the boundaries of play have included features such as enjoyment, open-endedness, spontaneity, voluntariness and active engagement. It is unlikely, however, that all of these would be present in all play situations. Moreover, since play is a form of behaviour, the same activity can be carried out in a playful or non-playful way. The boundaries of play are therefore fluid and it is difficult to provide a comprehensive definition.

As well as seeking to define the boundaries of play, educationalists have attempted to categorise it. Hutt *et al.* (1989) devised a complete 'taxonomy of play'. This categorises play into 'epistemic', 'ludic' and 'games with rules'; each of these is further sub-divided. Epistemic play refers to the acquisition of knowledge and skills, and ludic play refers to self-amusement and imaginative play. Other scholars have used the categories 'structured' and 'unstructured' (Manning and Sharp, 1977), and 'directed' and 'free' (Moyles, 1989).

Despite any differences, all these writers agree that play should be taken seriously, with Moyles commenting that: 'play has all too often been used to infer something rather trivial and non-serious – the polar extreme to work rather than, as in a child context, the essence of serious, concentrated thinking' (Moyles, 1989: 16). As this chapter will show, children's play is a serious business. It would therefore be helpful if it had a different name, one that became synonymous with a significant and valuable occupation.

While there is not the opportunity here to examine the issue in detail, it must be acknowledged that children live in a social context, and this profoundly influences the nature of their play across each of the areas that will be examined. An individual context may vary according to a multitude of factors, including gender, culture, religion, family make-up or ability/disability, and each of these will influence the child's play. Because children's experiences are central to their play, differing experiences will result in different play. It should be acknowledged that the discussion in this chapter is from Western European perspective, and within the 0–8 age range.

Children as active players

The following observations indicate that children are naturally active, both physically and mentally.

In a nursery class playground the following notes were made during a ten-minute observation:

> Three children are climbing on a climbing frame. One child has reached the top and is calling and waving to friends playing below. One child has climbed about half way up the climbing frame and seems unsure about climbing higher. She rests for a period then climbs carefully down. One child is running in and out of the climbing frame. Two children are on tricycles. One is pedalling and one is being pushed by a friend running behind. Two children seemed to be in a chase game. One runs away then the other starts chasing her. When the second catches her up they rest, then reverse roles. Three children are walking along wavy lines painted on the floor of the playground.

The following notes were made in an early years classroom:

> Six children are sitting around a table. Two are making necklaces by threading beads onto a lace. When complete they ask an adult to tie the ends together and wear the necklaces proudly. Four children are putting

pegs into a pegboard. Some are copying patterns drawn on cards, others are experimenting freely. On the carpet four children are playing with coloured wooden bricks. Following an adult's instruction, they are making towers and bridges. One child builds a tower of nine bricks before it tumbles over.

A three-year-old is playing a game on a computer. It involves placing pictures in a three by three grid by dragging pictures from a selection. Once compete, the computer hides the pictures. It then asks the child to find a particular picture by clicking on the correct box. This is repeated for each picture. The game is then repeated, the aim being to find the pictures using fewer attempts.

In the first observation, the children are developing their large (gross) motor skills through their activities. The illustration mentions climbing, running, pedalling and balancing. These activities and others, including, jumping, hopping, skipping, galloping, dancing and turning, enable children to take control of their bodies. From the time a baby lifts its head, it is starting to exercise control over its body. Movements that initially appear wobbly and jerky will gradually become more regulated. As Angela Anning points out, in addition to providing enjoyment and challenge, play promotes physical development. She writes:

there is evidently a spontaneous urge amongst young children to try out and practise physical activities for the sake of enjoyment and the sense of achievement they gain from progressive mastery of large motor skills such as running, jumping, climbing, kicking and catching balls, etc.

(Anning, 1997: 33)

In the second observation, children are improving their fine motor skills. Consider the dexterity needed to make a tower of bricks. Each has to be placed accurately, and with appropriate pressure, on top of the previous one if a tower is to be produced. Threading beads, putting pegs in small holes and building towers all require sophisticated control of the hand and fingers and accurate hand–eye co-ordination. In addition to playing, children are developing the techniques they need to write fluently and legibly. The skill required to put a peg in a small hole is comparable to that required to make marks with writing tools.

The final observation illustrates that children do not have to be physically engaged to be active, as Julie Fisher observes:

'being active' does not necessarily mean 'moving around'. Being active means that young children engage with experiences, actively (as opposed to passively) bringing their existing knowledge and understanding to bear on what is currently under investigation.

(1996: 9)

Fisher suggests that children can be active or passive, but when they are engaged in mental work they are active. Children use their existing knowledge and understanding when faced with a new or unfamiliar situation. In the final observation, the child is engaged in challenging mental processes. She is making choices about where to place pictures, attempting to remember where she put them and trying to improve on her success each time. She is using existing knowledge and understanding and applying it to a new context. She is active, not passive.

Following the discovery that children's play was valuable, the active nature of it was seen to be fundamental, as Froebel (1782–1852) recognised. Prior to Froebel, play was largely perceived to be a trivial activity that children carried out as a reward for 'working'; to relieve excess energy; to pass the time until adult maturity; to practise and prepare for adulthood. Froebel was the first to provide a structured curriculum where the development of physical and mental activity was catered for in a systematic way.

When the first Froebelian kindergarten was opened in Hampstead, England, the idea of 'active learning' was stressed. This occurred through exploration with highly structured educational materials called 'gifts of increasing complexity' ... These activities reflected the exploratory and active nature of the learning that was being encouraged through 'playing' with particular materials.

(Beardsley and Harnett, 1998: 20–1)

The 'gifts' that Froebel used involved children in an active way, and he had a huge influence on subsequent educationalists such as Margaret McMillan, Maria Montessori and Susan Isaacs. The ideas he developed about the place of play in active learning are still with us today; such theories are discussed in Bruce (1991: chs 2–3) and Anning (1997: chs 1–2).

In building up a picture of childhood, the first element we have is that children are naturally active players. It is difficult to think of a pre-adolescent child who remains inactive for more than a few minutes. Indeed, parents may often feel their young children are only inactive when asleep!

Children as learners

Children have a huge capacity for learning, and play, rather than formal teaching, is the natural medium through which they learn, since it is enjoyable and self-motivated.

Consider the following teaching situations, where play is being used as the teaching method. They were observed in an inner-city school where the majority of children have English as an additional language.

Three children (two female, one male, all aged four or five years in a Reception class) were playing in a water tray. The equipment available included the following: corks, sponges, coloured plastic boats, coins, plasticene balls, plasticene boat-like shapes, empty plastic bottles, metal teaspoons and golf balls. The children were left to play with the objects for about ten minutes and were asked to see which floated and which sank. The teacher then came and sat with the children. After a general chat about floating and sinking, the following conversation took place (T = teacher, C = child).

T: Does all of the plasticene sink?
C1:   Yes.
T: What about the plasticene shaped like a boat?
C2:   (Picks one up and tries it.) Well, it floats if you put it like this. (Like a boat.)
T: So the plasticene balls sink and the plasticene boats float. Why's that?
C1:   Well, because that's like a boat.
C3:   That's like a ball and that's like a boat.
T: But the golf ball floats.
C3:   That's, um, light.
C1:   Yes, the plasticene ball's heavy. The boat's a different shape.
T: Does the shape make a difference?
C3:   Yes.
T: Why?
C3:   Boat-shapes float.

Four children (two female, two male, all aged five or six in a Year 1 class) were playing in a role-play area designed to be a greenhouse. The area was cornered off using tables and shelving and a large plastic sheet hung out from the wall over the tables and shelving to create a greenhouse. The equipment available included flower pots, seed trays, seed packets (empty packets that the children had used in lessons), plant catalogues, soil, watering cans (the children were not allowed real water while playing in the greenhouse), trowels, forks, rakes and seeds at various stages of growth (that had been planted in class). The following play and talk was observed.

C1 Picks up a flower pot and chooses a seed packet by examining the pictures on the front. Goes over to the soil and uses a trowel to put some in the flower pot. Shakes the packet over the soil. Examines closely. Uses hands to sprinkle some more soil over the top. Goes to get a watering can and 'waters' the soil. Puts the pot on the windowsill.

> C2: Look at this bean. The roots are growing down and the shoot is growing up. It's only a tiny shoot. Do you think it will have flowers on it?
>
> C3: No. Beans don't have flowers on them.
>
> C2: No, they don't (*laughs*).

In the first observation, the children were learning about floating and sinking. Initially, they explored this using a range of equipment chosen by the teacher. After a period of playing freely with the equipment, the teacher joined the children and sought to enhance their learning through questioning. Through the teacher's intervention, the children were developing their understanding about why some objects float and some sink. In the extract above, they were thinking about the effects of the weight and shape of objects.

This is an example of the teacher 'scaffolding' children's learning (Bruner, in Wood *et al.*, 1976). The teacher is encouraging the children to move from their 'actual developmental level' to their 'level of potential development' (Vygotsky, 1978). Vygotsky argues that the role of the teacher (or more capable peers) is to lead children through the zone of proximal development (ZPD), that is, the distance between actual and potential development. (See also Chapter 5 in this volume for further comment on the concept.) The teacher supports children to do what they cannot currently do independently, the aim being ultimately a measure of autonomy.

Anning (1997: 23) has argued that the work of Bruner and Vygotsky has initiated a significant new paradigm in thinking about young children and learning. It is seen as a social process. This contrasts with the work of Piaget (1962), for whom learning is largely an individual process with children passing through stages of development when ready. The influence of Piaget encouraged teachers to set up learning opportunities and wait until children were ready to learn from them independently. The influence of Vygotsky, however, encourages teachers to set up learning opportunities and to support children through them in the belief that they would learn more quickly than if left until ready. A full discussion of learning theories, including those of Piaget, Bruner and Vygotsky, can be found in Wood (1990).

In the second observation, the children are playing using previously acquired knowledge and skills, and consolidating their learning. Child C1 is enacting the process of planting seeds, utilising what she already knows about what seeds need to grow. Child C2 is examining plants that the class has grown and is confidently using the terms 'roots', 'shoot' and 'flowers'. Moyles (1989) talks about directed and free play, and constructs these into a spiral. Through directed play children are taught knowledge and skills, and in free play they are consolidating this learning. Repeated directed and free play form a spiral of learning. Moyles uses a simile to explain this:

> Rather like a pebble on a pond, the ripples from the exploratory free play through directed play and back to enhanced and enriched free play, allowed a spiral of learning spreading ever outwards into wider experiences for the children and upwards into the accretion of knowledge and skills.
>
> (Moyles, 1989: 15)

Moyles's understanding of play is illustrated in the observation. Free play has been enhanced by previously directed play. Subsequent directed play could develop free play further: for example, Child C3 now could learn that bean plants *do* have flowers on them!

Play is believed to enhance all areas of learning, including problem-solving, creativity and language development. In today's educational climate, where standards and achievements are placed at the centre of the educational experience, play would soon be eliminated if it was not believed to be an effective learning strategy. However, whether learning through play occurs in or out of the school context, the second element we have in building up a picture of childhood is that children are learners.

Children as emotional beings

Children have strong emotions and feelings. As they progress, they learn to control their emotions and feelings and to express them in culturally acceptable ways. Play takes a significant role in this process. Consider the following observations:

For a number of weeks Dominic (male, aged three years) had been having nightmares about a lion coming into his bedroom. The following play situations were subsequently reported by his mother.

Dominic tucked rabbit, a favourite doll, up in bed. He then said, *A lion's coming. I'm telling the lion, 'Go out of the front door, go back to the jungle'* (with angry expression and pointing to the front door). *It's alright, rabbit. The lion's gone now. I told it to go down the stairs and go out of the front door and go back to the jungle. You'll be safe now.*

This was repeated on a number of different occasions, each time the wording being very similar.

Dominic was playing with a set of miniature animals and people. He picked up a lion and made roaring noises with it, directed towards a male figure. His mother asked Dominic, *Is the man frightened?* Dominic replied, *No, it's a friendly lion.* The play continued.

A family holiday had entailed driving through the night to reach a continental destination. The children, Rebecca and Eleanor (sisters, aged six and four years) engaged in the following play when they returned home a fortnight later.

R: Come on, get in the car, we're going on holiday. Get your suitcase.

(Two chairs had been placed next to each other to make a car.)

E: But it's dark. It's bedtime.

R: Yes, but we've got to go now. So that it won't be busy. So that we get there first in the morning. We'll have our breakfast in a service station in France.

E: I'll be Mummy. Here you are. *(Gives cushion to R.)* Lie on your pillow. Now, try to go to sleep.

R: OK. I'll be Daddy. I'm driving.

E: It's a long way. We've got a long way to go.

R: Yes, I'll tell the girls to go to sleep now. *(Turns round, addresses pretend children.)* Go to sleep, then when you wake up we'll be there.

E: They won't go to sleep. They're uncomfortable. They need their blankets.

R: Well, they can watch the lights until they fall asleep. Here, I'll put a tape on for them to listen to.

The play continued for over fifteen minutes and was returned to over the next few days.

Dominic's play illustrates how he was coming to terms with his nightmares. In the first observation, he is taking control of the situation. He makes himself bigger and stronger than the lion so that he can control it and not be frightened. In the second observation, he is acknowledging that lions can be friendly, in which case again it is not necessary to be frightened when meeting one.

Rebecca and Eleanor are playing out a scene in which, when it originally took place, they were anxious. Getting into the car and driving a long distance is far removed from their usual evening routine. Such deviation from routine caused anxiety. When they returned home, representing a return to familiarity and security, they play out the scenario and, like

Dominic, put themselves in control of the situation. Through repeated play, they gradually became familiar with the situation and are able to integrate it into their experiences. One could expect this to result in reduced anxiety should the situation be repeated.

Isaacs recognised that, through play, a child learns to understand everyday experiences and to deal with uncomfortable emotions. In opening the Cambridge Malting House School, she acknowledged the place of active play in teaching children cognitive concepts and recognised its importance for children's healthy emotional development, commenting: 'Active play can be looked on as a sign of mental health; and its absence, either of some inborn defect, or of mental illness' (Isaacs, 1929: 9). Today, Isaacs's terminology might not be used, but we can still have sympathy with the notion that emotionally healthy children play actively and that children who do not play, or who are not able to play constructively, have an emotional need.

More recently, Tina Bruce has acknowledged the importance of children's feelings. She refers to the 'whole child', who has physical, intellectual and emotional needs which must be met for healthy development. She devised ten principles of early childhood education and the second of these is:

> The whole child is considered to be important. Health, physical and mental, is emphasised, as well as the importance of feelings, thinking and spiritual aspects.
> (Bruce, 1991: 7)

Bruce's work supports that of Isaacs in the assertion that all aspects of a child's development – physical, intellectual and emotional needs – are equally important.

The third element we have in building up a picture of childhood is that children are emotional beings. Through play, children learn to understand everyday experiences and deal with their emotions. Observations of children playing indicate that they come to terms with their experiences and feelings by re-enacting situations in which they felt anxious or vulnerable until they have understood the situation and feel in control of it.

Children as social beings

Children live in a social world, and learning to live with others is an important part of childhood. Through play, children learn important lessons about making healthy relationships with others. This process has a developmental aspect to it which can be seen in the following observations:

Stephen, Connor and Michael (all aged two years, three months at time of observation) meet, with their mothers, for a couple of hours every fortnight. The mothers met in hospital having their babies, have become friends and meet together with the children on a regular basis. The following observation was made on one of these occasions.

Once each child had settled, they started to play with the toys in the room. Initially Stephen started to play with a Noah's ark toy. He put the animals in and out of the ark, sometimes making animal noises. Connor played with two cars. He pushed them along the floor, crawling along with them. Michael played with a teapot. He took the lid on and off. His mother gave him a teacup. He poured a cup of tea and took it over to his mother who pretended to drink it. They played happily for a few minutes. Stephen then decided he wanted to play with the cars that Connor had. He took one but Connor snatched it back. Stephen went to take it again. Connor's mother said to him, *Connor, share the cars, give one to Stephen*. At the same time, Stephen's mother found another car and gave it to him. They continued playing happily.

Laura and Victoria (both aged six years) are school friends and are playing at Laura's house. They play with a toy kitchen, equipped with typical kitchen equipment. The following dialogue is overheard.

L: I'm making supper for you. What would you like?
V: I'm putting this in the microwave. (*Baby's bottle.*) Can you hear it ping?
L: Here's the pizza. I'll put it in the oven.
V: Yes, I love pizza. What's your favourite? Mine is cheese and tomato.
L: Yes, mine's cheese and tomato too. This is a cheese and tomato pizza I'm putting in the oven.
V: My baby's bottle is ready now. I'm going to feed the baby. (*Goes to get a doll.*)
L: OK. I think my baby's getting hungry too. (*Goes to get another doll.*)
V: Oh, the milk's too hot. She'll have to wait for it. I'll wash up while I'm waiting. (*Goes over to sink.*)
L: I think our pizza will be ready now. Yes, it is. Here you are. Be careful, it's hot. (*Both girls have a slice and stand and pretend to eat it.*)

As children get older, they become more aware of others. Young children are largely egocentric, that is, their world consists entirely of their own feelings and emotions and they cannot see the world from another's perspective (rather like some adults!). In Stephen, Connor and Michael's play, illustrated above, they are happy to play alongside each other, but they barely acknowledge the existence of each other. The only person each child relates to is his mother. In addition, they have no skills to allow them to negotiate in a conflict situation. When two children want the cars, the mothers have to intervene to provide a resolution.

However, by age six, as illustrated in Laura and Victoria's play, children are usually able to form relationships with others and playing with friends becomes an important part of their lives. In their play, the presence of the other is critical. Rather than each playing with the kitchen independently, as younger children would, their play is inclusive. Furthermore, for successful play they need to utilise a number of skills which are required to make positive relationships. In the above extract, they exhibit communication skills (responding directly to each other's talk), and sharing skills (distributing the pizza slices). They also appear to recognise that friends need to have things in common to make friendship bonds. Laura, the less dominant player, agrees with Victoria about cheese and onion pizza, and she copies Victoria in feeding her baby. They are well on the way to developing sophisticated social skills, including clear and concise communication, conflict resolution and empathy. Such skills are not seen in Stephen, Connor and Michael

Children's play progresses through a number of stages. At the earliest stage, young children's play is solitary; they are largely unaware of others. Then children move to parallel play. Illustrated in the first observation, children are aware of others and will play happily alongside each other, although they are not likely to include each other in their play. Finally, they engage in associative and co-operative play, as illustrated in the second observation. Children, therefore, learn the skills of friendship. Such groups become very important and gradually a child's friends will probably exert a greater influence than any other.

Play enables children to find their own position, moving from an egocentric view to a more realistic picture of their place in a world where they have to co-exist peacefully with others. Isaacs writes:

> Much of it is social in direction, and belongs to the world of fantasy. He plays at being father and mother, the new baby sister, the policeman, the soldier; at going for a journey, at going to bed and getting up, and all the things which he sees grown-ups doing. Here also his play makes it easier for him to fit himself into his social world.
>
> (1929: 10)

Isaacs is suggesting that, through play, children can try out being other people and explore their social world. They can begin to acknowledge others' feelings and appreciate a network of influences. Fisher pursues this and highlights the place of social interactions in developing children's learning. She discusses the idea that young children learn by interacting with others:

The young child is a social being, playing, talking and living alongside others, watching what they do and imitating them, questioning what is seen and responding to questioning, drawing on the knowledge and expertise of others to interpret and make meaning of experiences.

(1996: 11)

That children are social beings is the fourth element in our picture of childhood. Through play with others, children develop social skills, derive pleasure from having friends, become aware of their place in the world, and learn from others. However, they are also autonomous players. Despite existing in a social setting, children nevertheless retain their individuality and uniqueness.

Children as autonomous players

In addition to being in a social world, each child is unique, with individual life experiences, knowledge, understanding, skills and personality. Children are fundamentally in control of their play and can take it in any direction they wish. They are also free to finish playing at any point they choose. Consider the following observation.

Hamzah, a six-year-old boy, was playing with a collection of 'small world' toys in a school classroom. The selection included human figures, animals, vehicles and home equipment. The following play was observed.

Hamzah put a suitcase in the hand of a grey-haired female figure and put her in the train. He then put the train on the track and moved it along the track, making train-like noises. The figure was then taken out of the train and moved towards a home area which had been created by putting the home equipment together. Hamzah then put four figures into a car and drove it along. As it drove, animals came up to the car. Firstly, tigers growled at the car, then monkeys climbed all over the car, then giraffes came up and looked into the car, then elephants walked past the car.

The observer interrupted at this point and the following dialogue occurred.

O: Who's this? (*Pointing at the grey-haired female figure.*)
H: My Gran. She came to visit us on a train.
O: Who else is in the car?
H: Me and my Mum and Dad. We're at the Safari Park. When you see the tigers you have to keep the windows shut. And the monkeys.
O: Why's that?
H: So they don't come into the car. The tigers might eat you, you know. They eat people.

O: Do they?

H: Yes.

O: What about the monkeys. Do they eat you, too?

H: No, but they jump all over the car. (*Laughs.*) They went on our roof. We could hear them on the roof.

O: Oh, have you been to the Safari Park in real life?

H: Yes. When my Gran came. We all went.

Hamzah was constructing his play based on his personal experiences of his Gran's visit, and on his knowledge and understanding of the world: tigers eat people and monkeys are playful. In addition, his personality influenced his play; he has good concentration and takes care with detail. But another interesting aspect of this scenario is that, presented with identical materials, no other child would play in exactly the same way. Hamzah's play was almost certainly stimulated by a recent real-life event. Another child presented with human figures, animals, vehicles and home equipment would develop its own play scenario, based on unique personal experience.

Moyles emphasises that the most important feature of play is that the child has 'ownership', that is, the child is in control of the play situation. In addition, she also recognises the central place of the experiences each child brings to the situation. Writing about play in a school context, she says:

> In play activities production may or may not be important; the emphasis is on children and their ownership of, and active involvement in, curriculum processes and on what they bring to learning which forms the foundation of knowledge, skills and understanding.
>
> (1994: 4)

The child is placed firmly in control of the play situation. This represents an interesting shift from adult to child control. Early play theorists, such as Froebel and Montessori, recognised the value of play but believed that children needed to be guided by adults through a predetermined set of play experiences. Moyles is placing children firmly in control of their own play experiences. It is in this way that the autonomous nature of children can be recognised through observing play. This said, it must be recognised that limits are imposed on children's play in fundamental ways, such as time, space and resources.

Conclusion

Analysis of observations of children's play has built up a comprehensive picture of childhood. Five contributory elements have been identified. Children are:

- active players, both physically and mentally
- learners, with a capacity for developing cognitively, linguistically and creatively
- emotional beings, learning to understand experiences and deal with their feelings
- social beings, who learn to live in the world alongside others
- autonomous players, all unique

For us, as adults, making time to observe children playing is both vital and a great privilege.

Appendix

Hints for observing children's play

When watching children at play it is helpful to have an observation schedule to focus the observation. Without this, it is possible to make pages of notes, yet have little relevant information.

General information may include any of the following, depending on the purpose of the observation:

- date
- time/length of observation
- type of setting (e.g., nursery class, school playground, childminder's living room)
- number of adults/children present
- resources/equipment available
- child/children being observed (this should be anonymous in all public documents).

Specific headings should then be identified, based on the focus of the observation. For example, the following headings could be used to observe social interactions during play:

- who focus child interacted with (adult/child, girl/boy)
- nature of interaction (e.g., asking an adult a question, playing with a friend)
- length of interaction
- summary/quotes from talk heard (ideally, using a tape recorder)

Two final points. It is very difficult to watch more than two children in one observation. A decision will need to be made about whether to sit apart from the children or with them. This will depend on the nature of the observation (but see also Chapter 10 in this volume).

Review questions and tasks

1   Attempt a brief written definition of children's play, incorporating the key elements described in this chapter.
2   Visit an early years setting. List the activities on offer to the children. Identify which are intended mainly to develop problem-solving, creative, or linguistic learning (most will develop more than one area).
3   Observe the social interactions of one child over a half-hour period. How many interactions does the child make? What is the purpose of each? Repeat for children of different ages (e.g., three years, six years).
4   Observe children playing in a playground/outdoor play setting. How does the children's play differ from that in a more formal setting?
5   Observe similarities and differences in the play of girls and boys. What do they play with and how do they play?
6   Investigate the work of Iona and Peter Opie and make a detailed assessment of their contribution to what we know of children's worlds.

Further reading

Anning, A. (1997) *The First Years at School*, 2nd edn, Buckingham: Open University Press.   Angela Anning starts with a useful review of the histories and ideologies behind early years education. There are then chapters on children learning and teachers teaching. These combine theory and practice in a way that makes them interesting and valuable to read. Anning then examines curriculum organisation and content before discussing the statutory National Curriculum. The second edition then concludes with a chapter on contemporary issues including assessment, children with special educational needs, the education of children under five and training teachers to specialise in early childhood education. This book offers a comprehensive and intelligent examination of the first years at school.

Bruce, T. (1991) *Time to Play in Early Childhood Education*, Sevenoaks: Hodder & Stoughton.   This book explores the importance of play in education, particularly what Tina Bruce calls 'free-flow' play. It starts by revising the ten 'Principles of Early Childhood Education' that were established in her previous book (Bruce 1987) and to which other authors frequently refer. There is a useful discussion of play theories over the last two hundred years and of educationalists who have influenced our thinking about children's play. Bruce emphasises the importance of firsthand experiences and how it acts as a catalyst for the development of games with rules, humour and representation. Finally, Bruce offers practical suggestions for assessing, evaluating and recording 'free-flow' play.

Fisher, J. (1996) *Starting From the Child?* **Buckingham: Open University Books.** Julie Fisher's starting point is what children know and can do when they come to school, an area which is often neglected. She moves on to discuss the importance of building on this and the role of parents and other adults in this process. Fisher then discusses, in a practical way, the nature of the curriculum, the role of the teacher and effective use of space and resources. A valuable chapter is offered on the importance of talk and ways to facilitate it. After a discussion about play, Fisher moves on to examine power and control in the classroom, and how children can be encouraged to organise their own learning. Finally, there is a chapter on evaluation and assessment. Overall, the real strengths of this book are that it discusses many crucial areas that are often overlooked and it offers many practical suggestions.

Moyles, J. (1989) *Just Playing? The Role and Status of Play in Early Childhood Education,* **Milton Keynes: Open University Press.** This book offers a comprehensive picture of play in early childhood education. In Part One, Janet Moyles discusses the value of play and examines the place of it in children's learning. She proposes the notion of a 'play spiral' in which children learn through the accretion of directed and free play. Part Two examines the place of play in developing language, problem solving and creativity. In Part Three, Moyles deals with making provision for play in the early years and includes chapters on curriculum organisation; assessment and record-keeping; children with special educational needs; and relationships with parents and other adults. The final chapter reviews children's and adults' play. Moyles offers a convincing case for putting play at the centre of early childhood education.

References

Anning, A. (1997) *The First Years at School*, 2nd edn, Buckingham: Open University Press.

Beardsley, G. and Harnett, P. (1998) *Exploring Play in the Classroom*, London: David Fulton.

Bruce, T. (1987) *Early Childhood Education*, Sevenoaks: Hodder & Stoughton.

—— (1991) *Time to Play in Early Childhood Education*, Sevenoaks: Hodder & Stoughton.

Fisher, J. (1996) *Starting From the Child?* Buckingham: Open University Books.

Garvey, C. (1977) *Play*, London: Fontana/Open Books.

Hutt, S.J., Tyler, S., Hutt, C. and Christopherson, H. (1989) *Play, Exploration and Learning: A Natural History of the Pre-School*, London: Routledge.

Isaacs, S. (1929) *The Nursery Years*, London: Routledge.

Manning, K. and Sharp, A. (1977) *Structuring Play in the Early Years at School*, London: Schools' Council.

Moyles, J. (1989) *Just Playing? The Role and Status of Play in Early Childhood Education*, Milton Keynes: Open University Press.

—— (ed.) (1994) *The Excellence of Play*, Buckingham: Open University Press.

Piaget, J. (1962) *Play, Dreams and Imitation in Childhood*, London: Routledge & Kegan Paul.

Smith, P.K., Takhvar, M., Gore, N. and Vollstedt, R. (1986) 'Play in Young Children: Problems of Definition, Categorisation and Measurement', in P.K. Smith (ed.), *Children's Play: Research Developments and Practical Applications*, London: Gordon & Breach.

Vygotsky, L.S. (1978) *Mind in Society: The Development of Higher Psychological Processes*, Cambridge, MA: Harvard University Press.

Wood, D. (1990) *How Children Think and Learn*, Oxford: Basil Blackwell.

Wood, D., Bruner, J.S. and Ross, G. (1976) 'The Role of Tutoring in Problem-Solving', *Journal of Child Psychology and Psychiatry*, 17 (2): 89–100.

Chapter 5

Language and thought

Alison Johnson

Summary

In this chapter, concepts of language and thought are defined and the work of Piaget and Vygotsky on the origins and development of thought are outlined and evaluated. The issue of whether language is universal or relative is raised. In the second half of the chapter, examples of children's language are explored to see what they can reveal about the nature of childhood thought.

> When I was a child, I spake as a child, I understood as a child, I thought as a child: but when I became a man, I put away childish things.
>
> (I Corinthians 13: 11)

So writes Paul to the Corinthians, in this verse from the Bible, as if it is a simple truth known to everyone. But are things so straightforward? As children, do we speak and think differently from adults?

It would be misleading to suggest that any discipline, whether psychology, linguistics, sociology or philosophy, has discovered all the answers to the question of how children's thinking develops. Since ancient times, this has been an active area of research: the philosopher Socrates sought to discover the form of thought in people's utterances, and the twentieth-century thinker Wittgenstein was still grappling with the same topic when he commented:

> Everyday language is a part of the human organism and is no less complicated than it. It is not humanly possible to gather immediately from it what the logic of language is. Language disguises thought. So much so, that, from the outward form of the clothing, it is impossible to infer the form of the thought beneath it, because the outward form of the clothing is not designed to reveal the form of the body, but for entirely different purposes.
>
> (1981: 4.002)

No straightforward answers in philosophy, then. Therefore, this chapter now encourages you to engage with the questions posed and answers put forward by psychologists and psycholinguists who study language and the mind.

In seeking to understand how children think, and if, indeed, this is different from the ways in which adults think, we should consider the writings of two key figures in the psychological field: Jean Piaget and Lev Semenovich Vygotsky. Many reviews and critiques of Piaget and Vygotsky's work on language and thought have been written (see Donaldson, 1978; Tryphon and Vonèche, 1996; Wood, 1988), but it is to their own writings that we will go to see what they have to say on the subject of the relationship between language and thought.

First, though, we should define *language* and *thought*. There are four fundamental questions we should ask:

1   What is language?
2   What is thought?
3   How are language and thought related?
4   What does children's language reveal about their thinking?

What is language?

What it means to know a language and to be able to use it has, in psycholinguistics, traditionally been described in terms of *competence* and *performance*. Competence refers to 'people's knowledge of a language, the knowledge that enables them to produce and understand utterances in that language'; performance refers to 'the production and comprehension of utterances, whether in speech or writing ... which may include slips, errors and misunderstandings' (Greene 1986: 17, 20). In short, competence relates to knowledge and ability, and performance to actual use of language.

So what does this knowledge or competence look like? Types of linguistic knowledge include:

*   a vocabulary, or mental lexicon (Aitchison, 1987), and associated meanings and classes (for example, knowledge that dogs, cats, pigs and elephants are all classes of animals that can be subdivided into domesticated and undomesticated animals; knowledge that *wee-wee* is allowable as a request to go to the toilet in the pre-school days, but that more formal words are needed after this);
*   syntax (i.e., knowledge of how words combine to make phrases, clauses and sentences in a particular order, for example in English we say, 'The cat ate its dinner' rather than, 'The cat its dinner ate');
*   social, cultural and world knowledge (for example, knowledge that in a particular culture, the time of day can be passed with a relative stranger by discussing the weather);
*   pragmatic usage (for example, knowledge that when a parent says to a child, 'How can you hear that music properly, when it's so loud?' they are not enquiring about acoustic capacities, but asking for less volume).

Language, then, can be defined as skills of knowledge, comprehension and communication, acquired initially in the pre-school years and added to over the course of a lifetime. It has both internal and external functions, with externalised speech developing first and, as we shall see, the internal linguistic processes of verbal thinking following. Early childhood is, therefore, the setting for this key area of linguistic development.

What is thought?

This brings us to our second question. Thinking clearly involves a large number of skills and processes, amongst which are memory and cognitive schemas (Bartlett, 1932), symbolising, reasoning, logic, information processing and metacognition, a complex cognitive skill defined by Meadows as:

> analysing and defining the problem at hand; reflecting upon one's own knowledge (and lack of knowledge) that may be required to solve the problem;

devising a plan for attacking the problem; checking and monitoring how the plan helps in the problem-solving ...

(1993: 78–9)

Thought, according to Vygotsky, begins as talk accompanying action, with the transition from speech to thought taking place in three stages: 'external speech, egocentric speech, inner speech' (Meadows, 1993: 78–9). An example of this monologue which is 'not communicative language' is reported by Crystal. Here is his two-year-old talking to herself while drawing:

Draw a coat down. Draw a ling-a-ling-a-ling. Draw a little thing – little ear squeer – big eye – little eye here – eye! A little girl called Sinky and she's walking. And there's Humpty Dumpty – pull him down!

(Crystal, 1998: 166)

Thinking for pre-school children, as in this example, is largely an external phenomenon.

For Piaget, individual action, rather than talk, is the basis of later thinking. Vygotsky, on the other hand, argues in favour of the social construction of thought, involving the notions of scaffolding and the 'zone of proximal development' (ZPD), as Susannah Smith pointed out in Chapter 4 of this book. Scaffolding of children's writing is currently being applied in Britain with the introduction of a Literacy Hour. Teachers model writing, lead guided writing groups and provide writing frames to support initial writing of new genres. Vygotsky characterises the ZPD as the difference between the child's 'actual developmental level, as determined by individual problem solving [and] potential development, as determined through problem solving under adult guidance or in collaboration with more capable peers' (Vygotsky, 1978: 86, cited in Tryphon and Vonèche, 1996). This has important implications in tests of children's thinking, which usually assess unsupported rather than supported thinking, thereby failing to gain a complete picture of the child's capacity for thought.

Vygotsky, Piaget and Dewey, among many others, discuss the centrality of play in developing thinking, as seen in the previous chapter. Vygotsky maintains that, 'the most spontaneous form of thinking is play which, up to the age of seven or eight ... dominates in child thought' (1962: 13) and Piaget says that, 'play, when all is said and done, is the supreme law of egocentric thought' (1924: 276).

Thought can, therefore, be simply defined as an effort in which language plays a major part, whether inwardly or outwardly. It occurs at the intersection between activity (either concrete or verbal) and some kind of problem motivated by curiosity.

For Piaget, formal thought develops slowly, although, in noting its delay until the age of seven or eight, he is in broad agreement with Vygotsky, for whom inner speech begins 'when egocentric talk subsides' (1962: 15) around seven or eight or 'approximately at the beginning of school age' (1962: 18), when egocentric talk is observed to drop quickly. However, we should note that contemporary commentators dispute this late development of formal thought. Wozniak (1996: 20) argues that to suggest 'the use of speech for thinking awaits the ultimate fate of egocentric ("private") speech at ages 5, 6, 7, or later seems … highly implausible', and Van der Veer (1996: 46) suggests that both Vygotsky's and Piaget's research investigations, by today's rigorous standards, 'were somewhat crude and inadequate'.

To summarise Vygotsky's position, he sees egocentric speech as an early form of thought, similar to that of adults, in that it can be used at this very early age of two or three to plan solutions to problems. From this perspective, Piaget is seen to subordinate early childhood thought to that of older children and adult thinkers, over the age of eleven, whereas Vygotsky attributes prototypical thought to egocentric speech. Second, whereas Piaget sees the origins of thought as biological, developing out of the period in which the child explores the world through senses and actions, the sensori-motor stage, Vygotsky sees thought as having social and functional origins, developing out of socio-cultural contact. It is, therefore, not surprising that Vygotsky, writing in the Stalinist era of Russian history, is influenced by the Marxist theory that environment determines consciousness. Marx (1859) said that 'it is not the consciousness of men that determines their being, but, on the contrary, their social being that determines their consciousness'; Vygotsky firmly believed that 'thought development is determined by language' and that 'thought and language, which reflect reality in a way different from that of perception, are key to the nature of human consciousness' (1962: 153).

These beliefs represent one side of an important debate in linguistics about the relationship between language and thought: linguistic relativity versus linguistic universals.

How are language and thought related?

The two sides of the language and thought debate – the relativity or universality of language – have received much attention from psychologists and linguists. If we examine the index of any major work on psychology and language, the terms 'linguistic universals' and 'relativity' (this latter notion linked with the names of Sapir and Whorf) will be found. What is held by these dichotomous positions is:

1   that language affects the way that we perceive the world around us – it is relative;
2   that our representation of the world is encoded in ways that are common to all languages: it is universal.

Piaget, as we have seen, sees action as the origin of thought; Vygotsky sees thought as determined by language and thus takes a contrasting position. Brown (1956) and Pinker (1994) mount vigorous attacks on Whorf's ideas. Others (Clark and Clark, 1977; Montgomery, 1995) consider both sides or prefer a weak form of Whorf's hypothesis. Many now conclude 'that language and thought mutually influence each other' (Siegler, 1998: 170). Brown's and Pinker's stance, though, avoids sitting on the fence and uses the logic that languages are based on general cognition which means that 'people do not think in English or Chinese or Apache; they think in the language of thought' which 'probably looks a bit like all these languages' (Pinker, 1994: 81).

The debate has stimulated many questions, like those asked by Siegler:

> Everyone agrees that people have concepts within which they categorize objects and events. Everyone also agrees that they have words for describing the objects and events. But how are the words and concepts related? ... Do people throughout the world think in basically similar ways? Or are languages a sufficiently strong lens that people who speak different languages see the world differently? Similarly, does children's learning of new words trigger the formation of new concepts, or does ability to understand new terms demand that the relevant concepts already be in place?
>
> (1998:169)

Some answers to these questions have been put forward. On the relativist side of the debate, Whorf (1956) said that:

> We dissect nature along lines laid down by our native languages ... We cut nature up, organise it into concepts, and ascribe significances as we do, largely because we are parties to an agreement to organise it in this way – an agreement that holds throughout our speech community and is codified in the patterns of our language.
>
> (1956: 213–14)

Relativists, therefore, say that people who speak different languages do see the world differently, and that having one word or four words for snow is evidence of this. Euphemisms and politically correct language which assigns positive terminology to previously negatively viewed concepts has also been seen as evidence of the relativity of language: examples include 'passing away' instead of 'dying', or describing a car as 'pre-owned' rather than 'second-hand'.

On the universalist side of the debate, people such as Chomsky have argued that all languages have universal grammar and that vocabularies have equivalent linguistic cognates. Rosch (1977) argued also for semantic universals with her prototype theory that states that when we hear a word, e.g. 'bird', we all have a similar image of what that is and that this image is more likely to be 'robin' than 'penguin'. And Berlin and Kay (1969) found that all languages divide the colour spectrum similarly, although some languages have fewer categories. Universalists, then, say that we can generally agree on our descriptions of an event, representing it in the same way, although using different languages.

It is answers to Siegler's questions that we will look for in the next section.

What does children's language reveal about their thinking?

By adulthood, most thinking is silent. In fact, when thinking aloud is required, of the kind found in football commentaries or the running commentary accompanying an advanced driving test, it is far from effortless. Not so, however, are children's egocentric monologues, which accompany activity from the time they begin to use language until the early school years, at which point teachers and parents prompt children to 'think quietly' or 'stop talking'. Thought takes a while to go fully inwards, though, and sometimes re-emerges at times of stress, such as when talking to oneself is jokingly referred to as the first sign of madness. These words, said in jest, have, however, an aspect of truth. Mental illness and some of the conditions associated with senility are characterised by the kind of egocentric non-interactive speech used in our early years. (Caporael *et al.*, 1983, discuss judgements of speech disorders in the elderly as 'secondary baby talk'.)

We see something of what this might mean in Ruth Weir's recorded monologues from children. In the example below, Anthony, aged two and a half is talking to himself in his cot before going to sleep:

> Where you going? I'm going. Shoe fixed. Talk to mommy. Shoe fixed. See Antho. Anthony. Good night. See morrow morning.
>
> (Weir, 1962, cited in Siegler, 1998: 139)

What can we say about what this reveals of the child's thought? First of all, any interpretation is subjective, since the speech of children at this stage is telegraphic; it leaves out most of the grammatical words and connectives that make meaning clear and logical. So, when the child says, 'I'm going. Shoe fixed', the meaning could be: 'Tomorrow, I'm going to get my shoe fixed' or 'Tomorrow, I'm going to get mummy's shoe fixed'. Parents, of course, confidently interpret these kinds of utterances from their offspring, since they have contextual knowledge gained from being present for much of the child's waking time. That said, we, too, can fairly confidently say that this child is thinking about the next day's activities, because this is often part of the parent and child bedtime ritual (i.e., talking over the day's activities and previewing the next). Here, the child seems to be previewing for himself.

On the other hand, this speech may not be evidence of the child's previewing activity but may merely be echo-like repetition of a conversation just carried out with his mother. There is some evidence of this, since the child refers to himself by name and seems to be repeating the mother's parting comment. However, the conversation is not merely echoing his mother. She has gone and it has been internalised. Also, his use of the personal pronoun 'I' seems to discount mere imitation. The mother would use 'we' or 'you', as the question, 'Where you going?' seems to demonstrate. We can, therefore, suggest that the child is talking and thinking for himself by saying, 'I'm going'. This child is at the stage of using both his own name and the personal pronoun to refer to himself, but has clearly moved on from the earlier stage of referring to himself solely with his name (Peccei, 1994). This also suggests development of an early self-concept.

Another kind of speech event that is important is verbal play. Interesting writers on this subject include Weir (1962), Farb (1974), Garvey (1984) and Crystal (1998). Garvey writes of 'socially constructed sound play' that it:

> is distinctly different from other kinds of talk ... because the content comprises sounds or nonsense words. In such episodes turns are alternated promptly and rhythmically, but each child successively repeats and/or slightly modifies the form, rather than the content, of the previous turn.
>
> (1984: 162)

She gives an example of a conversation between Judy (32 months) and Tom (33 months):

JUDY: Well, someday you can see the dada, but not for a long time.
TOM: I have a dada too.
JUDY: I have a dada, too.
TOM: I have a real dada.
JUDY: I have a special dada.
TOM: I have a real dada.
JUDY: I do too.
TOM: I do too.
JUDY: I have a special dada, too.
TOM: I do too.
JUDY: I have a special dada doo. Da daaa. (*Starts to chant.*)

(Garvey, 1984: 162–3)

Crystal (1998: 165), remarks that 'from around age two ... sound play emerges, in which children start to manipulate their growing inventory of vowels and consonants'. He uses an example from Bryant and Bradley (1985: 48), recorded from a pre-school child:

I'm a whale
This is my tail
I'm a flamingo
Look at my wingo
The red house
Made of strouss

These examples demonstrate a productivity and creativity in children's language that can only occur through growing linguistic competence, which involves knowledge of rhyme and the internal structures of mono-syllabic words, described as 'onset' and 'rime' and demonstrated in *strouss*. Here, the onset of the word *straw*, *str-*, is retained and the rime of *house*, *-ouse*, is added to it. This takes a special kind of conscious mental acrobatics that can sometimes occur by accident in spoonerisms such as *berry vig* for *very big*, and blends like *tummach*, blending tummy and stomach (Aitchison, 1987: 167).

Outside this period of natural thinking aloud, there are still ways of collecting evidence of children's thinking. At times of emotion or anxiety, even as adults, we find it extremely difficult to keep our thoughts to ourselves and they tend to come spilling out, often interpreted as accusa-tions levelled at whoever happens to be in the vicinity: one's partner or children, for instance. One of these emotional vocalisations occurred in my young son, Richard, when he was being wheeled into the anaesthetist's room for an operation. As the doors closed I heard him shout, 'No mummy bye-bye'. Although delayed and uncommunicative in his speech, as a result of autism, the frightening situation provoked language in him. Positive emotional experiences also provoke outbursts, as anyone who has ever taken a toddler to see Postman Pat's stage show will testify.

Children's acquisition of morphology is important in the development of thought and language. (Villiers and Villiers, 1973, and Brown, 1976, discuss the order of development for morphemes which are the grammat-ical markers in words, for example, the plural *-s* in *dogs*.) This development starts around age three but continues beyond six, with interesting errors and coinages noted by and Bloom and Lahey (1978), Peccei (1994) and Clark (1995). For example, when a child uses the word *unsqueezed* in the sentence 'How did you unsqueezed it', while trying to open a clip (Bloom and Lahey, 1978), could it be evidence that words are stored in the mind 'disassembled into morphemes and then put together when needed' rather than as whole words? (Aitchison 1987: 107). The child who uses this word does indeed seem to know that the negative prefix *un-* means: the opposite of, and can be used to signal the reverse of actions when attached to a word. When the child encounters a lexical gap (i.e., a gap in vocabulary), a word is coined for the purpose, thereby demonstrating linguistic compe-tence.

In another example, where a child of three and a half says, 'You be the storyer, daddy' (Clark, 1995: 401), the suffix *-er* is added to the noun *story* to

105

coin a noun with an agent, not far from the appropriate words *storyteller* or *reader*. Creative coining of this kind is evidence of logical thinking on the part of children. Once they have a basic lexicon which includes a whole range of morphemes and their meanings, children have all the tools to fill any lexical gaps they encounter. Many of the resulting neologisms are viewed by adults with humour and treated as errors, because they are sometimes illogical – we open rather than unsqueeze something – but this ignores their true significance in the development of intelligence and logic.

Bilingual children demonstrate evidence of syntactic thinking in their mixed language speech, as can be seen in the following example from a three-year-old child:

I can't sleep. Khala Parveen noise karni ha.

(Word-for-word translation: I can't sleep. Auntie Parveen noise making is.)

This mixing of Mirpuri and English, far from being ungrammatical, as its literal translation would suggest, shows evidence of applied grammatical competence. The child begins her utterance in English, but, in selecting the word *noise* as the object of Khala Parveen, has chosen the subject–object–verb word order of Mirpuri and, in order to avoid an ungrammatical English sentence, completes it in Mirpuri with the verb at the end. This child's language use shows developed knowledge of two grammatical systems and the ability to use these intelligently.

It is not just in the monologues prior to silent thought that we can see evidence of children's thinking. There are many aspects of children's language, including verbal play, word use, creative word-coining, blending and errors that help us look at childhood thought. Adults, too, have long-established folk views about children's thinking, which have surfaced recently in television advertisements for drinks. Here are three examples of adult–child interactions:

FATHER: Do you know what the capital of England is?
CHILD: E.

CHILD: Do Mummies have girls and Daddies have boys?
MOTHER: Ask your father.

CHILD TO GRANDFATHER: Granddad, when Wally dies, will he go to Devon?

These examples, exploiting the humorous side of children's inexperience of the world, and their thinking, demonstrate the potential for using children's speech as a basis for interpreting their thought. These examples, though fictional in that they are created for humorous purposes in order to sell drinks, are far from being merely stereotypical. In fact, they demonstrate some of the comprehension errors that children make when faced with real language: failing to recognise homonyms ('capital'), jumping to inventive childlike conclusions – females produce females and males produce males (see Donaldson, 1978: 76–85 on child logic in problem solving) – and mis-hearing or mistaking similar words, resulting in child malapropisms such as 'Devon' for heaven.

Consider the following joke, heard recently, which depends on fairly sophisticated adult knowledge of the world:

> Two men were arrested earlier today, one for drinking battery acid and one for eating fireworks. The first man was charged and the other was let off.

As adults, it is clear that the humour centres around the dual meaning of 'charged' and 'let off'. From an interpretative point of view, let us examine what this evidence might suggest about children's thinking. There are two possible conclusions: first, that children think in ways that are different and inferior to adults and older children; or second, that children think differently but only because of inexperience in language and world knowledge. Either way, and the second is more 'contemporary' (Meadows, 1993: 197), what it does suggest is that language influences children's thought and comprehension. Processing of input is influenced by the vocabulary used.

Conclusion

In this chapter, we have examined children's language to see what this can tell us about their thinking. We have seen that children's competence in language quickly develops and that verbal thinking appears as soon as children begin to use meaningful language. Psychologists are divided as to whether a maturational model of development as proposed by Piaget, which suggests that children have deficits or are incomplete thinkers, is preferable to the notion that children's thinking is very similar to adults, but that they lack experience (Meadows, 1993). Siegler acknowledges Piaget's contribution to research in setting out the extent of children's abilities and describes children's thinking as 'limited' but nevertheless 'flexible' (1998: 66). Milestones in children's thinking are observable, from understanding that words refer to things, to understanding jokes and constructing identity. Names, classes and categories at first develop as a mental lexicon and are then transformed in the construction of self.

Psychologists are also still assessing the influence of biological factors over social ones in the development of thought. We have seen that Piaget's theory embodies the former, whilst Vygotsky's entails the latter. In looking at children's language, we have seen that language has strong social functions, but we also have to recognise the biological foundations of language and thought, as children the world over begin to talk and think in very similar ways.

Children's thought is still subject to a great deal of research. Questions are by no means entirely answered. It is up to us to interpret snapshots of children's language and to decide what these can tell us about the ways in which children think. What we can say with certainty, however, is that they show that children have remarkable abilities from an early age, which elevates the human child's capacity to reason and reflect in relation to animal counterparts.

Review questions and tasks

1 Do you agree with Piaget that formal thinking is slow to develop, not maturing until after the age of eleven? What evidence do you have to support your opinion?

2 If you have access to children of different ages, investigate Vygotsky's 'zone of proximal development' by giving two children of the same ability the same task. Support one of the children and get the other child to carry out the task unaided. Make sure that the task contains a degree of challenge, but ensure that it is not so difficult that it is frustrating to the unsupported child. You could, for example, provide a text to be read aloud and ask one child to read it through to themselves and then read it to you. With the other child, you could first read it together, pausing and analysing problematic words, before asking for it to be read to you.

3 To understand how thinking develops, reflect on how children of different ages – say, three, seven and eleven – might respond to the same problem-solving task (for example, thinking of a way to get an elephant on to a lorry). If you have access to children, try this out and analyse the results in terms of enhanced logical thinking in older children.

4 Do you think language influences the way we view the world? For example, is politically correct language evidence that differences in labels indicates differences in the way we perceive them? Evaluate the relativity/universality debate.

5 Investigate homonym and homophone jokes and riddles. At what ages do children 'get' these? For example: 'What's black and white and read all over?' Answer: 'A newspaper.'

6 How does children's thinking develop? Collect your own examples of children's language, or have a look at Donaldson and Elliot's examples of children's explanations of events, in Grieve and Hughes (1990).

Further reading

Aitchison, J. (1987) *Words in the Mind*, **Oxford: Blackwell (Parts I and IV and Chapter 8).** Jean Aitchison, Rupert Murdoch Professor of Language and Communication at the University of Oxford, looks at how words are stored in the mind and how we retrieve them when needed. This book, subtitled *An Introduction to the Mental Lexicon*, helps us to see how our use of words reflects the way words are organised in the mind. Evidence from natural errors and the difficulties of aphasics are discussed in terms of how these help us examine the structure of the mental lexicon. In Chapter 8, Aitchison looks specifically at the question of whether children store and retrieve words in the same way as adults.

Donaldson, M. (1978) *Children's Minds*, **London: Fontana.** In this early but still very important book, Margaret Donaldson examines Piaget's work in the light of the results of her own experiments with children. She reinterprets Piaget's conclusions about the ways in which children think while engaged in problem solving.

Grieve, R. and Hughes, M. (1990) *Understanding Children*, **Oxford: Blackwell (Chapters 2, 3 and 11).** These chapters by Eve Clark, Morag Donaldson and Alison Elliot, and Robin Campbell and David Olson look at children's language, children's explanations and children's thinking, and are dedicated to Margaret Donaldson, who inspired much of the work.

Meadows, S. (1993) *The Child as Thinker*, **London: Routledge.** This book is a very comprehensive review of current research in the acquisition and development of cognition in childhood. Chapter 5, which looks at causes of change and variation in cognitive development in children, is particularly useful for considering social and cultural as well as biological factors affecting difference.

Siegler, R.S. (1998) *Children's Thinking*, **3rd edn, London: Prentice-Hall International.** Siegler discusses complicated psychological processes and theories surrounding the development of thinking. He also clearly describes and evaluates Piaget's theory. He looks specifically at six aspects of children's thinking: perception, language, memory, conceptual representation, problem solving, and the development of the academic skills of reading, writing and number use.

Wood, D. (1988) *How Children Think and Learn*, **Oxford: Blackwell.** This book contains further evaluation of Piaget's theories and compares him with Vygotsky and Bruner and other leading researchers. This is essentially a book for those interested in applying this work to teaching issues. There are useful chapters on the literate and mathematical mind.

References

Aitchison, J. (1987) *Words in the Mind*, Oxford: Blackwell.

Barrett, M. (1995) 'Early Lexical Development', in P. Fletcher and B. MacWhinney (eds), *The Handbook of Child Language*, Oxford: Blackwell.

Bartlett, F.C. (1932) *Remembering*, Cambridge: Cambridge University Press.

Bergvall, V.L., Bing, J.M. and Freed, A.F. (eds) (1996) *Rethinking Language and Gender Research*, Harlow: Longman.

Berlin, B. and Kay, P. (1969) *Basic Color Terms: Their Universality and Evolution*, Berkeley and Los Angeles: University of California Press.

Bloom, L. and Lahey, M. (1978) *Language Development and Language Disorders*, London: Macmillan.

Brown, R. (1956) 'Appendix: Language and Categories', in J.S. Bruner *et al. A Study of Thinking*, New York: Wiley.

Brown, R. (1976) *A First Language: The Early Stages*, Harmondsworth: Penguin.

Bruner, J. (1956) *A Study of Thinking*, New York: John Wiley & Sons.

Bryant, P. and Bradley, L. (1985) *Children's Reading Problems*, Oxford: Blackwell.

Caporael, L.R., Lukaszewski, M.P. and Culbertson, G.H. (1983) 'Secondary Baby Talk: Judgements by Institutionalised Elderly and Their Caregivers', *Journal of Personality and Social Psychology* 44 (4): 746–54.

Clark, E.V. (1995) 'Later Lexical Development and Word Formation', in P. Fletcher and B. MacWhinney (eds), *The Handbook of Child Language*, Oxford: Blackwell.

Clark, H.H. and Clark, E.V. (1977) *Psychology and Language*, New York: Harcourt Brace Jovanovich.

Crystal, D. (1998) *Language Play*, London: Penguin.

Donaldson, M. (1978) *Children's Minds*, Fontana.

Farb, P. (1973) *Word Play: What Happens when People Talk*, London: Jonathan Cape.

Fletcher, P. and MacWhinney, B. (eds) (1995) *The Handbook of Child Language*, Oxford: Blackwell.

Frith, U. (1990) *Autism*, Oxford: Blackwell.

Garvey, C. (1984) *Children's Talk*, Fontana.

Greene, J. (1986) *Language Understanding: A Cognitive Approach*, Milton Keynes: Open University Press.

Grieve, R. and Hughes, M. (1990) *Understanding Children*, Oxford: Blackwell.

Marx, K. (1859) *Contribution to the Critique of Political Economy*, http://csf.colorado.edu/cgi-bin/mfs/24/csf/web/psn/marx/Archive/1859-CPE/cpe0.txt780\mfs.

Meadows, S. (1993) *The Child as Thinker*, London: Routledge.

Montgomery, M. (1995) *An Introduction to Language and Society*, 2nd edn, London: Routledge.

Peccei, J.S. (1994) *Child Language*, London: Routledge.

Piaget, J. (1923) *Le langage et la pensée chez l'enfant*, Neuchâtel-Paris: Delachaux & Niestlé.

—— (1924, 1959) *The Language and Thought of the Child*, Routledge & Kegan Paul.

—— (1972) 'Language and thought from a genetic point of view' in P. Adams (ed.), *Language in Thinking*, Harmondsworth: Penguin.

Piaget, J. and Inhelder, B. (1969) *The Psychology of the Child*, trans. H. Weaver, London: Routledge & Kegan Paul.

Pinker, S. (1994) *The Language Instinct*, London: Penguin.

Rosch, E. (1977) 'Human Categorization', in N. Warren (ed.), *Advances in Cross-Cultural Psychology*, vol. 1, London: Academic Press.

Sapir, E. (1921) *Language*, New York: Harcourt Brace.

Siegler, R.S. (1998) *Children's Thinking*, 3rd edn, New Jersey: Simon & Schuster.

Tryphon, A. and Vonèche, J. (eds) (1996) *Piaget – Vygotsky: The Social Genesis of Thought*, Hove: Psychology Press.

Van der Veer, R. (1996) 'Structure and Development: Reflections by Vygotsky', in A. Tryphon and J. Vonèche, J. (eds) *Piaget – Vygotsky: The Social Genesis of Thought*, Hove: Psychology Press.

Villiers, J. de and Villiers, P. de (1978) *Language Acquisition*, Cambridge, MA: Harvard University Press.

Vygotsky, L.S. (1962) *Thought and Language*, trans. E. Hanfmann and G. Vakar, Cambridge, MA: MIT Press, and London: John Wiley & Sons.

Weir, R. (1962) *Language in the Crib*, The Hague: Mouton.

Whorf, B.L. (1956) 'Science and Linguistics', in J.B. Carroll (ed.) *Language, Thought and Reality: Selected Writings of Benjamin Lee Whorf*, Cambridge, MA: MIT Press.

Wittgenstein, L. (1981) *Tractatus Logico-Philosophicus*, trans. C.K. Ogden, London: Routledge.

Wood, D. (1988) *How Children Think and Learn*, Oxford: Blackwell.

Wozniak, R.H. (1996) 'Qu'est-ce que l'intelligence? Piaget, Vygotsky, and the 1920s Crisis in Psychology', in A. Tryphon and J. Vonèche (eds) *Piaget – Vygotsky: The Social Genesis of Thought*, Hove: Psychology Press.

Chapter 6

Moral and spiritual growth

Jack Priestley

Summary

This chapter explores the growth of the moral and spiritual awareness of children through an analysis of various research programmes over the past thirty years. It begins by discussing and rejecting the dominant idea of development which has been transferred from the cognitive to the affective domain without thought to its relevance. It then looks in some detail at what is termed the 'Kohlberg Story', which includes the work of Carol Gilligan and Robert Coles as well as that of Lawrence Kohlberg himself, as a way of raising what are regarded as the fundamental questions surrounding the whole sphere of growing moral awareness. Finally, the discussion moves into the related area of spiritual growth with particular reference to the work in England associated with such names as Alister Hardy, Edward Robinson, David Hay and Rebecca Nye, and attempts to show that this empirical work serves to confirm a tradition well documented in English literature.

> In the sandpile I learned, 'Share everything. Play fair. Don't hit people. Put things back where you found them. Clean up your own mess. Don't take things that aren't yours. Say sorry when you hurt someone. Wash your hands before you eat. Flush the toilet.'
>
> (Fulghum, 1989: 6)

I have deliberately used the word 'growth' in the heading of this chapter rather than the more commonly used 'development', because I believe that one of the reasons for the difficulty we seem to experience today in dealing with moral and spiritual issues can be attributed to the way in which we have become bewitched by a certain type of language which has the effect of shutting us off from past wisdom. Indeed, 'wisdom' itself, once central to the whole educational enterprise, has all but disappeared. One will look in vain for any mention of it in current government literature.

Yet, traditionally, it is wisdom, rather than intellect, which has formed the basis of the areas with which I want to deal, unless we are to take the view that those most highly educated in terms of intellect and academic achievement are *ipso facto* the most moral and spiritually adjusted members of society. It takes no more than a second's reflection to realise that this seems unlikely to be the case.

This 'bewitchment of language' (a phrase borrowed from the philosopher Wittgenstein) is, I would argue, a very subtle form of indoctrination because it forces us to think along certain lines without questioning or confirming their validity. Let me, then, first explore the notion of development and analyse just why it gets in the way of a serious discussion about the moral and spiritual growth of children.

The limitations of 'development'

The use of the word 'develop' in general, and of the phrase 'child development' in particular, have become so commonplace that we often overlook the fact that they are of comparatively recent usage (see Richard Mills' passage on 'children as apprentices' in Chapter 1 of this volume). For a long time the word was recorded in dictionaries only in the form of what we would now take to be the past participle and used as an adjective, 'developed'. It meant, simply, 'unfolded' or 'laid open', the opposite of 'enveloped'.

We still use it in that way in connection with one very common everyday activity, namely photography. We talk of, 'having a film developed'. Only very rarely, however, do we use the word in this sense when we come to education. Without realising it, educationalists have, over the past two or three generations, begun to borrow related but subtly different usages from two academic areas which have long been with us but which, in recent times, have emerged as discrete disciplines in their own right and within that process have created their own specific use of language. They are psychology and economics.

Psychologists use the word 'develop' to denote what is often a slow, natural unfolding of an innate potential such as intelligence, but no value judgement is involved. Intelligence and conceptual awareness can be shown to develop along certain well-documented lines, but so can dementia, which might be perceived as their opposite.

Economists, on the other hand, use the term rather differently and tend to take certain value judgements for granted. They talk of a developing economy and of underdeveloped or developing countries. It is here that the danger creeps in unawares. Such a description usually refers strictly to finance and overlooks the fact that rapid economic progress may actually be destroying a country's art, its culture, its language, its traditions and its self-identity, all of which may have gone into rapid decline as a result of foreign investment and the incursion of new, alien ways of doing things, but all of which become hidden, and consequently devalued, by our use of language.

This, I want to suggest, is equally the case with the moral and spiritual dimensions of education. The word 'development', with all the connotations of improvement, is present in a host of official documents. To take as examples just two influential publications, we might note the titles of the discussion paper of the Schools Curriculum and Assessment Authority, *Spiritual and Moral Development* (SCAA, 1995) and the draft guidance document of its successor, the Qualification and Curriculum Authority, *The Promotion of Pupils' Spiritual, Moral, Social and Cultural Development* (QCA, 1997).

These have to be seen now in the context of further policies to promote what is called *Preparation for Adult Life* (PAL), which would seem to assume an apprenticeship model of childhood without any consideration of the other five models described by Mills in Chapter 1. That this is being promoted specifically in the areas of the personal, social, moral and spiritual domains should be a matter of some concern. It is, in fact, rather worse than an apprenticeship model and it has a direct bearing on the moral and the spiritual. By this, I mean that there is a whole world of difference between the cultivation of a living, growing organism like a tomato plant or a child, and the building of an inanimate object like a motor car. The latter has no meaning and no value until it is finished; the former is a whole throughout all stages of its growth. To build educational policies on assumptions that we are not fully human beings until we reach maturity is to create a seventh model in addition to the six outlined by Mills: the child as an unfinished product.

All of these issues are implicit within the very notion of moral and spiritual growth because whenever we talk of the child, we are, in effect, talking about ourselves. We have to try, as the Danish thinker Sören Kierkegaard attempted nearly two hundred years ago, to be objective to self and subjective to all others, a process which stands current investigation and research practice on its head.

How then can we proceed? Because I would maintain that story is the key form of transmission for moral and spiritual growth (see Chapter 3 in this book), I shall attempt to tell as narrative what has been perhaps the most influential movement in moral educational theory over the past thirty years, and in so doing, to raise what I see as the key questions as well as highlight some of the confusions which continue. That story, because it has all emanated from the same university campus, might be called the Harvard Story, but it would be more appropriate to call it after its originator and to refer to it as the Kohlberg Story, even though the other two figures who are involved have emerged into greater prominence since his tragic and untimely death a decade ago.

Lawrence Kohlberg and the idea of moral development

Lawrence Kohlberg's work, which he himself regarded as being innovative (see Kohlberg, 1978: 10), was based on two explicit foundations. The first was a philosophical judgement about what constituted the high point of morality. Kohlberg argued, very properly, that unless we know where we are heading it is not possible to measure how far we have got. From his own philosophical background he argued that this high point was what he termed 'disinterested justice' when, leaving personal feelings and emotions aside, we can make moral judgements of a totally objective sort on the basis of principle. When pushed for an example, he cited the Stoic philosopher and Roman Emperor Marcus Aurelius (121–80) as an exemplar.

Kohlberg's second foundation lay in his methodology, which he consciously built on the already established stage development theories associated with the Swiss philosopher Jean Piaget (Kohlberg, 1981: 6ff; Piaget, 1958). It was Piaget who had shown that we do not grow intellectually in some sort of upwardly slanting straight-line continuum but rather in a series of stages, suddenly surging forward between periods of relative stability. Every parent knows that there is a certain truth in this in terms of physical growth; Kohlberg wanted to show that it was also the case in terms of our ability to grasp and employ moral concepts. In addition to these two explicit starting points, Kohlberg also made an assumption. Having decided that justice was the pinnacle of moral development, he repeatedly emphasised his belief in a natural sense of justice within the young child.

It was this belief, allied to his foundational criteria, which then allowed Kohlberg to argue that his approach went beyond the relativism of mere values clarification without being in any way indoctrinatory. There would be no need for any imposition of moral values. The educator's task would be to permit and to encourage the unfolding of what was a natural development towards the known outcome of disinterested justice.

Taking a sample of seventy-five children for his longitudinal study, Kohlberg embarked on the task of monitoring their responses to a range of moral questions at various ages. He found what he was looking for as he closely followed the threefold Piagetian model in terms of pre-conventional, conventional and post-conventional reasoning.

This presents no surprises, and Kohlberg went on to subdivide each Piagetian category into two, thus presenting us with his well-known six stages (1981: 17–20):

Stage 1   the punishment and obedience orientation.
Stage 2   the instrumental relativist orientation.
Stage 3   the interpersonal concordance or, 'good boy–nice girl' orient-ation.
Stage 4   society maintaining orientation.
Stage 5   the social contract orientation.
Stage 6   the universal ethical principle orientation.

However, his attention then focused on the movement, or lack of it in a very large number of cases, between Stage 4 and Stage 5. This marked the transitional point between the conventional and post-conventional Piagetian categories and, in his own stages, between following rules and following the principles which lie behind those rules or, in more common parlance, between the letter of the law and the spirit of the law.

It was what he perceived as the social and educational necessity of reaching Stage 5 which became Kohlberg's driving passion for a number of years. His problems were twofold. First, his sample began to fail him in that a disconcertingly low proportion seemed to be making the transition. Second, the world outside, far from supporting him, also seemed to be undermining the process. That world was the American world of the Vietnam War and then of Watergate in both of which Kohlberg felt that many of the political and social leaders of his own nation were showing themselves incapable of operating beyond a very conventional form of morality. Their attitudes of right and wrong were clearly formulated, but according to law and current conventions and not to any higher principle on which those laws might have initially been created.

Kohlberg decided to step outside of his sample and investigate what he termed 'examples from literature', citing in particular the cases of Mahatma Gandhi and Martin Luther King. Such figures, Kohlberg decided, showed evidence of Stage 6, a morality which went beyond the idea of a social contract into realms of a universal ethic. Not content with that, he then began to speculate about the possibility of a Stage 7 in which certain such individuals began to sense themselves as a finite part of an infinite whole. He had by this point begun to cause alarm among some of his most ardent followers such as the British scholar Robert Carter, who published an article entitled simply, 'What is Lawrence Kohlberg Doing?' (1980).

117

Carter's reaction signifies something of why Kohlberg's work was beginning to cause great interest in England and Wales. It was, first and foremost, a thoroughly secular approach to morality, and therefore seemed an attractive replacement for religious education which, for historical reasons, had traditionally been assumed to be the main vehicle for moral education in schools. Consequently, the alarm bells began to ring loudly when Kohlberg's pursuit of moral development began to leave the empirical and enter the sphere of the mystical. Gandhi and King were both recognised religious figures, one a devout Hindu, the other an American Baptist minister.

But by this stage, other questions were also beginning to be asked. In the first place, was Kohlberg's enquiry to do with moral development as such or just with the development of moral reasoning? Knowing the difference between right and wrong is one thing; doing it is quite another. Which is the aim of moral education? In fairness to Kohlberg, he himself had never hidden the fact that he was as concerned with the reasons for a moral stance as with the moral stance itself, although in terms of high politics he had argued that the way certain leaders, including teachers, publicly reasoned was of itself a moral action.

A third weakness concerned the whole notion of indoctrination. He became actively involved in a tough Boston secondary school, and was soon drawing clear and somewhat embarrassing distinctions between educational research and practice, acknowledging that:

> I realise now that the psychologist's abstraction of moral cognition from moral action ... are necessary abstractions for certain psychological research purposes. It is not a sufficient guide for the moral educator.
>
> (Kohlberg, 1978: 14)

and adding later in the same passage:

> I believe that the concepts guiding moral education must be partly indoctrinative. This is true by necessity in a world in which children engage in cheating, stealing and aggression and in a context wherein one cannot wait until children reach the fifth stage to deal directly with moral behaviour ... I now believe that moral education can be in the form of advocacy.
>
> (1978: 15)

These three modifications threw up deep and central questions not only about the nature of moral education but also about the whole central notion of development. Moreover, two other research projects, both on the same university campus, were beginning to offer an even greater challenge to the whole Kohlbergian hypothesis. These were the work of first, Carol Gilligan and second, Robert Coles. I will deal with them in that order.

The different voice of Carol Gilligan

Carol Gilligan also worked within the School of Education at Harvard University, but in a different department from Kohlberg. However, she came to work closely with him in a relationship which was co-operative and supportive but, at the same time, dynamic and challenging. She has recently given a full account of that relationship (Gilligan, 1998), and in doing so has re-opened all the key questions about the very notion of development in moral education. But it was the publication of her earlier book, *In a Different Voice* (1982), which first provoked a fascinating debate, one which must cause us to re-assess not only our attitudes to moral education but to all aspects of values education and, indeed, to ways in which we can learn which are other than the purely cognitive/intellectual.

Gilligan's 'different voice' is the voice of women. At the time, in the mid-1960s, Kohlberg's sample raised few eyebrows but it consisted of seventy-five boys, all of whom were white and middle class. By 1980 this had become very questionable indeed. For her quite independent piece of research, Carol Gilligan had taken a small but all female sample and for a very good reason. They shared the same uniquely female moral dilemma. All were pregnant and all were questioning whether or not to have an abortion.

We feel immediately the emotional intensity within such a group. Kohlberg's moral dilemmas, by contrast, were what we might term 'bar stool' problems of the 'what would you do if?' genre. Discussion could be endless and even entertaining. What Gilligan managed to create for research purposes was a situation which bore all the ingredients of real moral decision making. These were that the emotions were involved every bit as much as the intellect; there was urgency about the need to act – the decision had to be made within a very strict timeframe – and, once made, it could not be revoked. The effects of the decision would be long lasting and must, of necessity, affect others.

All of this would seem to demonstrate that, in making value judgements of any sort, we acknowledge that feelings and emotions are sources of knowledge; the intellect is not enough and may not even be dominant. Carried over into stage development theories, we then have to ask just what is the justification for applying such theories to areas other than the strictly cognitive? Does our emotional 'development' automatically follow the same path as our intellectual one?

But Gilligan's research provided another crucial insight. Her women respondents did not see disinterested justice as the high point of moral attainment at all. The word 'relationship' occurred again and again, and with it came the notion that loving kindness and compassion were more important than cold justice. Often there simply was no 'right' answer:

Women were saying, 'I'm in this dilemma of relationship and I can't see a way of acting that will not cause hurt. So I don't know what to do. There is no good thing to do here.'

(1998: 130)

We have, then, two contrasting perspectives on morality. One claims that detached justice is the high point; the other that it is loving kindness and mercy. But surely we have been here before. Kohlberg was from a strongly Jewish background, a refugee from the Holocaust, and had come to psychology via philosophy. Gilligan came to assist in his work from a literary background. Neither, however, as far as I am aware, has fully recognised the deep significance and the irony of the point at which they arrived. The clash between justice and mercy as the highest moral virtue is, as we all know, the central theme of Shakespeare's *Merchant of Venice*. But the issue goes back much further even within the same tradition, to the Hebrew prophets of the eighth century before Christ. While Amos was proclaiming, 'Let justice roll down like water and righteousness like an ever flowing stream', his contemporary, Micah, was asking, 'What does the Lord require of you but to *do* justly, to love mercy and to walk humbly with your God?'

In brief, the arguments about the nature of morality and moral growth are very old, and they have not changed fundamentally over nearly three millennia. Kohlberg's claim for innovation can hardly be sustained. Gilligan, for her part, now explicitly argues that 'psychologists have discovered in the last twenty years that the story they told about development was a wrong story' (1998: 137).

There are, however, at least two other lessons to be learned from the Kohlberg–Gilligan dialogue before we move on, and both are now explicitly recognised by Gilligan herself. The first concerns the absence of any real connection between intellectual development and moral growth. It had dawned slowly on Kohlberg that the Jewish Holocaust should never have happened in Germany of all places. Was this not the very centre of the Enlightenment which had produced Kant and Hegel? 'That the holocaust happened in Europe', writes Gilligan, 'meant that the assumption that civilisation led to moral development could no longer be held. Education, social class, culture and civilisation were not necessarily associated with higher stages of moral reasoning ' (1998: 134).

Second, there are the implications for our whole approach to research. It is the obsession with the idea of objectivity which is being challenged as soon as it is suggested that feeling is a source of knowledge and that being human means being relational. To isolate the variables in the human, as opposed to the physical, sciences is to run the risk of destroying the essential nature of what it is to be human in the first place. It is akin to studying a brick wall by looking only at the bricks and ignoring the mortar which holds them together and links each to the whole. This, in Gilligan's eyes, is where Kohlberg's whole approach faltered and the lesson for all of us is contained.

> The dissociation from relationship ... hid the experiences, the thoughts and feelings of all people who were considered to be lesser, less developed, less human and we all know who these people are: women, people of colour, gays and lesbians, the poor and the disabled. It was everyone who was 'different' and the only way you could be different within a hierarchical scheme was, you could be higher or lower, and all the people who had historically been lower turned out – surprise, surprise – to be the people who did not create the scheme.
>
> (1998: 134)

What is being voiced here is only one of the many calls now being heard for a greater degree of subjectivity to be involved in the study of human beings, a recognition that the researcher is himself or herself a part of the enquiry. This modern reaction to two hundred years of Enlightenment influence is to be seen most clearly in those areas identified by Gilligan – in women's studies, racial studies, disability studies and the like – but it has never wholly died. (For a survey of recent literature across these areas, see Mark Priestley (1999: 13–17).) It was Carl Jung who reminded us that where human beings are concerned, the observer has a different relationship with the observed than with any other species or range of objects. 'Only the psyche can penetrate the psyche' (1937: 3), he comments, while in 1925 a former Principal of Westhill College, Basil Yeaxlee, quoted as if it were an adage of the time, 'Spiritual things are spiritually discerned' (1925: vii).

We have moved from the moral to the spiritual. It is no coincidence that the recent growth of interest in what is termed the 'spiritual dimension of education' has coincided with demands for a re-adjustment of research methodologies and it is to that area that we now turn.

Robert Coles and the story of Ruby Bridges

Ruby Bridges was six, and Ruby Bridges was going to school. The only trouble was that no-one else was going to school with her apart from the sheriff, while the Louisiana National Guard held back the mob who were jeering at her and threatening to lynch both her and her family.

It was 1956, and Ruby was the first black child to be admitted to the Frank's School in New Orleans, as a result of which all the white parents had decided upon a school boycott. The whole story is fully documented by Robert Coles (1986: 22–7) whose subsequent career was determined by it.

As a young, newly qualified doctor intent on a career as a psychiatrist, Coles witnessed the events while serving in the army. He observed Ruby endure this treatment over six months and interviewed her and her family on several occasions. He discovered that she was not showing what he had expected to be the normal signs of stress and tension such as nightmares or enuresis. He also discovered that she had a clear, articulate rationale. When seen speaking to some of the crowd, he asked her what she had said. The reply was, 'Father, forgive them. They don't know what they are doing.' Her mother endorsed the statement when interviewed. She had told Ruby the story.

Coles concludes that Ruby, now a middle-aged woman, became the first member of her family ever to go on through secondary education and to become a college graduate. She has had three children of her own and has never had to consult a psychiatrist, nor has she ever had any recognisable psychological problems.

Coles went on to spend his working life looking at children in crisis (Coles 1978, 1992) and developing his theories from that basis (see Coles 1989, 1992). The sequence is highly significant. The theories are an attempt to make generalisations from observations, not a preconceived framework into which the experiences were fitted. It is probably for this reason that Coles, working on the same university campus as Kohlberg and Gilligan, is only now coming to be known. Without a grand theory to proclaim and attract research funding, his work has long been ignored by the academic world, particularly as he seems to be saying that, far from being new, this whole area of moral growth and awareness is quite uninfluenced and unchanged by modern scientific enquiry. The answer lies not in grand theories of development but rather in what another critic of Kohlberg's pinpointed as 'vision' and 'character' (see Dykstra, 1981).

Cole's interest drew him to dozens of other instances where children and teenagers had taken moral leads, often, like Ruby, volunteering to be the first black child to enter an all-white school. Whereas Kohlberg and even Gilligan seem to have assumed that morality had to be gauged by the way in which their sample responded to moral challenges, Coles's interest is equally in those young people who take a moral initiative and force a response from others. Morality is proactive, not just reactive.

If that is the case, it follows that morality comes as much from inner resources as from external stimuli. This 'inner vision' has its roots in the sensing of a greater story of which one feels to be a part and its application emerges from a deep sense of self worth or 'character'.

Notwithstanding this outcome to what I have termed the Kohlberg story, officialdom in England and Wales remains firmly committed to an assumed developmental line of which Clive Erriker (1998) has recently offered a detailed critique in an article entitled 'Spiritual Confusion'. Robert Coles's work has led us from moral into spiritual growth, but much thinking on the latter has gone on in Britain over recent years, much of it unacknowledged outside of a very small group of thinkers.

The spiritual dimension of education in England and Wales

There is a strong tradition within English culture that, far from developing, spiritual awareness declines with age. This is a very strong feature of the Romantic poets, but this romanticism need not be identified with the notion of childhood innocence.

The 1970s saw a significant resurgence of interest in the concept of the spiritual which Edward Robinson (1977) entitled *The Original Vision*, borrowing the phrase from Edwin Muir whom he quotes as the frontispiece to his book: 'A child has a picture of human existence peculiar to himself [*sic*] which he probably never remembers after he has lost it: the original vision of the world.' Muir then goes on to talk of the vision as containing for the child, 'a completer harmony of all things with each other than he will ever know again' (Muir, 1938: 3).

Robinson's work was, in fact, a continuation of that begun by the eminent biologist Sir Alister Hardy, who, by simply placing an advertisement in a national newspaper, had encouraged people to write in describing any event by which they, 'felt that their lives had in any way been affected by some power beyond themselves'. No mention was made of any particular age range, but one of Robinson's significant findings when he came to analyse the material was that some fifteen per cent of the four thousand experiences recorded took place in childhood. Moreover, they were often accompanied by statements such as, 'The most profound experience of my life came to me when I was very young, between four and five years old', and, ' I just know that the whole of my life has been built on the great truth that was revealed to me then' (at age six) (Robinson, 1977: 11).

This 'completer harmony' constitutes a real sense of knowing and directly relates to the moral. Robinson's penultimate chapter is entitled 'Morality and Significance', and consists of examples of knowledge of right and wrong derived from early childhood. They prompt Robinson to ask some of the all important questions with which we have been concerned. While acknowledging the huge contribution to our understanding of the acquisition of concepts by such developmentalists as Piaget, for example, he points out (1977: 9) that the starting point of such researchers is always the incapacity of children to see the world as adults see it. As we have seen with Kohlberg, measurement of development requires prior assumption of the route and the high point. 'Reality' in such systems, however, is simply how adults see the world. Children are assumed to get better, or develop, insofar as they can be measured along the line of their relative incapacity to see adult 'reality'.

When we turn to morality there is an additional factor. Later in his *Autobiography* (1938: 25) Muir talks of a feeling of immortality in our early years because, for the young child, time hardly exists. But, Robinson comments:

> One of the problems when we come [as adults] to look at the sense of right and wrong in childhood is that we tend to judge it in terms of our own notions of morality; and this morality is essentially time-bound. A moral act involves an act of calculation.
>
> (1977: 131)

Nevertheless, faced with the examples before him, he goes on to state that, 'It seems certain that children are capable of deliberation and a sense of responsibility long before they can find words to formulate these feelings and capacities', and then to ask, 'is there native to childhood some *timeless* imperative, independent of the categories of thought and calculation?' (1977: 131).

Robinson's work on the spiritual dimension of experience has been continued by David Hay (1982, 1985, 1996), assisted most recently by Rebecca Nye (Hay and Nye, 1998). Working as an academic psychologist, Nye has demonstrated through its methodologies what literary figures such as Wordsworth and Muir have long maintained from their own experience, namely that the core of what we understand by the spiritual is what she has termed 'relational consciousness'. It is that sense of wholeness of which one is oneself a part. It is felt before it can be articulated. Moreover, in our modern world the learning to articulate is itself the process most likely to destroy it as we are taught to differentiate and analyse. As young children we are at one with the physical world of nature, with the past as much as with the present and with other people by whom we are surrounded. In short, space and time are not important to us.

They cease to be important again in old age, which is perhaps why that period has long been referred to as second childhood. There is, I would argue, nothing wrong with the notion of development provided we get the model right. We have long abandoned any idea of a straight-line development from birth to death. The stage developmentalists, in particular, substituted a staircase model, but its deficiency is that it leaves childhood behind as it ascends, making a tacit assumption of continuous improvement. Coles, in his accounts, also gives examples of sudden shifts of perception in which, for example, a white child suddenly and for the first time sees a black child as a fellow human being and instantaneously changes in attitude – what we might term an insight rather than a development (see, for example, Coles, 1986: 27–9).

One problem with all of these models is that they tend to assume that progression to a new stage causes us to leave behind an earlier one. I have myself for many years taken with me into lectures a cross-section of the trunk of an old pine tree cut down in my garden. The rings which had formed over some sixty years are clear and distinct. At least, they are near the core. They become fudged as the eye moves out to the perimeter where they have started to decay. As it is with nature so I believe it is with us. Childhood remains at our core and never leaves us although the years of later experience grow round it and dull its sharpest experiences only to fall away first as we start to age and decay mentally and physically.

Conclusion

I began with talk of wisdom. It was T.S. Eliot who, in his poem 'The Rock' (1928), asked, 'Where is the wisdom we have lost in knowledge? Where is the knowledge we have lost in information?' We have seen how, in the cases of Kohlberg, Gilligan and Nye, modern forms of research have served not so much to make new discoveries as to confirm ancient wisdom. Part of the ancient wisdom with regard to moral and spiritual growth is that they are 'caught not taught'. More accurately, it is to suggest that we teach values through what we are, more than through what we simply say. Parents probably know this better than teachers among whom it has become anathema to suggest that what they are as persons is of professional significance.

Nor, of course, is this a matter only for parents and teachers. While these may still be the most significant persons in their lives, the moral and spiritual growth of children depends on the whole group and society in which they live. It has become a commonplace for politicians, journalists and even inspectors to berate parents and teachers for moral faults in the young while demonstrating in their own lives that cheating, lying and deception are no barriers to social advancement and fortune.

'Our moral lives', writes Stanley Hauerwas (1974: 74) 'are not simply made up of the addition of our separate responses to particular situations. Rather we exhibit an orientation that gives our lives a theme through which the variety of what we do and do not can be scored.' A little later, he says:

> Our character is the result of our sustained attention to the world which gives coherence to our intentionality. Such attention is formed and given content by the stories through which we have learned to live our lives. To be moral persons is to allow stories to be told through us so that our manifold activities gain a coherence that allows us to claim them for our own. The significance of stories is the significance of character for the moral life as our experience itself, if it is to be coherent, is but an incipient story.

But story is the subject matter of a separate chapter.

Review questions and tasks

1 Think of various ways in which the word 'develop' is used. When does it denote improvement? When is it value-free?

2 Can a methodology which claims to be value-free ever be employed to promote values?

3 Is moral education to do with promoting moral reasoning or moral behaviour? Is morality itself taught or caught?

4 Why be good? Is it possible to answer this without asking religious questions?

5 Investigate the moral teaching of a religion you know little about. Compare and contrast this teaching with your own beliefs.

6 Try and write your own spiritual autobiography, going back as far as you can into your own childhood. What were the key experiences in your childhood which might most have influenced what you now are as an adult? (This exercise may best be done in private without any compulsion to reveal it to others.)

Further reading

Fynn (1974) *Mr God This is Anna*, **London: Collins.** First published anonymously in 1974 and illustrated by Papas, this little classic has been in print ever since. It tells the story of a young stray girl in the east end of London by the man who unofficially adopted her and took her into his family. Anna has had little education but her insights into moral and spiritual situations are sharp and penetrating. Nothing in this account can be proved; the author has never revealed his identity. But does it read as authentic, especially considering the ending?

Golding, W. (1956) *Lord of the Flies*, **London: Faber & Faber.** Golding's novel posits what might happen were a group of children (boys) to be left without any adult supervision over a sustained period of time. It is a graphic comment on the question of how far morality is imposed from outside or whether there is an innate sense of justice within us. Its theme links up with Kohlberg's experience, described above, in the Cluster School in Boston when he experimented with the idea of a school administered by pupils themselves.

Hughes, T. (1970) 'Myth and Education', in G. Fox (ed.) *Celebrating Children's Literature in Education*, **London: Hodder & Stoughton, 1995.** This essay was first published in 1970, but has been reproduced in a number of publications since such as G. Fox *et al.* (eds), (1976) *Writers Critics and Children*, Heinemann, London and in a Faber collection of Ted Hughes's essays *Winter Pollen* (1994). It should be compulsory reading for anyone training to become a teacher. It is concerned with the nature and power of story, especially that form which we know as myth. In this essay, Hughes explores the contrasting nature of the Christ

Story and the Hitler Story, but also gives some insight into what he felt lay behind some of his own writing for children, particularly *The Iron Man*.

Sereny, G. (1998) *Cries Unheard: The Story of Mary Bell*, London: Macmillan. This book documents in detail the story of Mary Bell who, in 1968 at the age of eleven, was tried and convicted of manslaughter following the death of two small boys in Newcastle on Tyne. In 1998 Mary Bell's new identity and whereabouts was published by elements of the press. This book raises a whole host of questions about the relationship of morality and law, especially in the context of a young child's lack of awareness of right and wrong following a harrowing upbringing in an appalling social context. It also shows society's confusion about the relationship between punishment and care in such situations. The account has similarities with the later James Bulger case.

Wordsworth, W., 'Ode: Intimations of Immortality', to be found in any collected works. In this poem, which can be read with the opening parts of *The Prelude*, Wordsworth explores the experience of losing the deep sense of spiritual relationship with the natural world as he gets older until he reaches the point where he sees it 'die away and pass into the light of common day'. It can be read against our current assumptions of education as development.

References

Carter, R. (1980) 'What is Lawrence Kohlberg Doing?' in *Journal of Moral Education*, 9 (2).

Coles, R. (1978) *Children in Crisis*, 5 vols, Boston: Atlantis Press.

—— (1986) *The Moral Life of Children*, Boston: Atlantis Press.

—— (1989) *The Call of Stories: Teaching and the Moral Imagination*, Boston: Mifflen.

—— (1992) *The Spiritual Life of Children*, London: HarperCollins.

Dykstra, C. (1981) *Vision and Character*, New York: Paulist Press.

Erriker, C. (1998) 'Spiritual Confusion: A Critique of Current Educational Policy in England and Wales', *International Journal of Children's Spirituality* 3 (1).

Fulghum, R. (1989) *All I Really Need to Know I Learned in Kindergarten*, London: Grafton.

Gilligan, C. (1982) *In a Different Voice*, Cambridge MA: Harvard University Press.

—— (1998) 'Remembering Larry', *Journal of Moral Education* 27 (2): 125–39.

Hauerwas, S. (1974) *Vision and Virtue: Essays in Christian Ethical Reflection*, Indiana: Fides.

Hay, D. (1982) *Exploring Inner Space*, London: Penguin.

—— (1985) 'Religious Experience and its Induction', in L.B. Brown (ed.), *Advances in the Psychology of Religion*, Oxford: Pergamon.

Hay, D. (1996) 'Memories of a Calvinist Childhood', in W.G. Lawrence (ed.), *Roots in a Northern Landscape*, Edinburgh: Scottish Cultural Press.

Hay, D. and Nye, R.(1998) *The Spirit of the Child*, London: Fount.

Jung, C. (1937) 'The Phenomenology of the Spirit in Fairy Tales', in B. Campbell (ed.), *Spirit and Nature: Papers From The Eranos Year Books*, Princeton NJ, Princeton University Press, 1982.

Kohlberg, L. (1978) 'Moral Education Re-appraised', *The Humanist*, 38 (6).

—— (1981) *The Philosophy of Moral Development*, San Francisco: Harper & Row.

Muir, E. (1938) *Autobiography*, London: Faber.

Piaget, J. (1958) *The Child's Construction of Reality*, London: Routledge & Kegan Paul.

Priestley, M. (1999) *Disability Politics and Community Care*, London: Kingsley.

QCA (Qualification and Curriculum Authority) (1997) *Promotion of Pupils' Spiritual, Moral, Social and Cultural Development*, London.

Robinson, E., (1977) *The Original Vision*, Religious Experience Research Unit, Oxford: Manchester College.

SCAA (Schools Curriculum and Assessment Authority) (1995) *Spiritual and Moral Development*, London.

Yeaxlee, B., (1925) *Spiritual Values in Adult Education: a Study of a Neglected Aspect*, Oxford: Oxford University Press.

Part Four

Cultural studies

Chapter 7

Race, class and gender

Neill Thew

Summary

The sociology of childhood has a relatively short history, but work in this field has proliferated rapidly over the past decade or so. This chapter begins by outlining some of the major trends in contemporary sociological thinking about gender, race, class and identity, and then moves on to explore these theories from a standpoint committed to the creation of a more nuanced and subtle way of theorising childhood varieties and experience. The chapter aims to open up a dialogue between often implicitly essentialist and homogenising theories of childhood and/or 'the child', and theories of difference and identity circulating in sociological theory (which is, however, overwhelmingly predicated upon adult identities).The chapter argues that many theories of childhood have implicitly become particular points of resistance against characteristic sociological ways of thinking. Overall, the chapter seeks to enable readers to develop the critical skills needed to interrogate childhood theories from a variety of intellectual viewpoints and in the light of a wide range of different personal histories.

I wait. I compose myself. My self is a thing I must now compose, as one composes a speech. What I must present is a made thing, not something born.

(Margaret Atwood, *The Handmaid's Tale*)

That first night of their dreaming, asleep beneath the Tree,
God said, 'Let meanings move,' and there was poetry.

(Muriel Rukeyser, *The Sixth Night: Waking*)

One of the central theoretical problems in childhood studies is that the objects of our study – children and childhood – exist at very different levels of enquiry. When we are thinking about children, we are often thinking locally about particular individuals, families, schools or communities, whereas childhood is more often thought of in global, sweeping terms. While each level of thought necessarily depends upon the other – theories of childhood must surely be referred back to, and rooted in, the experiences of actual children, while our observations of these individuals' experiences are also most fully understood and interpreted in the context of theorising about childhood – something seems to be missing from the centre, namely a more robust way of distinguishing groups of children and of understanding childhood's many, interlocking subcultures. Jacqueline Rose, writing about children's fiction, poses the challenging question, 'but to which child are we speaking?' (1984: 7), and adds that if we think that the answer is that we are speaking to, or for, all children, then our response is dangerously self-deluding because:

the idea of speaking to *all* children serves to close off a set of cultural divisions, divisions in which not only children, but we ourselves, are necessarily caught … class, culture, and literacy – divisions which undermine any generalized concept of the child.

(Rose, 1984: 7)

So, on behalf of which children *are* we speaking, writing, studying and thinking? This chapter aims to help you begin to address this question by exploring the relatively new and rapidly developing field of the sociology of childhood. In order to do this, we shall begin by looking at a set of wider sociological issues to do with race, class, gender and human identities.

Sociology is primarily concerned with the study of human societies and groups. It is a way of attempting to understand how societies operate, what influences social relationships, and how people come to perceive themselves and behave towards others. It is concerned with what produces continuity and what makes for social change and upheaval; it looks at customs and beliefs as well as structures and institutions in society, in fact, anything that helps to explain the relationship between individual lives and experiences, and the societies and groups to which we all belong. In much recent work in both sociology and cultural studies, gender, race and class have often been highlighted as central concerns in attempting to understand these processes of identity formation.

That phrase 'identity formation' gets to the heart of one of the central debates in sociology, that between essentialism and constructionism. One of the central tenets of sociology is that institutionalised social forces are assumed to play the major part in shaping human actions, understandings and identities. Most human behaviour is consciously learnt or unconsciously transmitted and absorbed through a range of social relationships and settings (like families and schools), and not just governed by instincts, biology or nature. Such ideas as these are constructionist. They run contrary to essentialist views that human nature is fixed, incontestable and unaffected by changes in history or across cultures. Take, for example, the question of who is best suited to looking after small children, men or women? An essentialist argument would develop along the lines that women are naturally intended for this role, due to their genetic and hormonal makeup, and due to the fact that they both give birth to babies in the first place and are strongly predisposed to nurturing and caring, unlike much more aggressive and competitive men. Furthermore, essentialism would suggest that to alter, or interfere in, this naturally ordained order of female childcare will have dire social consequences.

A socio-cultural enquiry which takes a constructionist approach will treat the fact that, in the recent history of the West, childcare has been overwhelmingly seen and practised as a female concern, not as a piece of 'data' confirming the natural, pre-given order of things, but as something itself in need of explanation, and as the starting point for a series of questions: Why has this been? What social forces have contributed to this state of affairs? Why do things seem to be changing right now? What might this also tell us about the changing natures of motherhood, fatherhood and childhood, as well as changing family structures, labour markets, governmental childcare policies and local council nursery provision?

I ran into a real-life example of the difference between essentialist and constructionist thinking last Christmas. My sister and I were staying with our uncle. We are very close to him, and very fond of him, yet the running joke in our family is that his social beliefs predate Noah's Ark. On Christmas Eve, we needed to do some last minute shopping, and he also wanted to exchange cards with some friends at his golf club. Since my sister and I are not members of the club, we had to wait for him outside. He emerged from the clubhouse looking perplexed. 'There are a lot of women in today', he remarked. 'Why's that odd?' I asked, wondering what lay behind his surprise. 'Well', he thought, 'You'd expect them all to be at home making lunch for tomorrow'. When my sister and I both pointed out that this was, to us, an outrageous statement, my uncle defended his comment by protesting, 'Well, that just can't be sexist, because it's true!' Now, this seems to me to be illustrative of a key feature of essentialist thinking – it tends to dress itself up in the language of nature as a way of ending debate and of denying the possibilities of difference. In this way, the essentialist language of description often functions also as a form of control.

While I find the constructionist line of enquiry the more useful and productive, it is important not to dismiss essentialism as having no insights to offer. A consideration of the complexity of class, race and gender identities is surely enriched by drawing from both traditions and understanding their respective domains. Gender provides a useful paradigmatic example here.

Much recent work on gender and identity draws a distinction between *sex* and *gender*. Sex is the domain of biology, genetics and the body. Your sex refers to the body with which you were born. Gender is in the domain of the social; it refers to the meanings given to that sexed body in society. These meanings are not natural but are open to being contested, and this contesting, or argument, about the meaning of gender underlies our sometime confusion about gendered identity in the modern Western world.

It is worth noting that there are some critical objections that this model oversimplifies the complex relationships between sex and the body, and gender and identity. One objection is that we can have no prior access to understanding the sexed body outside of language and culture, so therefore both sex and gender should be seen as culturally constructed. Another related objection is that even if we are supposed to have any kind of immediacy of understanding our own bodies, these bodies are almost inevitably read through already inscripted social codes. So, for example, when it is argued in psychoanalysis that the little girl feels envy and lack in relation to the phallus, the phallus has already been assigned a privileged status and meaning outside of any single individual's experience and thought. I take these objections as both important and valid, but maintain that the basic model proposed in this chapter is a vitally productive starting point for your thinking. This does not preclude you from going on to explore other models, of course.

Having our own identities caught up in and questioned by these arguments is inescapable. The making of these meanings begins at birth. What, after all, is the first question we ask about a new born baby: is it a boy or a girl? One of the hospitals in my area was recently called to task for the way in which the new born babies were tagged. Little boys were given a wrist band reading, 'I'm a boy', whereas girls had one proclaiming, 'It's a girl'. This might appear trivial, were it not that the implicit idea underlying this – that boys are assumed to have ready access to active social agency and girls are not – is so powerfully encoded in many other areas of gendered life. It is not, in other words, either accidental or unimportant, but rather one minor example of a regularly present form of social engendering.

It is sometimes easier to see the constructed and contingent nature of identities in cultures removed from our own, because locally specific ideas about identity in our own cultures are often talked about in the language of 'the normal', 'the natural' and 'common-sense', and thereby tend to become invisible to analysis. Given this, consider this Victorian account of race. The version here is taken from the entry on 'Ethnology' in the 1889 edition of *Chamber's Encyclopaedia* (reproduced in Yeo and Lovell, 1998: 108), which, after all, was striving to offer an objective account of contemporary knowledge and truth.

The article proposes three fundamental human types: Caucasian-European (subdivided into pale and dark types); Ethiopian-African and Mongolian-Asian. It begins with a description of the physical characteristics of each type, which we might find unremarkable were it not for the fact that the language of description becomes heavily value-laden (even though the author appears quite unaware that he is well outside the bounds of descriptive objectivity). Thus, the Mongolian-Asian type is said to have skin which is 'rough in texture, often with a washed-out look' and hair which is 'dull, black, coarse, lank and lustre-less'. The link between these physical characteristics and the description of the Mongolian-Asian temperament as, 'sluggish, gloomy, uncommunicative, passive and having little initiative', is implicit but perfectly clear. Mongolian-Asians are predisposed to their temperament by their very physical make-up, and cannot therefore act against their inevitable, nature-given types. From here, it is but a short step to evaluations of the cultures of each racial type which rank Caucasian-European culture (and it is, of course, no coincidence that this is the culture both of the writer and the culture within which, and for which, the *Encyclopaedia* was produced) as having 'science, art and literature' which are 'highly developed', and which describe the 'science' of Mongolian-Asian culture as being only 'slightly developed' with 'art and literature' little better in their state of 'moderate development'.

I am assuming that we post-Victorian readers will find ourselves, in a variety of ways, at odds with these ideas about race. But it does not seem enough to say that the writer of that article was 'racist' whereas we are now 'enlightened'. What seems more pertinent is to say that ideas and identities stemming from discourses of race, class and gender are endlessly contested and re-mapped, always being shifted back and forth in the interests of competing social groups and causes, and that there is, therefore, no final, definitive version of what these ideas and identities ought to mean to all individuals. It remains absolutely crucial to remember, however, that while, against essentialism, constructionism would argue that there is no correct, singular reality of race, gender and class, but, rather, competing constructions, narratives and stories, nevertheless these things are all very real in our lives, and have material consequences in the world. To say that identities are constructed is absolutely not to say that they are unimportant, evanescent, or easy to change and manipulate. They are not. However we theorise race, black youths are still fighting white gangs on the streets of many cities; however we theorise gender, women are still being forced into lower paid jobs than men and to bear the brunt of childcare, whereas, conversely, the paternity leave arrangements of many companies deny men the opportunities of spending time with their babies. The 1999 nail bombings in Brixton, Brick Lane and Soho must serve as sober reminders of this truth: socio-cultural research may very well put forward powerful arguments for the constructed and contingent nature of identity, but our lives still too often bear the inescapable impact of essentialist forces.

Within the British social context especially, it is impossible to think meaningfully about identity without considering class. Strangers will judge us according to their perceptions, and stereotypes, of our class status. My accent is a curious hybrid, because it has developed while I have lived in places all around Britain. One of its features is that I use short 'a' sounds, typical of Northern English speech, in words like 'grass', 'glass' and 'class'. At a reception in London recently, a fellow guest overheard me asking for a glass of wine. 'I love the way you say glass,' he drawled, 'It's so delightfully working class'. I would like to be able to say that I came up with a devastatingly witty reply to that patronising 'delightfully', but, although several rejoinders occurred to me afterwards, at the time I was made oddly tongue-tied and awkward. Thinking about why this was is interesting, and leads us into a consideration of several key features of class and identity.

A traditional Marxist approach to class looks at the individual's relationship to the means of production (of capital and goods) in their community. Marx looks at the differences between the working class, the bourgeoisie (which is more or less equivalent to the middle, managerial class) and the owning class. Members of the owning class are those who own the resources (for example, land, plantations or factories) from which wealth is produced. They do not, however, produce that wealth themselves; that task is performed by the members of the working class. Because the capitalist system depends on making a profit, members of the working class are never paid as much as their work is worth. To give a current day example, a worker in a Third World country might sew up fifty footballs in a day. In the UK, these footballs could sell for twenty pounds each, but that labourer, that person who made them, will earn only the equivalent of pennies. In this way, the worker is 'alienated' from her or his labour, and the owner (today more likely to be a large corporation producing profits for its shareholders rather than some individual) benefits from others' work. The owner exchanges capital for more capital; the worker tries to exchange labour for capital, and in this equation the worker always, of necessity, loses out. In this structure, it becomes the task of the middle class to manage the worker for the benefit of the owner, and, while managers never reap profits to the extent of the owner, the rewards of managing are nevertheless enough to give them a powerful interest in maintaining the status quo.

The problem with thinking our way through this model is that patterns of work and ownership have become increasingly complex (how many of us now own shares in privatised utilities, for example?). Also, in much

popular discourse, class is now increasingly defined (even if only implicitly) in terms of what we own and consume, rather than in terms of our
relationship to the means of production. It is noticeable that in my lessons,
my students find it much more difficult to think about and describe their
own classes than they do to consider their races, genders and even sexuali-
ties. Class is an oddly mobile concept at the beginning of the twenty-first
century, and yet it is nonetheless a powerful determinant of social identity.

There are many themes and ideas which can be taken from this sociological work and brought to bear on childhood studies. Most obviously, it is
important to notice that children as well as adults have races, genders and
classes, and that these dimensions impact on children's lives and experiences. It is also important to remember that we are no longer children, and
that in many ways we do not have immediate, if any, access to children's
own cultures, ideas and experiences. As students of childhood, we would
do well to see ourselves in the role of ethnographers, trying to be aware
that our understandings of our observations may well be quite different
from those of the children being observed, and that (bearing in mind the
example of Victorian views on race cited above) we need to be especially
careful not to blur the line between data and interpretation.

A further consideration is the absolute importance of remembering the
proper domains of the physically given and the socially constructed,
because speaking across or muddling these domains leads to some quite
alarming misunderstandings. To talk about the sexed body is different from
talking about our own – and social – constructions and understandings of
gender, even if the two discussions are intimately linked. Similarly, skin
colour belongs to a different realm from discourses of race; and, crucially
for us here, the period of biological immaturity in the human infant is not
the same thing as childhood. When Ariès famously claimed in his book
Centuries of Childhood that in medieval society the idea of childhood did not
exist, he was most certainly not saying (despite repeated critical misread-
ings of this work) that there were no such things as children in the Middle
Ages – to suggest such a thing would self-evidently be ludicrous.

Aside from these concerns, I would argue that there are two absolutely
crucial ways in which sociology and childhood studies must now come to
terms with one another, and that any attempt at developing a sociology of
childhood will be seriously compromised if it fails to take account of these
debates.

The first is that there is an imperative to open up a dialogue between the
often implicitly essentialist and homogenising theories of childhood
and/or 'the child' and the theories of identity and difference circulating in
sociological theory (which is, however, overwhelmingly predicated upon
adult identities). As Karin Lesnik-Oberstein points out, a confusing situation exists where:

> 'children' in (children's) literature, criticism, and history ... are still, and tena-
> ciously, placed at the centre of an on-going debate revolving around the basic
> question of whether identity is constructed or essential at all, while, in the mean-
> time, 'children' in much of sociology, and at least several approaches within
> anthropology, psychology, and psychoanalysis – fields supposedly much more
> closely concerned with 'actual' children – are much more generally accepted as
> constructed.
>
> (Lesnik-Oberstein, 1998: 7–8)

It is key to the debates about the constructionist nature of, say, gendered identity (parallel arguments can be found for other kinds of identity) not only that these identities are constructed and open to contest, rather than naturally inevitable, but also that identities are not somehow self-defined, but are constructed precisely in relation to other identities. Identities are both relational and differential, open to slippage due to both internal and external pressures. If I am what you are not, then it is little wonder that our identities are often experienced as problematic or precarious.

In the light of the above, we may begin to see why childhood studies remains a field often resistant to the insights of constructionism, and this is the second consideration important in the development of a sociology of childhood. It is part of many constructions of childhood precisely to separate childhood from these painful and difficult vicissitudes of adult identity. Views which see childhood as a lost state of natural grace offer the possibility of a redemption from constructionism, instability and the perils of the social. If adulthood is seen as constructed, then childhood, as adulthood's 'other', is claimed as essentially natural. As Jacqueline Rose puts it, childhood takes on the social function of offering us:

> a pure point of origin in relation to language, sexuality and the state ...
> Children's fiction emerges, therefore, out of a conception of both the child and
> the world as knowable in a direct and unmediated way, a conception which
> places the innocence of the child and a primary state of language and/or
> culture in a close and mutually dependent relationship.
>
> (Rose, 1984: 8–9)

In other words, many theories of childhood have implicitly become particular points of resistance against characteristic sociological ways of thinking, and have actually staked themselves against an acceptance of constructionism's consequences, whether these are the explicit terms of their debates or not.

These are certainly difficult ideas, and they are just now taking root in this field of study. They may well seem unfamiliar ideas upon first meeting them, but we should not be daunted by this. The essential argument here is just that childhood, like adulthood, is a battleground of constructed, shifting, arguing identities and that, painful as it might be to acknowledge it, there is no human escape from the conflicts of the social into a realm of the natural.

Conclusion

By way of a conclusion – by which I mean not an end to this chapter, but rather a new point of departure – I would like to refer you again, as in Chapter 1 of this book, to the work of Allison James and Alan Prout, who have written about the establishment of a 'new paradigm' for the sociology of childhood (James and Prout 1990: 8–9). They make six key points about children, childhood and the development of the new sociology:

1 They distinguish childhood from the developmental phase of biological immaturity, and suggest both that childhood is socially constructed and that it provides an interpretive frame for understanding the first years of life.
2 They remind us that childhood is just one sociological variable, and that it is interwoven with other factors such as class, gender and race.
3 They insist that children's social relationships and cultures are worthy of our study and attention in their own right, quite independent of our other intellectual concerns and interests.
4 They warn that children are not just passive social subjects, but are active agents involved in constructing and determining both their own social lives and those of people around them.
5 They suggest that ethnography is an important methodology in studying children and childhood, because it allows children a direct voice in our research.
6 Finally, they affirm that to create and operate a new sociological paradigm is also to play a part in the never ending process of constructing and reconstructing childhood.

It is surely our responsibility in relation to this final point, above all, that will best guide and drive our attempts to create a nuanced and sophisticated socio-cultural and sociological understanding of childhood that remains alive to the lives and aspirations of the very children who may, one day, as adults read and judge our efforts.

Review questions and tasks

1   Look again at the Margaret Atwood epigraph which began this chapter and think about the different personas which you present to the world. Why, when and how do you change?

2   Headlines such as these regularly appear on the covers of magazines aimed at girls:

   10 Tricks to make Him fall for You.
   Find your Perfect Summer Love.
   Boyzone Poster Special Inside!!
   Shape up for a Bikini Summer.
   Free gift – Body Shop Eau de Toilette.

   Look at some magazines for girls. How are girls constructed in and by these magazines? What are their concerns assumed to be? What role models are they offered? What do these magazines have to say about such topics as appearance, the body, diet, sexuality, school and education, careers, sport, leisure time, clothes, cosmetics, being popular, socialising? How are these messages being delivered: explicitly, implicitly, in words, pictures, adverts, advice columns, factual articles, stories? Who is writing for these magazines?

3   This activity can also usefully be undertaken by looking at magazines for boys, or for particular racial and ethnic groups. How do the magazines for boys and girls compare to those aimed specifically at men and women?

4   A further variation is to apply appropriate questions (in no. 2) above:

   • to children's television programmes;
   • to adult television programmes;
   • to television advertisements.

5   Pick one of the following topics: gender, race, class, sexuality or intelligence. In small groups, discuss how you first became aware of this aspect of your own identity. In the light of your discussions, how did/do you feel about your own sense of identity, and about how you feel you were/are perceived?

   (Note: this can be a very powerful exercise. It is wise to undertake this with a group whom you trust, with one person in the group not taking part directly in the activity but acting as a 'gate-keeper', ensuring that all participants are behaving sensitively. A useful way to ensure equality of participation is to choose a topic, and ask each group member to write down their memories. All contributions can then be read out, without comment, before opening up a general discussion.)

6   Native American cultures use the expression 'standing in your moccasins' to refer to the respectful exercise of attempting to understand someone else's experiences and perspectives. To think clearly and sociologically, we need to develop the ability to look as objectively as possible at other cultures and at our own. The fastest way to uncover your own, possibly unexamined and unacknowledged, assumptions about class, race, gender and childhood is to find yourself in alien contexts and cultures with different norms from yours. Last year, three of my male students gained a whole new series of perspectives on gender and sexuality when they came to college and attended lectures for a day dressed as women. So, swap childhood stories with someone you perceive as being very different from yourself, and seek opportunities to experience other cultures, be these racial, classed or gendered.

Further reading

Connolly, P. (1998) *Racism, Gender Identities and Young Children: Social Relations in a Multi-Ethnic, Inner-City Primary School*, London: Routledge.   This book explores the role that schools, and the relationships children form at school, play in shaping young children's attitudes towards racial and gender identities. There is a good balance of detailed observation and careful data collection, with socio-logical theory, where each is examined and understood in the light of the other. Parts of this text make for disturbing reading, especially where the impact of racism on the lives of young children is explored. The author also makes inter-esting and convincing links between the children's ideas about race and their gender identities. This is an excellent example of sociology in action.

James, A., Jenks, C. and Prout, A. (1998) *Theorizing Childhood*, Cambridge: Polity Press.   This is a challenging book by three leaders in the field. It outlines some of the recent major developments in the sociological study of childhood, which is a relatively new but very rapidly advancing area of study. The authors take on the idea that childhood has two dimensions – it is both a structural feature of societies and also at the heart of children's real, everyday lives – and explore the socially constructed character of childhood. Interestingly, they move away from some of the more traditional categories of childhood sociology (like play, the home, school and the family) and they discuss childhood in the light of such key contemporary themes in sociology as space, time, culture, the body and work. The focus here is not specifically on gender, race or class issues, but the book usefully suggests a wider set of sociological concerns.

Jenks, C. (1996) *Childhood*, London: Routledge (Key Ideas Series).   This is a particularly useful introduction to the general field of the sociology of child-hood. Jenks argues that the study of childhood in the social sciences has tended in the past to be seen as the domain of disciplines like developmental psychology which have a broadly essentialist or naturalistic bias, seeing childhood and children as a natural rather than as a social phenomenon. Jenks challenges this by highlighting key social factors and suggesting that childhood is essentially a social construct. The implication of this is that human understanding of children and childhood has varied considerably between cultures and across history. This is a forceful statement of the arguments for social constructionism, which are still generally more widely accepted in race and gender studies than they are in theories of childhood.

Lesnik-Oberstein, K. (ed.) (1998) *Children in Culture: Approaches to Childhood*, **London: Macmillan.** This book is most suitable for more experienced readers, and repays patient attention. It is a collection of interdisciplinary essays which all explore aspects of new theoretical approaches to childhood. Contributors are drawn from the fields of psychology, history, literary criticism, children's literature, film and drama. There are many interesting individual essays, but the overall impact of the book comes from encountering such an excitingly wide variety of ideas and approaches side by side.

Yelland, N. (ed.) (1998) *Gender in Early Childhood*, **London: Routledge.** This is a very useful source book for exploring how young children perceive themselves, and others, as gendered. The book is divided into two sections: the first examines children within the family and the general community, while the second looks specifically at school contexts. A wide range of interesting topics is covered, from analyses of play and art-making, to the influence of popular culture and young children's experiences of technology. It is particularly good to see work here on children's understandings of sexual orientation, which is a very under-explored area of research and knowledge.

International perspectives on childhood help us both to learn about and encounter other cultures, and to reflect on the particular constructions of our own culture, which might otherwise remain invisible to us. Two internationalist sources on childhood that can be recommended are D. Ransom (ed.) (1998) *Eye to Eye: Childhood*, Oxford: New Internationalist (reviewed at the end of Chapter 1 in this volume), and C. Sweetman (ed.) (1998) *Gender, Education and Training*, Oxford: Oxfam.

Compelling literary sources about childhood abound and are amply covered in other chapters of this Reader. For powerful, and interestingly contrasting, accounts of growing up as girls in the mid-twentieth century (and as excellent reads), I would also highly recommend Margaret Atwood, *Cat's Eye*, and Audre Lourde, *Zami*. What legacy does the child bequeath the adult?

References

Ariès, P. (1962) *Centuries of Childhood: A Social History of Family Life*, trans. R. Baldick, New York: Vintage Books.

James, A. and Prout, A. (1990) *Constructing and Reconstructing Childhood*, Basingstoke: Falmer Press.

Lesnik-Oberstein, K. (ed.) (1998) *Children in Culture: Approaches to Childhood*, London: Macmillan.

Rose, J. (1984) *The Case of Peter Pan or The Impossibility of Children's Fiction*, Basingstoke: Macmillan.

Yeo, A. and Lovell, T. (1998) *Sociology for Childhood Studies*, London: Hodder & Stoughton.

Chapter 8

_____

Children in film

Stuart Hanson

Summary

The intention of this chapter is to alert you to some of the key
issues involved in considering the 'reality' of film representations, the ways in which childhood is constructed in films and
the meanings which appear to lie behind some of those
constructions. Four films are discussed in detail: *Lèon, Walkabout,
Stand By Me* and *Salaam Bombay!* Common themes are identified,
such as the nature of innocence, the transition from childhood to
adulthood, and the relationship between children and adults.
This last theme reminds us that, while investigating the nature
of childhood construction, we might also consider the notion of
how adulthood is constructed.

> The figure of the child ... reflects the condition of civilization, its health or sickness, as projected in the values and aspirations of its art.
>
> (Wood, 1976: 155)

Films about and representing children, in which children play a key part in the narrative, have existed in the cinema almost since it began in the last years of the nineteenth century. As Sinyard (1992) observes, 'childhood is the great universal theme'. I do not want to argue with Sinyard's analysis of the importance of childhood to film makers, but I do want to explore how this universal theme has been represented in more particular ways, across a diversity of film cultures and styles. In looking at childhood in the cinema I want to do so in relation to three linked themes.

First, we need to think about the notion of representation, since the cinema, like all media forms, does not re-present 'reality' despite the connotations of the term 'representation'. Implicit in this consideration of cinema and childhood is a sense that the cinema is not concerned with a straightforward presentation of the world and of the relations between people within it.

Second, I want to consider how childhood is constructed and represented through cinema and the medium of the single fiction feature film. Here there will be a focus on a series of themes that are prevalent in the social constructions of childhood. These include:

- the notion of the child as nature;
- the child as en route to adulthood, the so-called 'incomplete adult';
- the child as vulnerable and in need of protection;
- gender identity and transgression;
- the condition of children and childhood as comment on contemporary society.

Third, it is important to recognise the ways in which the social construction of childhood and the meanings attributed to it through the process of representation are given popular expression through ideas and values, which in turn operate as ideology (Briggs and Cobley, 1998).

Like the notion of childhood, I want to suggest that a film's images and sounds, and the social realities portrayed in a film, are constructions as well. We need to recognise that the representations are both selected and selective, and that they offer a version of the world that relies to a larger extent on familiar or dominant images and ideas (O'Sullivan *et al.*, 1998). Indeed, we might more profitably think of the ways in which the cinema represents the world to the viewer rather than reflecting it, since representation is an active process of selection and the structuring of meaning (Hall, 1982).

It is in this realm of making meaning through representation that ideology operates, providing a 'framework through which we represent, interpret, understand and "make sense" of some aspect of social existence' (Hall, 1981: 31). The function of ideology in relation to representation provides the key to the importance of media forms like the cinema, since the media's main sphere of operation is the production and transformation of ideologies. They are the dominant means of ideological production, and what they 'produce' is, precisely, representations of the social world. Or rather, a *version* of the world in which particular images, and images of particular groups, are offered to us, the viewers, along with descriptions, explanations and frames for understanding how the world is and why it works as it is shown to work (Hall, 1981).

The power of the media to represent and imagine certain groups can and does have material effects upon the members of those groups, both in terms of how they see themselves and, also, how others understand them. This power resides, not only in the media's various forms, but in its ability to represent some images and assumptions in multiple ways and, equally importantly, to *exclude* others or represent them in marginal ways. Here it is important to recognise that representations of particular groupings can actively obscure difference and diversity particularly in relation to identity. We can think of children as one such important example but, in doing so, I want to argue that there is no *one group* called 'children' or one *version* of childhood.

In order to get a sense of the diversity of representations of childhood, I will consider four examples of films in which children are located at the centre of the narrative. These are *Léon* (1994), *Walkabout* (1971), *Stand by Me* (1988) and *Salaam Bombay!* (1988). Implicit in the selection is a recognition that the category 'children' is a diverse social, cultural, ethnic and racial one and that there is a plurality across and within cultures.

Léon (France/USA, 1994; dir. Luc Besson)

> Mathilda: Is life always this hard, or is it just when you're a kid?
> Léon: Always like this.

Professional assassin Léon reluctantly takes care of twelve-year-old Mathilda (Natalie Portman), a neighbour whose father, stepmother, step-sister and brother are killed by a corrupt policeman called Stansfield (Gary Oldman). Upon learning about the introverted neighbour's strange profession – contract killing, or 'cleaning' – she seeks his help in taking revenge for her little brother.

There is a moment in *Léon* when the central character tells Mathilda that certain things will change when she grows up, to which she retorts, 'I am already grown up, I just get older'. *Léon* is a film about two people for whom the traditional boundaries between 'adult' and 'child' are both blurred and transgressed. Though worldly-wise and cynical, Mathilda yearns to be more childlike, while at the same time striving to hide her

147

desire to be looked after and cared for. When the headmistress from the girls' school she is enrolled at phones to inform her parents that she has not been attending, Mathilda pretends to be her stepmother, telling the teacher that the child is dead. For Mathilda, the reality is that the 'child' inside is dead.

She looks to the enigmatic neighbour Léon for affirmation, offering to run errands for him to the corner store. Léon is an adult who is a thoroughly competent killer but who is both emotionally and intellectually 'immature'. Mathilda is adult-like in terms of her outlook and experiences, whilst Léon is child-like in terms of his experiences and naïvety. Mathilda disavows her lack of years through confidence that she is 'grown up', particularly in the way she dresses and behaves when she is with Léon. He is complicit in this and, while he recognises that she is too young to be a 'cleaner', he does not treat her as a child might be expected to be, or indeed how we, an adult audience, might expect her to be treated.

Thus, in *Léon*, the notion of innocence traditionally embodied in children and issues around gender are rendered as deeply problematic by the relationship between the central male character and Mathilda. For the (male) viewer, she embodies a visible sexuality that is at odds with the dominant idea of innocence. Whilst there is no suggestion of a sexual relationship between the two, there is a tension between the expectation that this be disavowed and a clear impression that, for Mathilda at least, the relationship is more than simply one of daughter and (surrogate) father.

Of course, what is deeply unsettling about Mathilda for the cinema audience is not just her apparent maturity, or her apparent sexuality, but her preparedness to use violence. Again, this challenges accepted notions, not only about childhood and its supposed embodiment of innocence, but about gender roles as well. Again, for (male) audiences the representation of prepubescent sexuality and the gun, both deeply fetishised in our culture, is a not entirely unproblematic image. In Chapter 1 of this volume, Mills indicated that the movement out of childhood was a slow process in which knowledge and experience is gained, including what Postman (1983) called 'secret knowledges'. These 'secret knowledges', which include death and sexual relations, are usually hidden from children, but in *Léon* Mathilda is graphically presented with both, particularly violence. In one scene Mathilda takes a gun to Stansfield's office in order to kill him. She is unsuccessful but, in Mathilda's world, there are no unpalatable secrets from which she is protected.

Bazalgette and Buckingham (1995) suggest that we need to recognise that there is a false separation between childhood as asexual, as non-violent or as innocent, and adulthood as an achieved and fixed state. Indeed, for Qvortup (1994) the question is whether it is possible to recognise that children and adults are ontologically different and, moreover, whether age can be used to legitimately justify different treatment of children and adults. This comes into sharp focus around the construction of sexuality in *Léon*, as well as the ways in which the character of Mathilda seems to embody attitudes and characteristics of adult women. Neil Postman (1983) has advanced the thesis that childhood is disappearing, mainly as a result of television's non-discriminatory presentation of information to all age groups, and the plethora of child models modelling adult-like clothing (before acting, Natalie Portman was a child model). Mathilda might well be an emblematic figure for Postman and for our age.

Walkabout (Australia, 1971; dir. Nicolas Roeg)

That is the land of lost content,
I see it shining plain,
The happy highways where I went
And cannot come again.
(excerpt from A.E. Housman, 'A Shropshire Lad',
spoken over soundtrack at end)

A teenage girl (played by Jenny Agutter) and her seven-year-old brother (Lucien John) become stranded in the outback after their father drives them to a secluded part of the country and then kills himself (having attempted to shoot them). The girl and her brother set off into the desert miles from the nearest city, whereupon they meet an Aboriginal boy (David Gumpilil) who is on a 'walkabout'.

Walkabout is a film about the encounter between two cultures: 'primitive' and the 'civilised', traditional and modern. The film also seeks to place these two cultures, embodied in children, *in* nature while, at the same time, emphasising that the children are *of* nature. In *Walkabout*, it is the Aboriginal boy who symbolises the natural order and oneness with the land. The two children from the city, still wearing their grey school uniforms and with their sunburned pale skins, are manifestly alienated from their environment. Since we never learn their names, they can be seen as embodying a universal (Western) identity.

In many ways the film establishes a juxtaposition between nature, symbolised by landscape and the Aboriginal boy, and modernity, symbolised by the white children's civility. Underlying the film, though, is a view that all children are essentially innocent and pure. This is represented through the white children becoming more comfortable with their bodies, as they strip away their school uniforms, and find their place in nature. The tension here is in the developing sensuality that the girl exudes and which is picked up by the Aboriginal boy, especially in the scene where they both swim nude in the rock pool. Jenny Agutter was sixteen when she made *Walkabout* and director Roeg focuses on her body in several key scenes, especially in a scene where the three are playfully climbing a tree. Here he counterpoises her white legs and thighs with the branches of the tree, as if to symbolise her developing oneness with nature.

Walkabout speaks to two key but linked constructions of childhood in Western thought – that of the savage and the 'natural' child – both of which are informed by the passage of time (see Wartofsky, 1983). Jenks (1996) writes of the early anthropologists who felt they could identify a 'savage' through locating who was different from them. In the same way, children are seen as different, less well developed and not yet imbued with proper moral standards. Thus, we see a construction of the 'other' in which 'savage' and 'child' means the same thing, that is, 'different'. In *Walkabout* these two positions – metaphorically and literally – come together in the representation of the Aborigine boy. Moreover, there is a sense in which the white children, and particularly the young boy, are not only pre-adults but are also moving away from civilisation to a position of savagery.

There is a further sense that, having been removed from their familial social and secular world, the children are able to reveal some essentialist notion of the child as naturalised. In this conception, childhood is a journey from immaturity to maturity, from child to adult with the popular metaphor being growth, not just physical but social. This journey is punctuated with signposts, markers, rites of passage and valedictory moments. These moments vary from culture to culture, but in the world symbolised by the white children in *Walkabout* the route to adulthood is not a sudden ritual act as it is for the Aboriginal boy. His 'walkabout' will see him emerge unambiguously as an adult man. Van Gennep (1960, in James and Prout, 1997) suggests a framework for understanding social transitions and rites of passage in childhood, for which *Walkabout*'s narrative structure provides an interesting, if extreme, example. This threefold structure sees 'rites of separation', where children are stripped of their social roles; 'rites of liminality' where they inhabit an 'ambiguous zone out of social time and space' (James and Prout, 1997: 247); and 'rites of re-aggregation' whereupon they are conferred with new roles and identities.

Stand by Me (USA, 1986; dir. Rob Reiner)

> I never had any friends later on like the ones I had when I was twelve. Jesus, does anybody?

In a small Midwestern town during the summer of 1959, four twelve-year-old friends – Gordie (Wil Wheaton), Chris (River Phoenix), Vern (Jerry O'Connell) and Teddy (Corey Feldman) – decide to go on an adventure to find the dead body of a boy lying by the railway track some twenty miles away.

The main theme of *Stand by Me* is the rite of passage, with its accompanying stress on the theme of friendship and comradeship and the progress from innocence to the beginnings of adulthood in teenage years. Like all the films under discussion here, the main protagonists are looking for someone or something. In *Stand by Me*, the pursuit of the body of Ray

Brower is the focus of an adventure, but it is the journey itself that is the key, both in a literal and metaphorical sense. Along the way they undergo a variety of adventures, including encountering the violent proprietor of a scrap yard on which they have trespassed, camping overnight in seemingly hostile woods and emerging from a stagnant forest pool covered in leeches. When they find the body, each is forced to confront their own emotional baggage. The rite of passage in *Stand by Me* revolves around this death and is used as an arbiter that the move to adulthood will present its own inevitable problems and troubles.

Like *Walkabout* and *Léon*, the exploration of 'secret knowledges' in *Stand by Me* revolves around death, which is also used to symbolise the death of innocence. Besides that of Ray Blower, the film also pivots on two other deaths, of Gordie's older and popular brother (a promising sportsman, idolised by his parents) four months earlier, and Chris, who would subsequently be killed in a stabbing incident in adult life. A grown-up Gordie reads of that death in the newspaper and, recognising the significance of the events that summer, begins to recount them, narrating the story in flashback for the audience.

As in *Walkabout*, *Stand by Me* also places the children in a world with few adults, in which all are estranged in some way from their parents. Indeed, the representation of adults in the film seems to suggest that adulthood is not only a condition of pain but also of cruelty. As the academically oriented introvert, Gordie is struggling for recognition from his parents who had invested all their hopes and dreams in the older brother. They no longer see him or hear him emotionally. 'That summer', Gordie announces, 'I became the invisible boy at home'. Chris is intelligent, but is constantly beaten by his father, as well as having to live down his older brother's bad reputation. Teddy, the son of an emotionally disturbed man who has abused him all his life, lives in constant denial of his childhood pain and creates a fantasy world in which his father is a hero who fought on the beaches of Normandy.

In addition to the absence of parental love and the potential violence of parents and older siblings, there is a shocking story recounted by Chris about the potential dishonesty of adults. Chris's reputation as a delinquent boy was cemented by his theft of the milk money from school. However, he confesses to his best friend Gordie that he actually took the money back and gave it to the teacher, Miss Simmons, who nevertheless let Chris take the blame while she used the money to buy a new dress. In this story is a sense that innocence is not necessarily 'lost' but is taken by adults, particularly adults that children should be able to trust.

Though the teacher who betrayed Chris was a woman, the film is primarily concerned with masculinity and the themes of boyhood and manliness. The myth of the male hero on an adventurous quest is deeply rooted in Western popular culture, as articulated by Teddy's obsession with war. The exploration and articulation of boys coming of age through adversity, bravado, facing up to fear, loyalty and comradeship make *Stand by Me* a source of identification for many men. Moreover, one suspects that, given its range of nostalgic cultural references, the film might be especially appealing to American men. Many of the tests that the boys go through are symbolic of the passage from boyhood to manliness. As Miedzian observes:

> for most American boys manhood is achieved through a series of informal tests. By not crying or associating with girls, by being strong, tough, good at sports, and willing to fight, boys prove to their peers – and often to their parents, especially fathers – that they are real men.
>
> (1992, in Siann, 1994: 64)

The strength of *Stand by Me* is the way in which the film is prepared to hold these tests up to scrutiny and critique as well as to celebrate them. Moreover, scenes in which Gordie remembers Denny as a kind and loving brother (he gave Gordie his prized New York Yankees baseball cap) are counterpoised by their father's aggressive celebrating of Denny's sporting prowess and his ignoring of Gordie's academic writing.

Salaam Bombay! (India/France/UK, 1988; dir. Mira Nair)

> Forget them all. Mothers, fathers, brothers, sisters, friends, lovers ... useless bloody lot.

Salaam Bombay! details the lives of the 'street children' who live in Bombay. The main character Krishna (Shafiq Syed) works for a travelling circus. One day he is sent by his master to a neighbouring village to buy some food and, when he returns, the circus has packed up and disappeared. He goes to a nearby village and takes a train to Bombay, spending his time as a runner for a teashop (a Chaipau) in a poor neighbourhood of prostitution, brothels and the drug trade.

The starting point for the child in *Salaam Bombay!* is rejection and betrayal, as Krishna returns from the errand to find the circus – and his home – gone. Was this the intention of the circus manager, who sent him on the errand, or was he so unvalued that they simply moved on without thinking about him? Moreover, as the film progresses we learn that Krishna ended up in the circus after his mother threw him out when he set fire to a motorcycle that was being repaired by his bullying brother. Krishna's quest to amass five hundred rupees is the price demanded by his mother before she would have him back. Like the attempted infanticide in *Walkabout*, the shock of such a rejection is both disturbing and deeply antithetical to many of our beliefs about the value of children and parental love. Thus, the film establishes the naïve and innocent child adrift amongst the cynical and exploitative world of the big city.

One of the many ironies of the film is that Bombay is the centre of the

Indian film industry, known as 'Bollywood'; it is a magnet for budding actors anxious to realise their dreams. Indeed, when Krishna asks at the railway station for a ticket to the nearest city (Bombay), the ticket seller tells him to 'come back a movie star'. As he emerges from the train into the streets still carrying the food that he purchased on the errand, it is clear that his innocence and trusting demeanour are no preparation for life beyond his small village. Thus, the film is particularly concerned with innocence, what Ehrlich (1990: 13) called the 'fragility of childhood'. Robin Wood (1976) identified this through what he called 'neo-realist child' in cinema, in which children act as a kind of cipher for the ills and despair in society. *Salaam Bombay!* is also concerned with the social status of children and childhood and, in particular, the role of the state, since Krishna and his friend Manju (a young girl) end up in a state orphanage/detention centre, from which only Krishna is able to escape.

Salaam Bombay! is not a uniformly bleak film; it has moments of great warmth and occasional happiness, as well as a sense of camaraderie. Life in the neighbourhood in which Krishna moves is undoubtedly harsh and often cruel, but Nair creates a humble sense of community and interdependence, particularly amongst the children. However, the narrative does present Krishna with a series of obstacles and situations in which his innocence and naïve hopefulness are stripped away. In this sense the tone of the film is predominantly bittersweet and poignant, particularly in the way in which it eschews a 'happy ending'. The film ends with Krishna staring dejectedly off screen, in an ambiguous manner reminiscent of *The Four Hundred Blows* (*Les Quatre Cents Coups*, 1959; dir. François Truffaut). In many ways a 'happy ending' would have been fatuous, since we already know that the plight of Krishna and the other street children is virtually hopeless.

In *Salaam Bombay!* the lives of the children are shocking, and one does want to ask the question, 'What can be done?' However, the film is deeply critical of the state's response, which is to place children in institutions that offer children little more than they receive on the streets. In a poignant and heartbreaking scene, Manju's mother, who lives for the child but fears the authorities due to her life as a prostitute, is told by an impassive official at the orphanage/detention centre that she cannot have her child back. It is the ultimate irony that the only child in the film with a caring and loving parent is taken away by officials who, it seems, are working within this dominant discourse of childhood. At the end of the film the camera pulls up and away to show Krishna, having escaped from the orphanage, lost in a huge crowd, having become separated from Manju's mother with whom he has been reunited. Here Krishna is dissolved into the mass, his identity lost, his innocence gone and left to do what all the street children do: survive as best they can with no one to rely on but themselves.

The representation of childhood through the street children in *Salaam*

Bombay!, like that of the Aboriginal boy in *Walkabout*, acts as a powerful reminder that there exists what Jenks called the 'forced commonality of an ideological discourse of childhood' (1996: 122). Here Jencks refers not only to the structures that regulate children (such as school, laws and statutes) but also to customary practices associated with particular cultures. For Western children, according to Jencks, this is essentially a protectionist experience in which children are looked after and 'trained' but given no autonomy. This is, incidentally, the tension in *Stand by Me* as the boys are removed temporarily from their familial surroundings. Although this version of childhood belongs to a particular time and place it has come to be seen as pertinent for all children, establishing the context for the ways in which we judge parental 'failure' and recognise those children who do not conform to the norm. In the context of a discussion of representations of childhood in cinema, the key dimension is the globalisation of this Western discourse of childhood. As Jencks observes:

> As a post-colonial legacy, variation in the form which childhood might take is denied [as] one particular vision of childhood has been and continues to be exported as 'correct childhood'. Not only does this cast doubt, and comparative judgement, upon different family forms and parenting practices in the Third World through the misguided, and tacit, assumption of a uniformity of childhood in Western Europe, it also disguises the complex, socially-constructed character of 'the child' upon which it rests.
>
> (1996: 122)

Conclusion

So, what have we learned from these films about childhood? Three key points emerge.

First, all the films discussed represent children as essentially innocent. Here innocence is constructed around a kind of naïvety and initial incorruptibility. Though seeming to start from this point, all the films then proceed to 'strip' them of their innocence in various ways, as if to suggest that children are merely the product of what gets done to them. This is expressed through a whole series of tensions between innocence and the circumstances they find themselves in, which ultimately change them in some dramatic way. Indeed, all the films offer a challenge to what increasingly appears to be an *imagined* world of childhood innocence.

Second, there is a clear sense that the loss of innocence is directly related to growing up and that growing up, and the passage into adulthood, is represented as a painful transitional process. All the films highlight the ambiguities in marking out the passage from childhood to adulthood, especially around the absence of clearly defined markers. It is only the aboriginal boy in *Walkabout* who is engaged in a clearly defined process of status transition. The characters who are clearly signalled by their

'Western-ness' (the teenage girl in *Walkabout*, Mathilda, the boys in *Stand by Me*) are bound by a series of unwritten rules and conventions – related to age and time – associated with childhood, adolescence and adulthood.

Age is the major determinant of this progress, linked to institutions like school, since it is used both to determine symbolic and formal transitions. Moreover, it can be used to mark out those children who do not conform to the expectations adults have of someone their age, often through a system of age grading. James and Prout use the example of teenage mothers, constructed as a social problem since, as individuals, they are 'literally out of time with the expectations of their age grade' (1997: 237). All my chosen films place children 'out of their time', through the ways the various narratives both remove children from familial surroundings and put them in circumstances in which the traditional transitional stages are supplanted, pushed to extremes or telescoped by time.

Moreover, all seem to be suggesting that, in making the transition to adulthood, formerly innocent and incorruptible children become complicit and corrupted, and that it is largely adults who are responsible. This introduces the third point about childhood: the relationship between children and adults. All the chosen film narratives, to a greater or lesser extent, challenge the viewer to confront the notion of childhood, constructed and mediated by adults, as deeply contradictory. The twin constructs of childhood and adulthood reflect a set of power relations that are played out in the context of the media through the creation of texts produced by adults for children. It is here that the 'respective positions of children and adults are staked out and defined' (Bazalgette and Buckingham, 1995: 5). As these two writers go on to observe, many of the texts produced for children allow children to think through their own positions in relation to adult power. One might instructively think of the film version of Roald Dahl's *Matilda* (1996, dir. Danny De Vito). However, all the films under discussion here, and many others, are not stories about childhood aimed at children; rather, all are films about childhood aimed at adults.

All these films problematise childhood. In doing so, they say something important about being both a child and an adult, yet their dominant address is to an adult audience. They reflect Robin Wood's description of films that 'construct the adult spectator as a child' (1986, in Krämer, 1998: 295). This, in itself, says something instructive about both the representations of childhood *and* adulthood.

Appendix

Further viewing

My four films were chosen from a much wider range of possibilities. What follows is a selection of other popularly available films that offer something similar.

Stanley Kubrick (1962) and Adrian Lynn (1997) have filmed Nabokov's *Lolita*. Both films are concerned with male adult obsession with a female child and, in doing so, offer a particular representation of teenage sexuality. Louis Malle's controversial *Pretty Baby* (1978) is about a twelve-year-old girl (Brooke Shields) growing up in a New Orleans brothel. Martin Scorcese's *Taxi Driver* (1976), with which *Léon* shares some similarities, features a twelve-year-old prostitute, played by Jodie Foster, who befriends, and is ultimately rescued by, the film's central character, Travis Bickle (Robert de Niro).

Walkabout is a unique film. However, its themes of nature and childhood innocence find echoes in Peter Weir's *Picnic at Hanging Rock* (1975), which is also set in the Australian outback. The theme of English children removed from their familiar social and cultural milieu runs through Alexander Mackendrick's *High Wind in Jamaica* (1965). Perhaps the classic example of the complex relationship between children, nature and the breaking down of traditional forms of social control is *Lord of the Flies*, which was filmed in 1963 by Peter Brook and again by Harry Hook (though substituting British schoolboys with American army cadets) in 1990.

Stand by Me is, perhaps, the best in a popular genre known as the 'rites of passage' or 'coming of age' films, many of which are set in the past but narrated by one of the key protagonists from the present. Others include *The Go-Between* (1970, dir. Joseph Losey) and Woody Allen's comedy *Radio Days* (1987). More generally, the 'rites of passage' film might include *Running on Empty* (1988, dir. Sidney Lumet), *Rumble Fish* (1983, dir. Francis Ford Coppola), *Rambling Rose* (1991, dir. Martha Coolidge), *My Life as a Dog* (1985, dir. Lasse Hallström), *Welcome to the Dollhouse* (1995, dir. Todd Solondz) and *Fanny and Alexander* (1982, dir. Ingmar Bergman). All these films also draw heavily upon the notion of innocence lost, to which we might add Steven Spielberg's *Empire of the Sun* (1987) and *A World Apart* (1988, dir. Chris Menges).

Finally, the representation of children as both exploited and devalued is one that is less associated with Hollywood and more so with the convention of 'realism' characteristic of non-Hollywood cinema. The Italian neo-realist films *Germany – Year Zero* (1948, dir. Roberto Rossellini) and *Bicycle Thieves* (1948, dir. Vittorio de Sica) present children as tragic victims, while Louis Malle's *Au Revoir Les Enfants* (1987) details the lives of Jewish children in wartime France.

Review questions and tasks

1   Analyse the epigraph from Wood which began this chapter. Unpick its various parts and discuss the extent to which you agree with the sentiments.

2   Unlike the other three films analysed in the chapter, *Salaam Bombay!* offers a completely non-Western version of childhood. After viewing it on video, consider to what extent the representation of childhood confirms or denies 'Third World' stereotypes?

3   Choose two of the four films analysed in the chapter and, after viewing the videos, compare the representations of children, concentrating particularly on:

   • the construction of innocence;
   • the transition from childhood to adulthood;
   • the ways in which the representations of children comment on contemporary society;
   • the constructions of childhood which cut across cultures.

4   Most of the films mentioned in the chapter are for adults rather than for young children. Think about one or two of these films in particular and discuss their representation of adults and adulthood. In what ways do these constructions confirm or deny your own views of adults?

5   Choose a film of your own which involves some representation of children or childhood. Try to decide:

   • what themes and issues are significant in this version of childhood;
   • the ideological meanings in the film;
   • the relationship between children and adults;
   • how the different worlds of children and adults are portrayed.

6   Think about two films you have seen recently which are set in different continents. How do the two cultures compare and contrast, in terms of:

   • way of life of the people;
   • depictions of women, children, men?

Further reading

Bazalgette, C. and Buckingham, D. (eds) (1995) *In Front of the Children*, **London: BFI.** Though primarily about television, and children's television in particular, this collection of essays has much to say, not only about the relationship between children and the media, but also about their representation. The authors' introduction makes some incisive points about media constructions of childhood and the ways in which childhood has been conceptualised. Other essays, by both media practitioners and an array of professionals concerned with child development, variously discuss Walt Disney, the divergence between the classic European-style 'children's film' and the US-style 'family film', and ways in which generational differences are breaking down in popular film.

Branston, G. and Stafford, R. (1996) *The Media Student's Book*, **London: Routledge.** There are many books for students wishing to know more about the production, circulation and reception of media products. Written by two teachers of media studies, this is an introductory textbook aimed at students new to the subject. It covers cinema, television and other mass media forms in a series of clear chapters around key themes (for example, genres, narratives, representations and ideologies) with accompanying case studies.

Sinyard, N. (1992) *Children in the Movies*, **London: Batsford.** This is a large-format book from a broadcaster, lecturer and former deputy film critic of the *Sunday Telegraph*, and is the only widely available text on the subject of representations of children in the cinema. The book is essentially a collection of individual essays about an eclectic range of films collected under a series of thematic headings such as films about children and war, children and horror and children growing up. Drawing on a worldwide film culture, Sinyard limits his discussion to films made in the postwar era but seeks to demonstrate 'how the theme of childhood has persistently cut across period, genre and nationality' (1992: 15).

Wood, R. (1976) *Personal Views: Explorations in Film*, **London: Gordon Fraser.** A unique and acerbic critic of cinema, Robin Wood's 1976 collection contains a wonderful and challenging essay entitled 'Images of Childhood', in which he seeks to map out the development of cinema's representation of childhood across time and film cultures. Beginning with an exploration of the child in Italian postwar neo-realist cinema, the essay considers the work of Ingmar Bergman, Federico Fellini, Jean-Luc Godard and a range of directors working in both 'classic' and contemporary Hollywood.

References

Bazalgette, C. and Buckingham, D. (eds) (1995) *In Front of the Children*, London: BFI.

Bridges, G. and Brunt, R. (1981) (eds) *Silver Linings*, London: Lawrence and Wishart.

Briggs, A. and Cobley, P. (1998) *The Media: An Introduction*, Harlow: Addison Wesley Longman.

Ehrlich, L.C. 'The Name of the Child: Cinema as Social Critique', in *Film Criticism*, 14 (2): 12–23.

Gurevitch, M., Curran, J., Bennett, T. and Wollacott, J. (eds) (1982) *Culture, Society and Media*, London: Methuen.

Hall, S. (1981) 'The Whites of their Eyes: Racist Ideologies in the Media', in G. Bridges and R. Brunt (eds), *Silver Linings*, London: Lawrence and Wishart.

Hall, S. (1982) 'The Rediscovery of Ideology: The Return of the Repressed in Media Study', in M. Gurevitch, J. Curran, T. Bennett and J. Wollacott (eds), *Culture, Society and Media*, London: Methuen.

James, A. and Prout, A. (1997) 'Re-presenting Childhood: Time and Transition in the Study of Childhood', in *Constructing and Reconstructing Childhood: Contemporary Issues in the Sociological Study of Childhood*, London: Falmer Press.

—— (eds) (1997) *Constructing and Reconstructing Childhood: Contemporary Issues in the Sociological Study of Childhood*, London: Falmer Press.

Jenks, C. (1996) *Childhood*, London: Routledge.

Kessel, F. and Siegel, A. (eds) (1983) *The Child and Other Cultural Inventions*, New York: Praeger.

Krämer, P. (1998) 'Would You Take Your Child to See this Film? The Cultural and Social Work of the Family-Adventure Movie', in S. Neale and M. Smith (eds), *Contemporary Hollywood Cinema*, London: Routledge.

Miedzian, M. (1992) *Boys Will be Boys: Breaking the Link Between Masculinity and Violence*, London: Virago.

Neale, S. and Smith, M. (eds) (1998) *Contemporary Hollywood Cinema*, London: Routledge.

Nelmes, J. (ed.) (1996) *An Introduction to Film Studies*, London: Routledge.

O'Sullivan, T., Dutton, B. and Rayner, P. (1998) *Studying the Media: Second Edition*, London: Arnold.

Postman, N. (1983) *The Disappearance of Childhood*, London: W.H. Allen.

Qvortup, J., Bardy, M., Sgritta, G. and Wintersberger, H. (eds) (1994) *Childhood Matters: Social Theory, Practice and Politics*, Aldershot: Avebury.

Siann, G. (1994) *Gender, Sex and Sexuality: Contemporary Psychological Perspectives*, London: Taylor & Francis.

Sinyard, N. (1991) *The Films of Nicolas Roeg*, London: Letts.

—— (1992) *Children in the Movies*, London: Batsford.

Van Gennep, A. (1960) *The Rites of Passage*, London: Routledge & Kegan Paul.

Wartofsky, M. (1983) 'The Child's Construction of the World and the World's Construction of the Child: From Historical Epistemology to Historical Psychology', in F. Kessel and A. Siegel (eds), *The Child and Other Cultural Inventions*, New York: Praeger.

Wood, R. (1976) 'Images of Childhood', in *Personal Views: Explorations in Film*, London: Gordon Fraser.

Wood, R. (1986), *Hollywood from Vietnam to Reagan*, New York: Columbia University Press.

Part Five

Research

Chapter 9

Uncovering the history of childhood

Maxine Rhodes

Summary

This chapter provides an introduction to the history of childhood, not simply through an assessment of the expanding literature on the subject, but by an examination of historical sources and methods. Its principal objective is to encourage you to explore history for yourself, to think about the construction of historical discourse and to begin, or continue, research into the history of childhood at a local level. By relating individual, localised research projects to wider debates, you can learn much about the construction of knowledge, the nature of history, and the experience of childhood in the past.

The past is a foreign country: they do things differently there.

(L.P. Hartley, *The Go-Between*, 1953)

The way historians write about childhood changes over time and the history of childhood has provided differing interpretations of the lives of children at any one given moment. This is because history is not absolute truth; rather, it is interpretation, and therefore no history of childhood can be seen as fact. While many historians now agree that childhood is a social construct and not an immutable, common experience, they have not always thought in this way; indeed, arguments continue about the experience of the child and the concept of childhood. Such disagreements and changing perspectives are the essence of historical enquiry and result from the nature of history itself. Moreover, discussion and debate are what continue to make history a relevant and vibrant discipline.

This chapter considers elements of these themes and argues for an active, research-based approach as a way to develop an interest in, and understanding of, historical study. Placed within the context of the history of childhood, it illustrates how those with an interest in the child, but with a differing range of expertise in history, can begin to explore and contribute to historical debate through small-scale local research. This is not, however, an argument for local history, but rather for an approach that builds on academic interest in the child and uses this as a way of engendering enthusiasm and interest in history. Such an approach encourages active engagement with both the practice and nature of history, and an assessment of the theories and arguments presented by historians of childhood, through the practical exploration of some aspect of childhood itself. In this way, history becomes real and relevant.

Discovering history

The best way to learn about history generally (and the history of childhood in particular) is by combining active research (on small-scale local projects) with detailed reading of the existing literature. This approach encourages an understanding of the nature and purpose of history while, at the same time, allowing exploration of a topic that is of particular interest. This is a persuasive argument that has developed a strong following amongst some academics in universities: in particular, it lies at the heart of the Open University's course 'Studying Family and Community History'. Such an approach is linked to developments in intellectual history (such as the expansion of social, and later women's, history), which have changed the general focus of enquiry in history from the patrician to the plebeian (that is, from 'Great Men', national institutions and events to 'Ordinary Folk', community activity and personal relationships). This has resulted in 'the developing academic awareness of the significance of the small-scale, personal or local experience *and* an awakening recognition of how small-scale studies can extend and question aggregate generalisations through the illumination of local and personal diversities.'(Drake *et al.*, 1998: 3). History needs to embrace this diversity if it is to have meaning and validity.

This type of approach, often referred to as 'micro-history', is not simply a process concerned with the minutiae of history, but is rather an approach that attempts to express 'the complexity of reality' (Levi, in Burke, 1997: 110). At the same time, it is often associated with a desire to democratise history – through a commitment to give a voice to those who have been ignored in traditional historical representations – and with the wish to open up the discipline itself. By demystifying the process of historical research and embracing the range of interested researchers, this approach challenges the elitism of the 'professional' university historian. Such a movement, associated with the Left in British politics, has arguably resulted in the profession being 'quietly but seriously radicalised. [As] "History from below" ... is now a central plank of higher research' (Samuel, 1998: 219). However, while there is no doubt that there has been change in some arenas of 'professional' history, this approach is not solely concerned with the university as the locus of historical knowledge. Instead, it both reflects and encourages the rise of the 'amateur' historian.

Such an approach is, of course, not without its detractors (Samuel, 1998: 197). Those who have questioned the value of such small-scale activity argue that, by its very nature, micro-history has limited use: by definition, it cannot be applicable elsewhere and its narrow focus ignores larger questions of national/general importance. However, others would suggest that this is precisely its strength. If we accept the constructionist approach, which is predicated on an understanding of 'how different discursive practices produce different childhoods, each and all of which are "real" within their own regime of truth' (James and Prout, 1997: 26), it is possible to see how crucial small-scale studies are, if we are to convey the range of approaches to, and meanings of, childhood at various points in time and in various settings. Rather than obscuring the whole picture, micro-history allows the complexity and richness of this big picture to be understood.

Developments in the history of childhood

The study of the history of childhood is a fairly recent development in the discipline and one that has grown in popularity. Over the intervening years since the translation into English of Ariès's *Centuries of Childhood* in 1962 (Ariès, 1973; Wilson, 1980), the focus of researchers in this area has altered and historians now no longer simply concern themselves with the 'improvement' of childhood but with its range of experiences and meanings. Most historians would agree that, in general terms, children today are 'better off' than those alive in 1800, but here agreement ends. Historians continue to debate the continuities and changes in childhood experience and approaches to children and childhood by the adult society. They ask questions about the ways in which different groups of children experienced change in different settings, the forces that influenced shifts in approach and the impact these then had on the lives of individual (or groups of) children.

From the late 1960s and 1970s onwards, the notion that children's lives simply improved from one century to another began to be criticised as Whiggish (seeing history as gradual but inevitable progress) and as based on a limited understanding of economic and social change, class and gender relations. Influenced by developments in social history and historical demography, some historians began to challenge the idea that children's lives had been improved in the nineteenth century, for example, by the development of closer emotional ties between parents and children, the rise of free and compulsory education or through the removal of children from the labour force (Pinchbeck and Hewitt, 1972). Instead, new work suggested that such an analysis was based on assumptions about the development of British capitalism which were incorrect. Anderson (1980), for example, argued that the nuclear family predated the Industrial Revolution and, therefore, that 'loving relationships within nuclear families had a predurance in history and a power to withstand the onslaughts and intrusions of church, of state, and of economic change' (Cunningham, 1995: 15). Others suggested that the introduction of legislation (shifting children from paid employment to school) did not mean that all children attended school on a full-time basis (Rubinstein, 1969) or were removed from the labour force (Walvin, 1982).

Despite this, some historians still argue that childhood was transformed in the nineteenth century and that the 'basic cause of this transformation ... was the transition from life at work from an early age to life in school to the age of twelve or even beyond, to fourteen' (Hopkins, 1994: 320). Others, however, maintain that, although the classroom may have replaced the workplace for many children before 1901, the reasons for this are still contentious. Reform did not come about as a consequence of simple altruism, but rather, it is suggested, as a consequence of economic demands: 'For example, the early motive for half-time schooling laws was not to broaden children's minds but to "tame" them as child workers and make them more tractable *in their place of work*' (Rose, 1991: 6).

While this emphasis on the development of a distinct period of childhood (separate from the adult world of work and characterised by the experience of school) is still an important theme for research and very much influenced by the debates in economic and social history, historians have more recently encouraged us to widen our perspective and to explore the complexity of the child's world by focusing on the construction of childhood. Currently, the areas of home, school and work, are not regarded as the only sites where children can be found. However, it is not simply that historians have changed the location of their research; rather they have begun to explore childhood from a perspective that places the child at the centre of the investigation. As a result, historians can identify not one childhood or one child in any given period, but many different approaches to children and childhood, depending on who is doing the looking; for example, educationalists, medics, scientists, artists, the various religions and writers all see the child in a variety of ways (Hendrick, in Prout and James, 1997). Such approaches have led to a re-examination of the child's relationships with the state, school, parents and the labour market, and have tended to focus not solely on class and gender but also on how childhood and children have been regulated by changing ideologies of childhood (for example, see Hendrick, 1996).

Despite the range of theoretical approaches to the history of childhood, authors tend to adopt one of two standpoints and are, therefore, either essentialist or constructionist in approach. Essentialists (as Neill Thew has indicated in Chapter 7 of this volume) argue that childhood is a fundamental human experience defined by biology and one where common themes in its experience can be traced over time. Constructionists dispute this 'commonality of childhood', and instead argue that the child and childhood are shaped differently in various landscapes of space and time. Simply put, 'the child' and 'childhood' can mean different things in different cultures and at different moments in history (Lesnik-Oberstein, 1998). This chapter (as with others in this volume) takes a constructionist approach and asks how British childhood in the nineteenth and twentieth centuries can best be explored, given the variety of definitions of the child at any one moment in history.

Many of the recent changes in the historiography of childhood have resulted from the impact of two intellectual movements (feminism and postmodernism) which have encouraged some historians to readjust their gaze and to see history through a variety of lenses which allow the full range of experience to be explored. Harry Hendrick is an example of one so affected. He suggests that children have been missing from history in much the same way as women were. Furthermore, he argues that historians of childhood can learn from the development of women's history as a discipline by seeing age as a category of analysis, recognising that the 'omission of children is ideological: it is a consequence of a set of attitudes and power structures' (Hendrick, 1997: 4). In addition, he draws his analytical framework from the influence that postmodernism has had on historical enquiry (Porter, in Burke, 1997) and presents an understanding of the child which is not simply in response to outside agencies but which illustrates the redefinition of the child as a human being:

> The body, then, does not exist as a timeless entity, forever the same from the perspective of itself and from that of the observer. The body in relation to mind (defined as 'will, self, soul') differs notably according to century, class,

167

circumstances and culture, and societies often possess a plurality of competing meanings.

(Hendrick, 1996: 2)

These different approaches and developments, which have occurred over the last thirty years, can be explored through the range of literature that now exists on the history of childhood (Hendrick, 1997). However, whilst the debates and range of approaches has added greatly to our understanding of the position of the child in history – through an exploration of childhood experiences, of the development of childhood and of ideologies towards children – there is still room for further research which explores the not-so-well-trodden territories of childhood (for example, little attention has been paid to issues of childhood and race, to paediatrics, or to children's leisure) and which tests the validity of various historians' conclusions.

Basic tools

Having briefly outlined the philosophy behind the concept of micro-history and suggested how the history of childhood has developed, some understanding of the way history can be researched, written and evaluated, is necessary to enable a project to take shape. Agreement between historians on this matter has not yet been reached, and there are a variety of approaches to historical research (for example, see Marwick, 1989; Tosh, 1991; Kozicki, 1993; Evans, 1997). The ideas in this chapter are not presented as necessarily the 'right' path to 'good history' but as one way to proceed, and one that, as we have seen, is itself invested with certain assumptions and ideals. The general principles outlined here, however, can be seen as the basic tools of historical research. They apply not only to the history of childhood but are a necessary component of all historical investigations. Moreover, the skills learned can also be utilised within other subject disciplines. Although it is impossible to anticipate the range of ideas and projects you will want to explore or to highlight all the pitfalls you will experience, this chapter can be used as a template to help structure your approach to discovering the history of childhood.

In order to write history, we need to explore how history has been written and take advice from others who have trodden the path before us. This can be done by exploring the range of books now available on historical methodology (both generalist and those with a focus on local history) and by reading the work of historians of childhood with a critical eye to their methodology. However, while there are a variety of approaches to take and methodologies to use, there is one underlying truism about all history: that it is based on the selection and analysis of sources. Indeed, the process of researching and writing history can be seen as a dialogue between the researcher and the sources used to explore the past. While researchers come from a variety of perspectives, there are two basic types of source: primary and secondary. Simply expressed, primary sources are those generated during the period being studied, while secondary sources are those written after the event or period under investigation.

While there are hierarchies of sources and a huge variety of both primary and secondary sources, there is one important point to remember: all sources are problematic and need careful handling. Arthur Marwick in his book *The Nature of History* provides a comprehensive guide to the variety and types of sources and their evaluation, and concludes that all sources are imperfect and fragmentary (Marwick, 1989, especially ch. 5). In analysing primary and secondary sources, therefore, it is important to maintain a critical approach and to question what is being presented. Although the questions will differ, depending upon whether you are looking at a primary or secondary source and on what form these take, the principle is the same: ask questions. A good place to start is with the following list: who, what, where, when and why? Such basic information is only the beginning, as you will want (and need) to verify the source, place it in context, read and understand it (Drake and Finnegan, 1994).

For secondary sources, the principle is exactly the same, although the basic questions may differ. You may want to gather the basic bibliographical material (who wrote it, when, who published it and where) and then move on to ask questions about the author, the argument, the theoretical approach, the evidence used and methods applied. By maintaining a questioning approach to all sources, some consistency of method is possible, and this allows for greater comparability and the development of analytical skills. What is important is to remember that one type of source is seldom sufficient; rather, historians gather a range of sources to substantiate their claims. While this may seem to be simple common sense, 'it is common sense applied very much more systematically and sceptically than is usually the case in everyday life, supported by a secure grasp of historical context and, in many instances, a high degree of technical knowledge' (Tosh, 1991: 71). It is from this type of approach that you can begin to develop a historian's frame of mind: that is, one that combines narrative, descriptive and analytical techniques.

Having acknowledged the problematic nature of sources and argued for a systematic approach to assess their usefulness, some consideration needs to be given to the role of the researcher. How far is the process of research separate from the person doing the research? Can researchers easily and systematically apply historical methodology without bringing their own attitudes and assumptions with them? As we have seen, history is constructed through a dialogue between the sources and the historian. History is, therefore, not only dependent upon the type and range of sources used but also upon the researchers, on their own interests or biases. While the process of research (the methods and sources used) needs to be carefully considered by the readers of history, the role of the researcher also needs careful evaluation in recognition of the relationship between writer and text. As Tosh has noted: 'In approaching the sources, the historian is anything but a passive observer' (1991: 70).

Historians have yet to reach agreement on whether objectivity is possible or useful, and while answers to these questions will probably never be found, researchers need to be aware of the existence and implication of bias. A number of questions need, therefore, to be asked about the researcher's background, education, political persuasion and career development, and not just about their methodology, sources and presentation of the material. In this way, the particular approach of the author can be identified and commented upon. Awareness of various approaches is the key to successful analysis of material as, of course, no source is free from bias. However, such debates about objectivity lead historians into discussion of the nature of the discipline more generally, and arguments continue about whether the discipline can be regarded as a science or an art (see for example Evans, 1997, especially ch. 2). This debate can be clearly seen in the two key historiography texts utilised here, and bias can be detected in the writing; in Tosh's work, for example, there is an inclination towards a more instinctive/intuitive approach (1991: 71) while Marwick's argument is for a methodology which scientists could respect (1989: 155). However, this debate may be something of a red herring (Tosh, 1991: 141) and one which seeks to stifle rather than encourage vibrancy and diversity within history (Rabb, in Kozicki, 1993).

By applying a series of questions to any given text, be it primary or secondary, critical evaluation is encouraged and some assessment of the suitability of various sources, approaches, theories and methods can be gained. This process of analysis is vital, not only to show how the source was created and to highlight its weaknesses but also, in the case of secondary sources, to show how one piece of work relates to another, where divergence and convergence of opinions are found and where gaps and generalisations exist. Through this process, the important principle of seeing how historical works relate to each other and how new work might inform existing interpretations can be established. This principle of relating the local project to the wider literature is vital if the study is to move from simply being of interest to a local audience. Local history has itself changed dramatically over time (Tiller, 1998) and remains a lively arena within the discipline; but here, we are concerned with contributing to the wider historical debate about the nature of childhood and not simply with adding to the range of local history studies. To do this, small-scale studies must be placed within their wider historical context; that is, connections must be made with existing literature. In the next section I explore, in practical terms, how this can be done and hope to encourage you to get started on your own research.

Researching the history of childhood

Once you have developed some understanding of what is meant by the history of childhood and of the nature of historical methodology, the next step is to organise your research group, find a topic and develop a plan. It is only by applying and testing existing theories and approaches that we can begin to develop our own understanding and perspective, to contribute to the debates and to explore the many underdeveloped areas of research. The completion of a group project offers one way to proceed and working with a group gives an opportunity for ideas to be shared and skills to be practised in a combined effort to produce history. However, the benefits can be greater than this, as project work is not simply about telling a story about childhood in the past but also helps develop (and improve) analytical, communication, research and writing skills which can be utilised within other disciplines. The process of learning, of course, does not end with the completion of the project. Reflection on the nature and success of group working, on your own role and on the finished product, allows the process of learning to continue. With all these aims in mind, it is clear that planning of the project is vital, and careful thought and preparation needs to go into developing a research group and project plan.

Students of the history of childhood are at an advantage as we all have some knowledge of childhood in the past – we were all children once. Talking to friends and family about their experiences of childhood is one way of beginning to develop ideas for a research project. Indeed, oral history – 'the interviewing of eye-witness participants in the events of the past for the purposes of historical reconstruction' (Perks and Thomson, 1998: ix) – has developed as a legitimate way to investigate the past (Thompson, 1988). However, utilising the memories of others is only one way of investigating the history of childhood. There is a range of primary sources available to the researcher, some of which are obviously going to contain information about the child (for example, school logbooks), while others (such as the census) may not be immediately recognisable as relevant to the budding researcher (Drake and Finnegan, 1994).

You will probably have your own ideas about what you want to investigate as you read around the subject. No doubt you will have already identified some of the key texts in the history of childhood and are beginning to recognise a range of opinions and approaches. You can utilise these as starting points for your research. For example, if you are interested in child labour, a number of authors make statements about the changing nature and purpose of work for children over time. Within the nineteenth century, you could explore (by using the census, for example) whether similar patterns of employment as Davin found in London – 'Until the 1870s London children might enter full-time employment as young as six or seven, though between ten and twelve was more usual' (1996: 157) – exist in your area. For the twentieth century, Walvin's assertion that: 'Since 1914 children have tended to work for personal rather than family reasons'

(1982: 195) begs both an investigation of the type of work children were involved in and an exploration of their reasons for working during an era where their opportunities were restricted by legislation. Alternatively, the long-term and short-term impact of war could be investigated, for example, to see how true was Rose's claim: 'And in the First World War the long-term decline in child labour was reversed by temporary need. When the war was over and the men returned, the Fisher Education Act of 1918 located the under-14s firmly back in school again' (Rose, 1991: 6). While each area can be investigated locally using a range of sources, all projects will be located within the existing debates amongst historians on child labour, thus moving from a project that is purely of local interest to one that contributes to current historiography.

Instead of specific experiences, ideas about the child could be investigated, for example, by exploring the categorisation of childhood illnesses and approaches to children's bodies and minds. Again, the range of local sources is wide. For the nineteenth century, for example, the work of Crompton provides an opportunity to explore the medical treatment of pauper children. Projects could be devised which tested his conclusion that 'workhouses were generally much safer places for children to live in, as they had an independent water supply that was clean and monitored by rudimentary biological tests, thus protecting inmates from water-borne diseases' (Crompton, 1997: 104) and which explored ideas and assumptions about pauper children. The administrative and medical records from children's hospitals would provide another way of assessing approaches to child health. For instance, you could look at the development of paediatric services, of the categorisation and treatment of certain 'illnesses' and of society's attitudes to the sick child in your locale. In this way Hendrick's assertion that by 1918 'medicine took the child's body, in common with educationalists and moral entrepreneurs, and fabricated it as a distinct entity with its own peculiar dimensions and resonances' (1996: 127) could be evaluated.

To find out whether it will be possible to complete a project in the time available to you, preliminary research is needed and a basic plan should be developed which consists of:

- title
- aims
- primary sources
- secondary sources
- methods
- expected findings and argument

An outstanding example of the application of this approach can be found in Taylor's (1998) article, 'Bell, Book and Scandal: The Struggle for School Attendance in a South Cambridgeshire Village, 1880–1890'. Of course, you may not want to do something quite so ambitious, but her work does give an excellent insight into what is possible. What is important is to remain open-minded and flexible at this point, as the primary focus of your investigation will invariably change (either completely or subtly) as a result of the preliminary research.

Let us, therefore, take a concrete example and work through one approach that you can use as a template for your own ideas. You will already have noticed from your reading that attitudes towards the child's economic role kept changing throughout both the nineteenth and twentieth centuries, as did the perception of child labour as a 'problem'. Legislation was introduced to, among other things, exclude children from factories and encourage school attendance, but it took until 1918 for the half-time system to be abolished. Despite this, children were still regularly working in a variety of ways at the turn of the century, which suggests tension between the conflicting demands of 'reformers', parents and children. The unease over child labour was reflected in contemporary debates about the nature and experience of childhood, and:

> there remained a conflict between the child as school pupil; the child as wage-earning employee learning occupational discipline; the child of the poor, indispensable to the economic security of his or her family, and the child as damaged in its physical and moral development through 'excessive' labour.
>
> (Hendrick, 1996: 73)

While the subject of child labour as a whole is too broad to be considered suitable for a single project, further reading suggests ways in which this interest can be refined.

Davin, for example, explores the complexities of children's work and, in particular, its definition. She also highlights a number of useful primary sources, including Parliamentary Papers (Davin, 1996: 269). She argues that the 'most difficult to gauge is the extent of children's work, particularly girls'. The enquiries concentrated on paid labour and, in effect if not in intent, on boys ...' (1996: 173). Now we have a more manageable project idea, and one which links into debates not only about child labour but also about the gendered experience. By studying other secondary sources, we can identify that the debate about children's employment was, once again, especially vociferous between 1899 and 1903. We now have a focus, in terms of both topic and time, and can therefore devise a title, a research question and a list of secondary sources (see plan below).

Next we need to locate our research within a particular geographical area (in reality, somewhere local to you) and to investigate the availability of local primary sources. The project plan that follows is based on a fictitious locality and therefore includes some fictitious sources; the approach can however easily be adapted and similar material will exist for your local area. I chose the town of Southwick in the Midlands, and decided to study the period 1899–1905 because I wanted to look at a time when these issues were being discussed nationally in order to determine what impact such debates had at a local level. I also wanted to study a time when labour legislation was already on the statute book – this would enable me to explore its implementation locally. Furthermore, by identifying this period of seven years, I would be able to see any changes in girls' work over time; research stopped well before the First World War as I was mindful of Walvin's comments indicated earlier.

A visit to my neighbourhood library revealed a wide range of local history texts – a help in outlining the socio-economic position of Southwick at the turn of the century. I found that there was a Local History Society which published its own research and that the library also held information about the County Record Office. My visit to that Office revealed a wealth of information on the lives of working-class families. For example, I found the Fabian Society's 1904 'Investigation into the Condition of Women and Children Homeworkers in Warwickshire'; the Annual Reports of the Medical Officer of Health, containing information about health and housing in Southwick, with references to the type of paid work women and girls were doing; and log books from the local school, which gave information about absenteeism. In addition, I unearthed some photographs of local children and a couple of autobiographies recalling local childhood. Finally, I came across evidence about the activities of a local reformer (a Mr Nelson from Southwick) and the local library was able to supply his obituary from a local newspaper and a small book on his life and work. I made a note to look at the 1902 *Report of the Inter-Departmental Committee on the Employment of Children* to see if he gave evidence.

I now had a clear and precise plan which followed the framework outlined earlier and, while I was prepared to revise it in the light of other discoveries, I knew my proposal would be feasible.

Title:

'Invisible Workers: Girls' Work in Southwick at the Turn of the Century'

Aims:

To investigate the type of work undertaken by girls in the small Midlands town of Southwick in the period 1899–1905.

To explore the nature of work for girls and to test Davin's assertion (1996) that, by definition, girls' work was less visible than boys' work.

Primary sources:

(Since this section is based on initial data collection, it will not be complete. Once these sources have been analysed, you will need to search for other relevant sources.)

Parliamentary Papers:

(You should provide a summary of the relevance of each source.)

- 1899 Elementary Schools, Children Working for Wages, Return for England and Wales Lxxv (205).
- 1902 Employment of Schoolchildren, Inter-Departmental Committee: Report xxv (849) and Evidence xxx (895).

Local sources:

- School logbooks for Southwick school, 1899, 1903, 1904, 1905, (1900–02 missing);
- Medical Officer of Health Annual Reports, 1900–10;
- Fabian Society (1904) 'Investigation into the Condition of Women and Children Homeworkers in Warwickshire';
- Information on Mr Nelson: obituary and E. Nelson's *A Life in Chains* (1976) (fictitious).

Secondary sources:

The project is located within the wider debate about the regulation of children's work and is, in particular, informed by (and identifies the competing interpretations in) the work of Davin (1996); Hendrick (1996); Hopkins (1994); Pinchbeck and Hewitt (1972); Rose (1991); and Walvin (1982). It also draws on the wealth of research available on gender and work which now exists within the field of women's history. In particular, the work of Roberts (1986, 1988) and Lewis (1986) highlight the roles and responsibilities of girls which, in turn, reflect broader gender divisions in society.

(You will in addition need briefly to highlight the different approaches used by these authors, together with any other relevant pieces of local research such as journal articles and local history studies.)

Methods:

A 'questioning sources' strategy, following analysis of the above material, plus close textual analysis, along with discussion of the positive and negative aspects of each source.

(You should provide precise details here.)

Expected findings and argument:

Girls continued to be involved in both paid and unpaid work throughout the period 1899–1905. I will argue that both contemporaries and historians have been confined in their exploration of the subject by the definition of 'work' and, in particular, by the exclusion of unpaid work from the debate.

At this time, girls' work generally was not disappearing; rather, it was difficult for reformers to investigate and, therefore, has remained largely invisible. Furthermore, unpaid domestic work was a socially acceptable 'occupation' for young girls. In Southwick, economic and social change affected the opportunities for girls to work in paid employment but evidence is expected to confirm that domestic responsibilities, as well as opportunities for casual paid employment, remained part of their experience.

This plan should give you some insight into the first stages of the research, and much of this can be conducted in your own academic library, and on the Internet, with the guidance of your tutor. Initially, you will be exploring what others have written on the subject, collecting references in order to gain a working knowledge of the subject area. In addition, you will need to make a critical assessment of the primary sources in much the same way as you did with secondary sources. To locate sources, you will need to explore the location of repositories, access arrangements and opening hours (Mortimer, 1997).

In the beginning, you may only have a very general idea of the subject area which you are interested in. With additional work you begin to refine this, narrowing it down to a specific issue, debate, time, place or institution. This obviously becomes easier once secondary texts and primary sources have been identified and located, in the manner described above. However, you should ration your primary source research time at this stage; it is amazing how the hours can slip away in the archive. Sometimes this can be because you become engrossed in the wealth of material available or because you keep searching for something that is not there. Limit yourself to one or two visits in the first instance to establish whether it is going to be possible to research your idea. You may need to redefine it. If, however, adequate primary sources are available you are ready to go on to the next stage.

Your plan will be beginning to take shape as you refine it in light of your discoveries. Having visited the library, you will have some idea of the time-consuming nature of research (and the effort required by the group to complete the work) and it is at this stage that you should limit the scope of your project. Past experience would suggest that it is the small, narrowly-focused project that is most manageable: one, for example, that discusses one issue or debate in one location at a narrowly defined moment in time. Avoid trying to do too much and remember that this is a history project, so that comparisons with the contemporary scene are not always useful.

At this point, you should decide on the division of the work and allocate tasks so that all members of the group are actively involved. Once you have your plan and have divided up the tasks, research can begin. Planning and management meetings should be called regularly so that a process of reviewing the project work can be taken. While there is no required format for such meetings, individuals should take their responsibility to the group seriously and be prepared to listen to others and offer constructive criticism. Again, flexibility is important, as some modification may be needed in order to accommodate new ideas and findings. However, sticking to your basic plan throughout the research is important so as to avoid deviation from the issues and so that you know when to stop. Finally, remember that the collection and analysis of the material is only one stage of the research. You have still to write up your findings and be able to communicate them to others.

Conclusion

By placing local, small-scale research within the context of wider historical studies, three important aims can be achieved. First, much can be understood about children, their lives and their relationship with adult society in the past. At the same time, an understanding can also be gained of the practice and purpose of history. Finally, important transferable skills (of researching, analysing, collating and interpreting information) will be utilised and developed.

Through active participation in the creation of history, an understanding of the way history is written and, in particular, how historians now approach the history of childhood, can be realised.

Review questions and tasks

1. What are the main developments in the history of childhood?
2. Look again at the opening sentence of this chapter. In the light of this, how confident can we be that any representation from the past approximates even reasonably to the true state of affairs?
3. Look at Davin's *Growing Up Poor* (1996). List the range of sources she uses and assess the advantages and disadvantages of each.
4. What are the main differences between constructionist and essentialist perspectives? Identify some authors who take these approaches and evaluate their work.
5. Using Thompson (1978) as a guide to good practice, interview someone from a different generation about some aspect of their childhood. How different is their experience from your own recollections of childhood? Why do you think this is? Confer with others about the outcome of their interviews. Explain the reasons for common themes and divergences in these narratives. What problems does this exercise raise for using personal testimony as a source? What steps might you want to take to further investigate the evidence presented to you?
6. Write your own definition of history. Think about the form and function of history, the use of sources, and the relationship between the historian and her sources. How far do you think history is based on facts? How do you explain different interpretations or historical arguments? What are the implications of all this for our understanding of childhood?

Further reading

Davin, A. (1996) *Growing Up Poor: Home, School and Street in London, 1870–1914*, London: Rivers Oram Press. Davin's landmark text offers much more than an exploration of childhood in London (with a focus primarily on the experience of working-class girls). Not only does it provide, as its title suggests, an insight into the life of the child in a variety of settings, but it is also an example of exemplary scholarship. As such, it is a fine text to use to begin an exploration of the changing concept of childhood and the way history is written. In particular, the introduction provides an excellent starting point for students of the history of childhood when read in conjunction with Hendrick (1997), and the final chapter (on national identity and the state) explores how new ideas about childhood were played out and offers suggestions for future research. The book is well researched and the bibliography is very useful as a guide to the range of sources available on the history of childhood.

Drake, M. and Finnegan, R. (1994) *Sources and Methods: A Handbook, Studying Family and Community History*, vol. 4, Cambridge: Open University. This is an excellent practical introduction to sources and methods for historians. It covers everything from the preliminary stages, organising a plan and assessing primary sources, through a range of sources and methods, to presentation and dissemination. Written by a variety of academics (all with an interest in family and community history), it is both easy to use and extremely informative.

Hendrick, H. (1997) *Children, Childhood and English Society, 1880–1990*, **Cambridge: Cambridge University Press.** For those beginning a study of the history of childhood, Hendrick's survey is a concise introduction to current themes and issues in childhood studies. This text briefly explores recent approaches to the history of childhood and provides a good bibliography. Chapters focus on the social construction of childhood in the period 1880–1920 and changing approaches to the child within the family, school and social policy.

Marwick, A. (1989) *The Nature of History*, **Basingstoke: Macmillan.** This book provides a broad evaluation of the development, purpose and practice of history. It is accessible to those from a non-history background and can be used as a basic text. Chapter 5 (Historical Facts and Historical Sources) is a superb introduction to the basic principles of historical investigation. It serves as a useful comparison to Tosh (1991) and Evans (1997).

References

Anderson, M. (1980) *Approaches to the History of the Western Family, 1500–1914*, Basingstoke: Macmillan Educational.

Ariès, P. (1973) *Centuries of Childhood*, Harmondsworth: Penguin.

Burke, P. (ed.) (1997) *New Perspectives on Historical Writing*, Cambridge: Polity Press.

Crompton, F. (1997) *Workhouse Children*, Thrupp: Sutton Publishing.

Cunningham, H. (1995) *Children and Childhood in Western Society since 1500*, London: Longman.

Davin, A. (1996) *Growing Up Poor: Home, School and Street in London, 1870–1914*, London: Rivers Oram Press.

Drake, M. and Finnegan, R. (1994) *Sources and Methods: A Handbook, Studying Family and Community History*, vol. 4, Cambridge: Open University.

Drake, M., Finnegan, R. and Weinbren, D. (1998) 'Editorial', *Family and Community History* 1: 3–6.

Evans, R. (1997) *In Defence of History*, London: Granta Publications.

Hendrick, H. (1996) *Child Welfare: England, 1872–1989*, London: Routledge.

—— (1997) *Children, Childhood and English Society, 1880–1990*, Cambridge: Cambridge University Press.

—— (1997) 'Constructions and Reconstructions of British Childhood: An Interpretative Study', in A. James and A. Prout (eds), *Constructing and Reconstructing Childhood: Contemporary Issues in the Sociological Study of Childhood*, London: Falmer Press.

Hopkins, E. (1994) *Childhood Transformed: Working-Class Children in Nineteenth-Century England*, Manchester: Manchester University Press.

James, A. and Prout, A. (eds) (1997) *Constructing and Reconstructing Childhood: Contemporary Issues in the Sociological Study of Childhood*, London: Falmer Press.

Kozicki, H. (ed.) (1993) *Developments in Modern Historiography*, Basingstoke: Macmillan.

Lesnik-Oberstein, K. (1988) 'Childhood and Textuality: Culture, History, Literature', in K. Lesnik-Oberstein (ed.), *Children in Culture: Approaches to Childhood*, Basingstoke: Macmillan.

Levi, G. (1997) 'On Microhistory', in P. Burke (ed.), *New Perspectives on Historical Writing*, Cambridge: Polity Press.

Lewis, J. (1986) *Women in England 1870–1950: Sexual Divisions and Social Change*, Brighton: Wheatsheaf Books.

Marwick, A. (1989) *The Nature of History*, Basingstoke: Macmillan.

Mortimer, I. (ed.) (1997) *Record Repositories in Great Britain*, Norwich: PRO Publications.

Perks, R. and Thomson, A. (1998) *The Oral History Reader*, London: Routledge.

Pinchbeck, I. and Hewitt, M. (1972) *Children in English Society*, vol. 2, London: Routledge.

Porter, R. (1997) 'History of the Body', in P. Burke (ed.) *New Perspectives on Historical Writing*, Cambridge: Polity Press.

Rabb, T.K. (1993), in H. Kozicki (ed.), *Developments in Modern Historiography*, Basingstoke: Macmillan.

Roberts, E. (1986) *A Woman's Place: An Oral History of Working-Class Women 1890–1940*, Oxford: Blackwell.

—— (1988) *Women's Work 1840–1940*, Basingstoke: Macmillan.

Rose, L. (1991) *The Erosion of Childhood: Child Oppression in Britain, 1860–1918*, London: Routledge.

Rubinstein, D. (1969) *School Attendance in London, 1870–1914: A History*, Hull: University of Hull.

Samuel, R. (1998) *Island Stories: Unravelling Britain*, London: Verso.

Taylor, S. (1998) 'Bell, Book and Scandal: The Struggle for School Attendance in a South Cambridgeshire Village 1880–1890', *Family and Community History* 1 (November).

Thompson, P. (1978) *The Voice of the Past: Oral History*, Oxford: Oxford University Press.

Tiller, K. (1998) *English Local History: The State of the Art, Board of Continuing Education*, Cambridge: Cambridge University Press.

Tosh, J. (1991) *The Pursuit of History: Aims, Methods and New Directions in the Study of Modern History*, London: Longman.

Walvin, J. (1982) *A Child's World: A Social History of English Childhood, 1800–1914*, Harmondsworth: Penguin.

Wilson, A. (1980) 'The Infancy of the History of Childhood: An Appraisal of Philip Ariès', *History and Theory* 19: 132–54.

Chapter 10

Researching childhood

Jean Mills and Richard Mills

Summary

Following on from the previous chapter, the purpose of this section is further to encourage you to do some research into childhood and/or children, and to help you to be better equipped to do so. It offers advice about the role and persona of the researcher and about how to collect data. It suggests some dos and don'ts for prose style and reminds you of points about presentation and referencing. Useful sources and books are indicated, with projects for you to try out.

> In research the horizon recedes as we advance, and is no nearer at sixty than it
> was at twenty ... Research is always incomplete.
>
> (Mark Pattison, 1875)

Thinking of a topic

Are you frightened by the word 'research?' Some people are. It seems to
suggest a region far beyond them, where other-worldly academics try to
unravel the mysteries of the universe. Well, a tiny bit of research is like that
(and you may have read, or tried to read, as we have, Stephen Hawking's *A
Brief History of Time*), but most educational research you will be interested
in doing is very down to earth and practical. It is concerned with real children and adults, and current concerns and issues.

So, begin to think of yourself as an investigator, as somebody who wants
to explore something. Notice, we do not say 'discover', for that puts unfair
pressure on you. No doubt you will discover something, but it will not be
what you expect. What you discover will be something about yourself and
your own feelings towards research. Listen to the story of one final year BA
student, as follows.

As we write this chapter, one of our students, Sarah, is doing an investigation into young children and smoking. When she began thinking about
the project three months ago, her aim was to find out how television (both
in programmes and advertising) affected the smoking habits of children.
She intended to have a large circulation of questionnaires; to interview
many children and transcribe their tape recorded conversations; to seek
information from television and advertising companies; to contact pressure
groups; and to find out the views of teachers, psychologists and parents.
Her aim, in short, was to *discover the answers*. And all in twelve thousand
words.

Clearly, Sarah had much going for her: lots of enthusiasm; a capacity for
hard work; an awareness of various methods for data collection; and the
confidence to telephone and write to complete strangers. However,
unknown to her at the time, she was only preparing herself for disappoint-
ment. Given all the variables in the equation, there was no way in which
she could possibly reach definitive conclusions about the relationship
between television and young children's smoking habits. At our first tuto-
rial, one little piece of information helped to convince her of this. It was the
fact that, in over seven thousand studies, no one had satisfactorily been
able to establish unequivocally a clear relationship between television
violence and violence by children. Indeed, the findings from some studies
contradicted those from others.

Sarah was clearly disconcerted at this first meeting. As *she* saw it, her
wonderful plans were under attack; as *we* saw it, they needed to be modi-
fied. After much thinking and a couple of tutorials, Sarah began to think of
her project in terms of an *exploration* into the attitudes of some young chil-

dren towards smoking, both as seen on television and as observed in everyday life. Her methodology would now rest heavily on tape recorded interviews and discussions with children, sometimes observing television extracts together for scrutiny. In short, the whole enterprise has been scaled down into something which is manageable and interesting to do (as recommended by Maxine Rhodes in Chapter 9 of this Reader), and which should yield useful insights into the thinking of some children.

At the present time, Sarah is very enthusiastic, both about her topic and about herself as a researcher. She is now much more realistic about what she can accomplish and much more confident in her draft submissions. The signs are good. In one more month we shall know what she has achieved, and so will she. Our guess is that this will prove to be the start of her career as teacher–researcher.

This does not mean that every student should become a lifelong researcher. What it does mean is that every one of us in the caring professions should remain intellectually alive, continuing to ask questions, to sift evidence, to challenge prejudices and easy assumptions and received opinion.

Data collection

Human beings seem to like collecting things – antiques, beer mats, comics, dolls, penny whistles, photos, stamps, even traffic cones – and the psychology of collecting is well documented. Whatever they are, someone, somewhere, will be collecting them. It is not surprising, then, that research data collection is often very satisfying. As each completed questionnaire, each transcribed interview, each relevant quotation, each tape recorded telephone conversation, is gathered in, so the satisfaction level rises. It is almost as if you are taming the chaotic world and preparing the way for getting a grip on events.

This is the ideal. It needs to be set against your terror at not knowing what to do with the material you are accumulating. But, first things first.

Why did you produce a questionnaire originally? Is that what you thought research was about? Do you know the large numbers you would have to deal with for your resulting statistics to be in any way valid and generalisable? Did you remember to do a pilot study first, in order to check the wording and sequence of your questions? How did you decide on your respondents: were they random or selected? Were they all your relatives or friends? (Surely you didn't fill in any of the forms yourself?) Did you remember to decide your method of analysis *before* reaching your final questionnaire version?

It will be evident from these questions that using questionnaires is not risk-free; in fact, it is fraught with difficulties, as several of the books mentioned later will indicate. In our view, you should only use questionnaires if you are prepared to learn how to manipulate the statistics and if you have sufficient resources to deal in several hundreds, and if you do a great deal of preparation first. Failing that, what you will learn, if you do use them, is their limitations. However, there are positive advantages. You will find, for instance, that your former confidence in quantitative data takes a knock, and you should henceforth be rather wary of statistics. You will also find that the division between quantitative and qualitative research methods is not so cut and dried as you might once have thought. Both the selection and interpretation of questionnaire sections involves making qualitative judgements.

You are left, then, with three main sources of data: reading; observation; and interview/conversation (either one to one, or in focus groups). If you wish to achieve a measure of triangulation in your research, you may use all three methods in complementary ways. Suppose, for example, you are investigating some aspects of children's attitudes towards certain computer programs. Each of the three methods just mentioned could be valuable to you. You might even discover, in this instance, a fourth source of information, for example, that the computer company which produced or marketed the program had already conducted its own research profile as part of its strategy.

- For help with questionnaires (for those who are undeterred), see Malec (1993); Norusis (1992); Oppenheim (1992); Sapsford and Jupp (1996).
- For advice about interviewing, see Burgess (1985a); Lummis (1987); Powney and Watts (1987); Strauss and Corbin (1999); Thompson (1978); Warwick (1989).
- For insights into observation, see Graue and Walsh (1998); Greig and Taylor (1998); Hannabuss (1993); Hitchcock and Hughes (1995); Hopkins (1994); Mills (1988); Waksler (1991).
- For general advice on conducting research projects, including reading searches, see Anderson (1990); Bell (1987); Chester (1989); Cohen and Manion (1995); Hart (1998); Walker (1985).

A final point. One contact can often lead to others. In the computer project just suggested, it is not impossible that you might even get in touch with the program author via the Internet or e-mail. To contemplate such a possibility requires confidence and a sense of adventurousness which research can stimulate. One student, Alison, investigating the work of Roald Dahl, found herself in charge for half a day of Dahl's daughter's house in Oxfordshire. After a morning of coffee and chat, the daughter left Alison with some of Dahl's manuscripts while she herself went out shopping. That was quite a coup for anyone.

Style

Every essay or study involves a kind of storytelling. We do not mean that your research is pure invention – perish the thought – but that you have an account to give to a real reader. So ask yourself first of all: who is the audience I am writing for? What do I know about that audience?

It will always include yourself, but it will also include your tutor, whom you know, and perhaps another tutor or others whom you do not know. What effect does this have on you? Do you feel you have to write what you know they want to hear or what they would agree with? Do you feel that you have to write incomprehensibly so as to sound academic? Or do you feel that you can remain academic while still speaking in your own voice, directly and honestly?

That loaded last question will indicate our preference. You have your story to tell and should constantly imagine your readers. They will be helped by being reminded from time to time of the plot, of where you have reached and where you are going next. We suggest, too, that you write in the first person ('I'), just as we are doing now (in the plural form) in this chapter. This will give your text an immediacy and a humanity which should help your argument. Remember, though, that many tutors prefer the third person (for example, 'the researcher conducted a series of' or 'it is argued that') on the grounds of greater objectivity. Our view is that, as with quantitative and qualitative approaches, so with objectivity and subjectivity, the boundaries are not so clearcut as might be thought. Provided you guard against subjectivity of the low-level, descriptive, anecdotal kind, it should be acknowledged rather than hidden; it will be there, whether overt or covert.

So, to summarise up to this point, you need to develop your own distinctive voice which will clearly convey your story and satisfy the demands of your readers for a detached, but involved, account. What other features can help you to do this, in addition to intelligible first-person writing, with pointers en route?

- Emboldened sub-headings help to carve up your large text into chunks which are both manageable for you to write and digestible for your reader. At first, a total of perhaps twelve thousand words may seem massive, but in sections of two to three thousand words it is not so daunting and may help you keep to word length requirements.
- Avoid gender-specific language. Instead, use plurals where you can and 'she/he' where you can't. At the same time, choose terms which are all-inclusive (e.g. 'headteacher'; 'police officer') rather than exclusive (such as, 'headmaster'; 'policemen'). Similarly, take care with such ethnocentric phrases as 'our culture'.
- Be wary of making jokes. Your reader(s) may not share your sense of humour.

- Maintain the confidentiality of your respondents by changing names and any other identifying features. (However, we suggest you only do this when you are at the final writing-up stage. If you do it too early, it can be difficult to remember who is who.)
- Don't define technical terms which will be obvious to your reader(s), but show in other ways that you know what you are talking about.
- Observe all referencing conventions, (as indicated later), both within your text and within your bibliography.
- Avoid exclamation marks!
- Avoid such phrases as: 'I have discovered', 'My research shows' or 'My work proves that'. All these phrases are hostages to fortune. It is safer to claim less with phrases such as: 'My work would suggest that', 'My reading tends to show' or 'It seems to be the case that'.
- Have a care for ethical considerations. No person (and that includes children) should be tape recorded, or have their work quoted, without their permission.
- Finally, proof-read, proof-read and get a friend to proof-read also. Speling an gramatical erors can have an explosive impact on your readers and undermine your credibility as a serious researcher.

Presentation

A poor essay or special study is not redeemed by good presentation, but a good one can be spoiled by poor presentation. Ideally, your work should both *be* good, and *look* good.

We assume your study will be word processed and will have been composed directly on to the screen. Some of you will have a mental block about this but, once you have made the transition, you will not turn back. Instead, you will wonder how you ever used a biro, or pencil, or typewriter in the bad old days. Composing directly on to the screen (as is being done at this moment) enables rethinking, redrafting and repositioning to occur simultaneously with composition. It enables you to check spelling, grammar and word length en route. It enables you to see exactly how your work will look on the page before you print it out.

Here are some questions you will have to decide about your presentation preferences:

- What kind of font (i.e. print style)? (We invariably use Times New Roman).
- What size of print? (We use 12 point for manuscripts).
- What kind of headings? (We use 14 or 16 point for headings in bold type, sometimes underlined, and on the left of the page).
- Left or right justified, or both (i.e. lined up equally at the start or end of the lines)? (You will notice that Routledge books are left and right justified).

- Where is your pagination? (Left, middle, right top; left, middle, right bottom?)
- How have you shown quotations? (Below forty words can be shown in the running text by single quotation marks; above forty words should be set out from the text with each line indented to the same degree).
- Do you indent your paragraphs? (If you do, your text is easier to read).
- Single or double line spacing? (Only use double if you are advised to do so. If you have not written enough and want to fool your reader with double spacing, it will not work. You'll have to think of another strategy; there are some).
- Footnotes? (No. Better to use numbered references and include all information in a separate appendix).
- Colour photographs? (Yes, if you wish, with captions).
- Graphs? (Yes, if you wish, with explanation or commentary).
- Coloured paper? (Maybe, but certainly thickish, at least 70 gsm (grams per square metre)).
- Audio/video tapes? (Yes, if necessary, but only if clearly identified and marked).
- Appendices? (Yes. Certainly a bibliography. Possibly other appendices such as further reading, references, transcripts, statistical tables, graphs, children's work, and/or questionnaire samples).
- Chapters? (No, for an essay. Yes, for a study. They should be numbered, titled, shown in your contents list and begun on new pages).
- As for the structure of your study, you should consider the following sections: title; dedication; acknowledgements; abstract (summary); contents list, with pagination indicated; introduction; background reading; methodology; data collection; analysis; findings; conclusions; suggestions for further research; bibliography; other appendices. (N.B. Not every study needs all these sections, or in this sequence. You make your own decisions about what your study needs, but remember that analysis always carries more weight than straight description.)

Finally, in this section, those of you who are very relaxed will only keep one copy of your work as the study proceeds. Those who are highly neurotic will have half a dozen copies, spread around in several places should fire, theft or civil unrest threaten your treasure. Most will be somewhere in between, with a copy on the hard drive, backed up by a set of discs, and maybe a paper copy as well. We suggest that you *always* keep some kind of second copy of whatever you do, and that you always anticipate a deadline by two or three days in case your PC expires, or your printer jams, or you are called up for jury service, or the baby eats your data.

Referencing

First, remember why clear referencing is crucial in any essay or project or dissertation:

1   You need to be able to re-trace your own information.
2   Your tutor, or other reader, needs to be able to find it also.
3   You need, in all honesty, to acknowledge your debt to other authors.
4   You need to guard yourself against the possible charge of plagiarism, that is, using somebody else's work or ideas without acknowledgement.
5   You need to show evidence of support for all your hard effort.
6   You need to demonstrate appropriate sources which can be evaluated by others.

It is useful to separate your bibliography from further reading. In your bibliography, you include only books and articles from which you have quoted or which you have referred to directly in your text. In your further reading section, you include other material you have read (skimmed through?) which has had some influence on your thinking. Some students feel that the more references they include, the safer they will be, rather like the captain of a ship placing lifebelts every few feet around the deck. For the passenger, however, these lifebelts can inhibit the enjoyment of the voyage, so do not be too liberal in your provision.

However, don't get so hung up on referencing conventions that they dominate your thinking. We can both remember students who seemed so anxious about the minutiae of referencing that they almost forgot the primary importance of the content of their work. Referencing is a means to an end, namely, the identification of support material. So:

•   Check the style of referencing preferred in your institution. Most colleges and universities will have a handout of conventions.
•   Check the preferences of your own tutor. (Some tutors engage in guerrilla warfare with their colleagues, rather than relinquish their own system; you should not be caught in the crossfire.)
•   Be absolutely consistent, whatever system you decide on.

Our preference for bibliographical entries is the Harvard system, as follows.

Books

The sequence for details is as follows:

Author surname; comma; initial; full-stop; open bracket; date of publication; close bracket; title in italics or underlined or both; comma; place of publication; colon; publisher.

Here is an example:

Wullschläger, J. (1995) *Inventing Wonderland. The Lives and Fantasies of Lewis Carroll, Edward Lear, J.M. Barrie, Kenneth Grahame and A.A. Milne*, London: Methuen

Within the body of your text, a quotation from Wullschläger would give the name, date and page in brackets after your quotation. Here is an example: 'The symbolic association between childhood, innocence and regeneration is age-old, lying at the heart of the New Testament and of Christian thought' (Wullschläger, 1995: 17).

Articles

The sequence for details is as follows:

Author surname; comma; initial; full-stop; open bracket; date of publication; close bracket; title of article in inverted commas; comma; title of journal in italics or underlined; comma; volume number; comma; edition number; comma; month; pp.; page numbers.

Here is an example:

Benton, M. (1996) 'The Image of Childhood: Representations of the Child in Painting and Literature, 1700–1900', *Children's Literature in Education*, vol. 27, no. 1, March, pp. 35–61.

The bibliographical items, whether books or articles, are all listed in alphabetical order of surname (with anonymous agency publications treated as if the agency were the author, e.g. HMSO, NSPCC).

Internet

This presents different referencing challenges from books and articles. The same principles of identification, location and potential for retrieval apply, but web pages may change frequently, or even disappear; original sources may be unretrievable; a contributor may be virtually anonymous; technological modifications occur. In such circumstances, you take the common-sense course and include as much relevant information that is available, such as:

Author or editor contributor; title of the work or discussion posting; date and address of the work and/or other electronic publication information; pages or paragraphs; date when accessed; location of access.

Here is a relatively straightforward example, taken from guidelines of the Modern Language Association of America:

'Fresco', *Britannica Online*, Vers. 97.1.1. Mar. 1997, Encyclopaedia Britannica, 29 March 1997 <http://www.eb.com:180>.

For further advice, of interesting but arcane complexity, see the MLA web site: <http://www.eb.com:180>.

Childhood research sources

At the time of writing, Internet searches on AltaVista showed the following numbers of web pages:

Childhood Perspectives	383,180
Children and Television	1,019
Children and Advertising	44
Children and Media	7,090,740
Children and Magazines	1,598,130
Innocence	146,810
Children's Society	4,813,018
Museum of Childhood	940,330

Many entries will be found under these titles in the CD-Roms Encarta 95 and Britannica 99.

Other useful references include the following:

Amnesty International U.K., 99–119 Rosebery Avenue, London EC1R 4RE. Tel. 020 7814 6200. <http://www.amnesty.org.uk>

Barnardo's Offices include:

Barnardo's, Tanners Lane, Barkingside, Ilford, Essex IG6 1QG, Tel. 020 8550 8822. <http:///www.barnardos.org.uk>
Barnardo's Midlands, Brooklands, Great Cornbow, Halesowen, West Midlands B63 3AB. Tel. 0121 550 5271/6.
Barnardo's Northern Ireland, 542–544 Upper Newtownards Road, Belfast BT4 3HE. Tel. 028 901232 672366.
Barnardo's Scotland, 235 Corstorphine Road, Edinburgh EH12 7AR. Tel. 0131 334 9893.

Barnardo's North East, Orchard House, Fenwick Terrace, Jesmond, Newcastle-upon-Tyne NE2 2JQ. Tel. 0191 281 5024.

Lewis Carroll homepage:

<http://www.lewiscarroll.org/carroll.html>
<http://www.megabrands.com/alice/goalice.html>

Children's Literature in Education Journal, Human Sciences Press, 3 Henrietta Street, Covent Garden, London WC2E 8LU. Tel. 020 7240 0859.
Children's Rights Office, 235 Shaftesbury Avenue, London WC2H8EL. Tel. 020 7240 4449. Email: <crights@ftech.co.uk
Children's Society, Room 229, Edward Rudolph House, Margery Street, London WC1X 0JL. Tel. 0845 600 4400.
Thomas Coram Research Unit, Institute of Education, University of London, 27–28 Woburn Square, London WC1H 0AA. Tel. 020 7612 6957. Email: <tcru@ioe.ac.uk

For film references, consult: <http://imdb.com>

The following Museums of Childhood have varieties of artefacts and written materials:

Bethnal Green Museum of Childhood, Cambridge Heath Road, London E2 9PA. Tel. 020 8980 2415. <http://www.vam.ac.uk>
Edinburgh Museum of Childhood, 42 High Street, Edinburgh EH1 1TG. Tel. 01315 294142. <http://www.personal.u-net.com>
Highland Museum of Childhood, Strathpeffer, Scotland. Tel. 01997 421031. <http://www.cali.co.uk>
The National Trust Museum of Childhood, Sudbury Hall, Sudbury, Ashbourne, Derbyshire DE6 5HT. Tel. 01283 585305. <http://www.kidsnet.co.uk>
Museum of Childhood Memories, 1 Castle Street, Beaumaris, Anglesey, Gwynedd LL58 8AP. Tel. 01248 712498. <http://www.nwi.co.uk>

Opie Collection, Bodleian Library, University of Oxford, Broad Street, Oxford OX1 3BG. Tel. 01865 277180. Email: <admissions@bodley.ox.ac.uk
National Children's Bureau, 8 Wakley Street, London EC1V 7QE. <http://www.ance.lu/ncb.htm> and <http://www.ncb.org.uk/policy.htm>
National Children's Homes Action for Children, 85 Highbury Park, London N5 1UD. Tel. 020 7226 2033.
National Society for the Prevention of Cruelty to Children, National Centre, 42 Curtain Road, London EC2A 3NH. Tel. 020 7825 2500. Email: <helpline@nspcc.org.uk

NSPCC Child Protection Helpline Tel. 0800 800 500.

NSPCC Regional Appeals Offices include:

NSPCC Cymru/Wales, 9 Brindley Road, Cardiff CF1 7TX. Tel. 01222 230117/8.
NSPCC Northern Ireland, Jennymount Court, North Derby Street, Shore Road, Belfast BT15 3NH. Tel. 028 901232 351135.

Runnymede Trust, 11 Princelet Street, London E1 6QH. Tel. 020 7375 2101.
Salvation Army, 101 Queen Victoria Street, London EC4P 4EP. Tel. 020 7332 0022. Email: <thq@salvationarmy.org.uk
Save the Children, 17 Grove Lane, London SE5 8RD. Tel. 020 7703 5400. <http://www.oneworld.org/sef>
Save the Children, Scottish Education Office, Jordanhill Campus, 76 Southbrae Drive, Glasgow G13 1PP. Tel. 0141 950 3560.
UNICEF-UK, 55 Lincoln's Inn Fields, London WC2A 3NB. Tel. 020 7405 5592.
UNICEF-UK, Baltic Chambers, 50 Wellington Street, Glasgow G2 6HJ. Tel. 0141 204 1598.

Suggestions for project investigations

1   Explore some of the ways in which children appear in public life or rituals (for example, in religious or civic ceremonies, in community processions, as mascots for soccer teams.) What roles do they play? What actions do they perform? What special clothing do they wear? Why are they involved?

2   Observe a group of two or three children playing a computer game, and analyse the roles each one takes; the language used by each; the strategies adopted; and the attitudes revealed.

3   Expand on (2) above either by surveying the preferences shown by different age groups for particular computer programs, or by exploring the attitudes of parents towards their children's playing of computer games, or by analysing the claims made on the boxes of two or three popular games programs and comparing those claims with the reality of playing.

4   'Children, Parents, Shopping and Audio Tape.' Do a series of observations of children and parents in supermarket, shopping mall, large store or corner shop, taking note of the words and actions of the children and their parents. First, write up your observations in the form of journal notes, then analyse and categorise your data to produce a summary of your findings,

in terms of children's behaviour and the relationship between children and parents. (The informed consent of both parents and children would be needed for this project.)

5   Search through the work of one or more famous artists for paintings which include children. Decide, in each case, if their presence in the painting is integral or peripheral. Decide, also, which of the various constructs of childhood (found in Chapter 1 and throughout this Reader) each painting seems to fit.

6   Take a selection of broadsheet and tabloid newspapers for a few days. Cut out all the items, including advertisements, which have some reference to children. Compare your cuttings. What picture emerges of children or childhood? Is that picture consistent or various? What ideology or attitude seems to lie behind the way each newspaper presents children? Does the presentation fit your own experience?

7   Produce a report detailing the potential value of six named internet hits for one of the following areas:

   •   children and games
   •   children and violence
   •   differing educational attainment between boys and girls
   •   child employment in Third World countries

8   Contact several agencies which recruit children as models for advertisements. Consider what they say and write about:

   •   the range of their activities
   •   their policies and procedures
   •   how they safeguard the interests of children and families.

   Where possible, compare these claims with the real experience of a family involved with such an agency.

9   Societies differ in how they mark the transition from childhood to adulthood. Some have precise, formal rituals; others are less precise. How does your own society mark this change? Is it the same for girls as for boys? Investigate the transition in a culture very different from your own and, if you can, compare your findings with those of others in your group.

10 Produce a detailed report on this present volume for someone who has not yet read it, outlining what you perceive to be its strengths and weaknesses. As you do so, indicate the ways in which your own knowledge and awareness has been developed by each chapter.

Further reading

Cohen, L. and Manion, L. (1994) *Research Methods in Education*, 4th edn, London: Routledge.   This is one of the most comprehensive and accessible surveys of the whole field of the nature of educational research and the methods used to promote it. First published in 1980, it has benefited from a series of revisions and amendments. The first three chapters define different kinds of research, and this is followed by a consideration of research design and method, with information about case studies, surveys, interviews, statistics, experiments, role-playing, and ethical considerations. Boxed information is particularly helpful in providing examples from a range of real projects.

Greig, A. and Taylor, J. (1999) *Doing Research with Children* London: Sage.   The usefulness of this book for present purposes is twofold. On the one hand, it seeks to place investigation projects within a theoretical research framework, and on the other hand, it concentrates on how research of real children may be undertaken. To this end, there are useful case studies and check lists, with suggestions for many practical projects. A key underlying premise is the complexity of children's worlds and thinking, and how best to get near some understanding of that world.

Hopkins, D. (1994) *A Teacher's Guide to Classroom Research*, 2nd edn, Buckingham: Open University Press.   This is a book for the teacher as researcher and it offers solid, straightforward advice about how teachers can and should observe children and classrooms. Several case studies describe or record action research, data gathering, observation schedules, and focused conversations. The whole thrust of the book is for the heightened perception and understanding of individual teachers leading to overall classroom and school improvement.

Taylor, J. and Woods, M. (eds) (1998) *Early Childhood Studies: An Holistic Introduction*, London: Arnold.   Using the term 'educare', the editors and contributors to this multi-disciplinary anthology seek to encompass the areas of child development, education and pastoral provision (including family structure), with every section well referenced. It is ironic that the so-called 'holistic approach' includes quotations from United Nations declarations which seem to assume that all children are male, but the editors cannot be blamed for the insensitivity of earlier generations. Their own approach is genuinely inclusive and this is seen particularly in the fairly wide cultural context which they reflect and in their treatment of children as whole persons.

References

Books and articles to consult about research

Anderson, G. (1990) *Fundamentals of Educational Research*, Basingstoke: Falmer Press.

Bell, J. (1987) *Doing Your Research Project*, Milton Keynes: Open University Press.

Bernstein, B. and Brannen, J. (1996) *Children, Research and Policy*, London: Taylor & Francis.

Burgess, R.G. (ed.) (1984) *The Research Process in Educational Settings: Ten Case Studies*, Lewes: Falmer Press.

—— (ed.) (1985a) *Issues in Educational Research: Qualitative Methods*, Lewes: Falmer Press.

—— (ed.) (1985b) *Field Methods in the Study of Education*, Lewes: Falmer Press.

—— (ed.) (1985c) *Strategies of Educational Research: Qualitative Methods*, Lewes: Falmer Press.

—— (ed.) (1988) *Studies in Qualitative Methodology: A Research Annual*, vol. 1, JAI Press Inc.

Chester, T. R. (1989) *Children's Book Research: A Practical Guide to Techniques and Sources*, Gloucester: The Thimble Press.

Coffey, A. and Atkinson, P. (1996) *Making Sense of Qualitative Data: Complementary Research Strategies*, London: Sage.

Cohen, L. and Manion, L. (1995) *Research Methods in Education*, 4th edn, London: Routledge.

Finch, J. (1985) *Research and Policy: Uses of Qualitative Methods in Social and Educational Research*, Lewes: Falmer Press.

Graue, E. and Walsh, D. (1998) *Studying Children in Context: Theories, Methods and Ethics*, London: Sage.

Greig, A. and Taylor, J. (1999) *Doing Research with Children*, London: Sage Publications.

Hannabuss, S. (1993) *Biography and Children*, London: Library Association.

Hart, C. (1998) *Doing a Literature Review: Releasing the Social Science Research Imagination*, London: Sage Publications with the Open University.

Hart, W.A. (1993) 'Children are not Meant to be Studied,' *Journal of Philosophy of Education* 27 (1).

Hitchcock, G. and Hughes, D. (1995) *Research and the Teacher: A Qualitative Introduction to School-based Research*, London: Routledge.

Hopkins, D. (1994) *A Teacher's Guide to Classroom Research*, 2nd edn, Buckingham: Open University Press.

James, A. and Prout, A. (eds) (1990) *Constructing and Reconstructing Childhood: Contemporary Issues in the Sociological Study of Childhood*, London: Falmer Press.

Joseph, S. (1993) 'Childhood Revisited: Possibilities and Predicaments in New Research Agendas,' *British Journal of Sociology of Education* 14 (1): 113–21.

Lummis, T. (1987) *Listening to History: The Authenticity of Oral Evidence*, London: Hutchinson.

Malec, M.A. (1993) *Essential Statistics for Social Research*, Boulder, CO: Westview Press.

Mills, R.W. (1988) *Observing Children in the Primary School: All in a Day*, 2nd edn, London: Routledge.

Mills, R.W. and Mills, R.M. (1998) 'Child of Our Time: Variations in Adult Views of Childhood with Age', *International Journal of Early Years Education* 6 (1).

Norusis, M.J. (1992) *SPSS (Statistical Package for the Social Sciences) for Windows Professional Statistics Release 5*, Chicago: SPSS.

Oppenheim, A.N.(1992) *Questionnaire Design, Interviewing and Attitude Measurement*, London: Pinter Publishers.

Powney, J. and Watts, K. (1987) *Interviewing in Educational Research*, London: Routledge & Kegan Paul.

Punch, K.F. (1998) *Introduction to Social Research. Quantitative and Qualitative Approaches*, London: Sage.

Sapsford, R. and Jupp, V. (1996) *Data Collection and Analysis*, London: Sage Publications with the Open University.

Strauss, A.I. and Corbin, J. (1999) *Basics of Qualitative Research. Techniques and Procedures for Developing Grounded Theory*, London: Sage.

Thompson, P. (1978) *The Voice of the Past: Oral History*, Oxford: Oxford University Press.

Van Manen, M. (1990) *Researching Lived Experience: Human Science for an Action Sensitive Pedagogy*, Ontario, NY: The State University of New York.

Waksler, F.C. (ed.) (1991) *Studying the Social Worlds of Children: Sociological Readings*, London: Falmer Press.

—— (1996) *The Little Trials of Childhood and Children's Strategies for Dealing with Them*, London: Falmer Press.

Walker, R. (1985) *Doing Research: A Handbook for Teachers*, London: Methuen.

Warwick, D. (1989) *Interviews and Interviewing*, London: Industrial Society Press.

Indexes and abstracts to consult

British Education Index
British Education Theses Index
Child Development Abstracts and Bibliography
Children's Literature Abstracts
Multicultural Education Abstracts
Register of Educational Research in the UK
Special Educational Needs Abstracts

*   *   *

I am looking for something still more mysterious: for the path you read about in books, the old lane choked with undergrowth whose entrance the weary prince could not discover. You'll only come upon it at some lost moment of the morning … Then, as you are awkwardly brushing aside a tangle of branches … you suddenly catch a glimpse of a dark tunnel of green at the far end of which is a tiny aperture of light.

(Alain-Fournier, *Le Grand Meaulnes* (*The Lost Domain*), 1912)

Index